HENRY FIELDING
Justice Observed

HENRY FIELDING
Justice Observed

edited by
K. G. Simpson

VISION
and
BARNES & NOBLE

Vision Press Limited
Fulham Wharf
Townmead Road
London SW6 2SB

and

Barnes & Noble Books
81 Adams Drive
Totowa, NJ 07512

ISBN (UK) 0 85478 106 4
ISBN (US) 0 389 20591 5

Printed and bound in Great Britain by
Unwin Brothers Ltd.,
Old Woking, Surrey.
Phototypeset by Galleon Photosetting,
Ipswich, Suffolk.
MCMLXXXV

Contents

Introduction

by K. G. SIMPSON

In *Henry Fielding: A Biography* (London: Paul Elek, 1979) Pat Rogers suggested that Fielding would have made a splendid broadcaster in the manner of J. B. Priestley or C. S. Lewis. One can appreciate what he means, given the combination of an engaging personality and a multi-faceted career. These essays acknowledge the diversity of Fielding's experience as citizen, magistrate, political writer, and dramatist—varied aspects of the man that influenced the nature of his fiction. At the heart of this collection is a concern with the formation of the writer's values and their expression in his novels. What judgements does Fielding offer, why does he offer them, and what judgements does he elicit from his readers?—to such questions these essays are addressed.

Plenitude is the hallmark of Fielding. Both the life and the writing attest to a richness and range of interest; both abound with the sense of what Donald Low aptly terms Fielding's 'exceptional appetite for life', a quality which induces him to compare Fielding to Chaucer. In our own century it is difficult to find examples as telling as that of Fielding (or that of Smollett, for that matter) of the close inter-relationship of literature and life. The vigour with which he pursued his several professional activities is remarkable. Noting that while he was completing *Tom Jones* Fielding was also making strenuous efforts to become a magistrate in Westminster, Donald Low observes,

> In his eyes, the two activities were merely different sides of the same coin. As a novelist he was making a contribution to public life; and the same was true in his other line of work, as 'man of action'.

7

Fielding's are the teeming fictional canvasses of a man with a mission. The mission was the exposure and censure of vice (The Prologue to his first play, *Love in Several Masques*, includes the statement, 'Our bard at vice, not at the vicious, throws').

For his contemporaries, and Lady Mary Wortley Montagu pre-eminently, Fielding was notorious for 'raking in the lowest sinks of vice and misery'[1]; and Richardson, intent on damning his rival as a profligate, remarked, 'Do men expect Grapes of Thorns, or Figs of Thistles?'[2] In V. S. Pritchett's witty formulation Fielding was 'an old Etonian [who] let the side down'[3]. Yet while his experiences amongst the lower social orders plainly influenced Fielding as writer, he did not reproduce an exact replica of them in his fiction. In his introduction to the Penguin *Tom Jones* R. P. C. Mutter rightly draws attention to 'the selective nature of Fielding's realism'[4] in contrast to that of Swift, Smollett or Hogarth (with whom, as Donald Low shows, he shares various targets for social censure). Patrick Reilly pursues the point when he argues that

> [Fielding's] fictional world is a magistrate's dream in which the innocent are always cleared and the guilty always exposed. What the magistrate vainly aspires to, the novelist triumphantly achieves—Fielding is the magistrate as novelist, recruiting the genius of the second vocation to remedy the shortcomings of the first.

For Smollett, everything depends 'on the tossing up of a halfpenny'.[5] Much more comforting is the world of Fielding's novels where we can rely on the dispositions of a just Providence. Such fictional justice comes appropriately from a man who, as Morris Golden notes, defined the state as a 'grand Machine, which, like a piece of Clock-work in right Order, moves steadily and regularly by fixed and certain Laws'.[6]

In his essay Donald Low substantiates his claim that novel-writing 'provides [Fielding] with an opportunity to combine invention with morally alert investigation of the human heart'. And he examines Fielding's activities and achievements as magistrate—reading the Riot Act after 3,000 sailors rioted against bawdy houses; censuring street robbery, masquerades, gambling, vagrancy, and receiving; and

organizing an early version of the police force to pursue
hardened criminals. All such activity was motivated by a
desire to rid society of vice, much of which he saw as rooted in
the desire of the masses to emulate 'the great'.

Morris Golden deals firstly with the course of Fielding's
political career, then with his theories as they can be inferred
from the political writings, and then with the political
implications of the fiction. Golden points out that in Fielding's
view evil politicians, like those who mislead the young, try to
'inflame the minds of the People against their best and truest
Friends'.[7] Here, Golden makes plain, is 'one of the clearest ties
between his political positions and the themes of the novels . . .
[where] he is always concerned for the guidance of the young,
the ignorant, and the weak'.

On the question of philosophical influence on Fielding,
Lance Butler claims a stronger affinity between Fielding and
Shaftesbury than recent thinking has conceded. Though
agreeing with Martin Battestin that in the beliefs of the
Latitudinarians is part of the moral basis of *Joseph Andrews*,
Butler rejects Battestin's dismissal of Shaftesbury and marshals
six arguments to support the influence of Shaftesbury's ideas
on the values of *Tom Jones*.

The other essays are concerned primarily with the expression
of values and the direction of the reader's judgement within
specific works. Patrick Reilly approaches Fielding by means of
contrast with Swift. 'Swift traps his readers', he suggests,
whereas 'Fielding undeviously asks his to act as jurors'. Reilly
sees the question, 'What kind of judge are you?', as 'the most
important challenge that the reader of Fielding encounters'.
With the parody of *Pamela* as starting-point, Neil Rhodes
examines the versions of innocence exemplified by Joseph,
Adams and Wilson. He explains the resolution of *Joseph
Andrews* as 'an escape into fantasy' because Fielding had not
yet successfully embodied the various aspects of innocence in
one hero; that had to wait for 'his masterpiece, *Tom Jones*'. In
'The Story-telling in *Joseph Andrews*' Bryan Burns argues that
the interpolations are integral to Fielding's method of widen-
ing the reader's perspective and establishing a dialogue 'where
the "literary" is upstaged by the "actual", the remote by the
immediate, the abstract by the concrete'. Mark Kinkead-

9

Weekes challenges the widely held view that the 'Author's Appearance' in Book III, Chapter 7 of *Tom Jones* represents Fielding's own genuine advocacy of the importance of acquiring prudence. Fielding is teasing, he suggests, and he shows how the author creates a 'battlefield' in the reader's mind—'the trial to which the roads to Upton lead is of *the reader's* judgement'—before making it plain that what Tom has to learn is not prudence but 'the need to acquire wisdom through loving *more* and *better*'. By examining the presentation of lying and concealment in *Amelia*, Donald Fraser both illuminates their thematic significance and shows how Fielding encourages, indeed requires, alert attention to detail on the part of the 'sagacious' reader.

If these essays go some way towards familiarizing the reader with the range of Fielding's activities, the variety of influences to which he was subject, the effects of all of these on his writing, and their presentation therein, it is hoped that they will encourage our sagacious reader to pose one further question: were these richly diverse activities and experiences undergone by an integrated personality? Was that insistent and—for a humorist—sometimes rather heavy-handed endorsement of Providence the refuge of a man who was more beset by doubts than he would care to admit publicly? Certainly there are dangers in trying to find in Fielding the forefather of the modern divided self. Yet in his biography Pat Rogers, with justification in my view, presents Fielding as a deeply thoughtful, almost innately retiring, man who could not resist the lure of the vibrant world of mass society.

Several of the essays collected here point to dichotomies and tensions within Fielding. Morris Golden identifies precisely the central duality in Fielding when he writes of his 'desire for order in the state . . . complicated by a fascination with the vitality of disorder'. As reflected in the fiction this accounts for the disjunction of commentary from narrative action. Rightly, Bryan Burns comments that the reader of *Joseph Andrews* 'comes increasingly . . . to feel quizzical about the relationship between Fielding's wish to impute some general interpretation to his work, and his often contradictory delight in the vagary and singularity of human behaviour'. Also detecting a certain conflict of aims in that novel, Neil Rhodes remarks, 'part of the problem is that *Joseph Andrews* is in some ways a romance like *The Winter's Tale*, while Fielding was also aiming to write a realistic novel'. In my own essay I suggest that the application of heroic modes to ordinary life bespeaks a humane, realistic, and 'modern' attitude, whereas the handling of plot—in terms of both the experiences of the characters and the course of narrator-reader relations—points towards an authoritative exposition of an absolutist stance.

One of the most engrossing aspects of Fielding is the tension between his tremendous creative energy, his readiness to range widely through both experience and genres in the interests of his 'new species of writing', and a measure of uncertainty that is perhaps to be expected of the adventurer (for instance, Ronald Paulson and Thomas Lockwood claim, rightly I believe, à propos of *Joseph Andrews* that 'Fielding's own uncertainty as to both what he was writing and how it should be defended in terms of the neo-classical categories is evident in his preface').[8] Poised thus between the constraints of rules and the spirit of individualism which the long prose narrative encouraged and came to embody, Fielding is a fascinating figure.

In a recent essay, 'The Novel and Europe', Milan Kundera identified Cervantes as the founder of the modern era. Kundera claimed,

> To take the world as relative, as Cervantes did, to be obliged to face not a single absolute truth but a heap of contradictory truths (truths embodied in *imaginary thinking selves* called characters), to have as one's only certainty the *wisdom of uncertainty*, requires no less courage [than to take Descartes's 'thinking self' as the basis of everything and to be alone before the universe].[9]

There are elements in Fielding—admittedly only some, but sufficient, in my view—to warrant placing him in the tradition of Cervantes in this respect. Beneath that veneer of benign assurance is there not a man who exemplifies that 'wisdom of uncertainty'? And when Kundera lists among the challenges to which he responds that of 'serious play', may not Fielding take a place alongside Sterne and Diderot as one of its exponents?

Acknowledgements: for help of various kinds, all most generously given, I am very grateful to Donald Fraser, Morris Golden, Catherine MacLeod, Andrew Noble and Margaret Philips. To Professor Dennis Fletcher I am indebted for permission to reprint Mark Kinkead-Weekes's essay which first appeared in *The British Journal for Eighteenth-Century Studies*, III, i (Spring 1980).

NOTES

1. Cited Wilbur L. Cross, *The History of Henry Fielding* (New Haven: Yale University Press, 1918; reissued New York, 1963), Vol. III, p. 109.
2. *Henry Fielding: The Critical Heritage*, edited by Ronald Paulson and Thomas Lockwood (London: Routledge and Kegan Paul; New York: Barnes and Noble, 1969), p. 174.
3. V. S. Pritchett, 'The Ancestor' in *The Living Novel* (London: Arrow Books, 1960), p. 17.
4. *The History of Tom Jones*, edited by R. P. C. Mutter (Harmondsworth: Penguin Books, 1966), p. 18.
5. *The Letters of Tobias Smollett*, edited by Lewis M. Knapp (Oxford: Oxford University Press, 1970), p. 98.
6. *Champion*, 8 May 1740.
7. *Jacobite's Journal*, No. 45.
8. *Henry Fielding: The Critical Heritage*, p. 7.
9. Milan Kundera, 'The Novel and Europe', *The New York Review*, 19 July 1984.

1

Mr. Fielding of Bow Street

by DONALD LOW

Certain English authors have sought to express themselves in philanthropic action, as well as in words. Fielding's is a particularly interesting case. The pattern of his whole life strongly suggests that he always saw writing as a form of social action, and in that sense its own justification; yet such was his energy, and such the quality of his social concern, that he took every opportunity to involve himself also in practical, extra-literary matters.[1]

Had he met with more financial success, it is possible that writing for the stage would have claimed him for good. There is a sense in which he was cut out to be an all-round 'man of the theatre'; it could almost be argued that he was a good Victorian actor-manager born a century too soon. Yet, subject as it was to changing fashion and to other strong pressures, theatrical entertainment in London could scarcely have provided an adequate outlet for all of his ideas about society. When his play-writing was going well, and before Walpole put an end to everything in 1737 by curbing freedom of dramatic expression, Fielding's work for the London stage enabled him to communicate very directly with large groups of people. He clearly enjoyed this, just as, later on, he took pleasure in the stimulus of political and miscellaneous journalism. Fielding never made the mistake of looking on these forms as insignificant. His obvious love for drama—as well as the weight of classical tradition—prevented him from being patronizing about the stage; while the varied evidence of his

13

prose-writing for periodicals strongly suggests that he recognized a social need for informed debate through the practice of responsible journalism.[2] Even so, neither drama nor journalism was in itself enough for him.

In time, the writing of fiction became central to his life. *Shamela* perhaps did little more than signal that he felt himself capable of handling the novel form with confidence and humour; but both *Joseph Andrews* and *Tom Jones* show steady awareness of novel-writing as something much more than mere diversionary entertainment. Fielding's purpose can be variously defined, in literary historical terms, but whether we speak of 'the comic epic' in prose, or of the novel 'coming of age', his essential commitment to his creations is never in doubt. Novel-writing matters to him; it provides him with an opportunity to combine invention with morally alert investigation of the human heart. Moreover, thanks to the particular kind of solution he devises to problems of plot construction and narrative, the novel increasingly enables him to deal intelligently and connectedly with a *society*, rather than simply with an assortment of individual persons. Especially in *Tom Jones*, he writes with a view to accomplishing more than a successful piece of story-telling. Tom Jones, Sophia, Squire Allworthy, Blifil and the rest are lovingly created characters; and Tom's adventures are at the heart of the book: but Fielding's eye is on the interconnections and above all on the values of an entire society.[3]

Fiction offered more scope than other literary forms, but it still could not fulfil all of his aspirations. Although the ideas expressed in his novels are complex and wide-ranging, Fielding's wish to contribute directly to the life of his time remained. In 1740 he had qualified as an advocate and had since gained professional experience. He was now utterly determined to take whatever action might be in his power to serve his ideal of justice in the busiest part of the capital. This ambition complemented his literary commitment, and was not in his own eyes secondary to it.

Thus we have the astonishing fact that at the very time when he was intensely busy as a novelist completing and arranging to publish *Tom Jones*, Fielding was also exerting himself strenuously to become a magistrate in Westminster.

His career as a novelist and his other chief professional career reach their climax together in 1749.[4] The only explanation of this which makes complete sense is that Fielding conceived of the two as intimately related, and not only in the sense that the writing of fiction was a relief from embroilment in the affairs of a Justice of the Peace. In his eyes, the two activities were merely different sides of the same coin. As a novelist he was making a contribution to public life; and the same was true in his other line of work, as 'man of action'. In Fielding's judgement, the country faced a crisis.[5] The largest single threat to social stability came from a love of 'luxury', especially as manifested in such habits as theft and gin-drinking among the poor. The faulty philosophy causing such abuses of individual liberty must be tackled head-on by responsible commentators, while those in authority, including magistrates, must show real firmness. Only a combination of art and direct action held out real hope for the future.

There can be little doubt that a tradition of public service which surfaced in his family from time to time helped to create his strong sense of civic duty, as well as helping to give him confidence; his grandfather on his mother's side had been knighted as a justice of the King's Bench. Fielding believed that it was up to people with his background of experience and education to give a lead. Thus the former man about town, now prevented by gout from walking any distance, but agile in mind as ever, sought and obtained the office of magistrate.[6] The process by which he did so was the normal one in his time, involving the patronage of a wealthy property-owner with political influence, in this instance the Duke of Bedford. Fielding's Eton schoolfellow, George Lyttelton, interested the Duke on his behalf; hence the comment in the dedication of *Tom Jones* to Lyttelton:

> while my gratitude for the princely benefactions of the Duke of Bedford bursts from my heart, you must forgive my reminding you, that it was you who first recommended me to the notice of my benefactor.[7]

Fielding needed Bedford's support at every stage, and especially with regard to his Middlesex magistracy, for which there was a property qualification. Bedford leased property to the novelist, including the house on the west side of Bow Street which soon became his place of work. Moreover, Fielding was not in practice required to pay the ground rent. In return, Fielding threw his weight behind the Duke's candidate in the 1749 Westminster election. To that extent, he was implicated as an agent in the network of power and political influence in his part of the metropolis.[8] He sincerely supported the Pelham administration, and the surviving evidence points to his having acted very willingly to promote the government interest on this occasion.

Fielding's work at Bow Street ranged from quite trivial instances of the abuse of law by London's less adequate citizens to serious crime and street rioting. Tenacity and coolness were both needed, particularly when unlawful conduct threatened to become completely out of hand. On 3 July 1749, for instance, Fielding wrote to his patron, shortly before a very large number of sailors rioted for the third successive night, ostensibly at least against the bawdy-houses in the Strand:

> I think it my Duty to acquaint your Grace that I have recd repeated Informations of upwards of 3000 Sailors now in Arms abt. Wapping and that they threaten to march to this End of the Town this Night, under Pretence of demolishing all Bawdy Houses. I have an Officer and 50 Men and submit to yr Grace what more Assistance may be necessary. I sent a Messenger five Hours ago to the Secretary at War but have yet no Answer.[9]

On this particular occasion, which severely tested his magistracy, reading the Riot Act and calling out the Guard enabled Fielding to disperse a 'mob' which contained many former fighting men who had lost their livelihood with the coming of peace after the war of the Austrian Succession (no fewer than 40,000 had been demobilized). He had to face an unlooked-for sequel, however, when a public outcry arose on behalf of the single individual, Bosavern Penlez, who went to the gallows as a result of offences under the Riot Act. Late in 1749, Fielding published a pamphlet entitled *A True State of the Case of Bosavern Penlez* defending his actions as magistrate. Not everyone was satisfied that his decision to read the utterly uncompromising Riot Act had been necessary, however; and his firm determination to put down tumult and protect property remains a subject of controversy.[10] A distinction clearly has to be made between a rough-and-ready law, the eighteenth-century Riot Act, and the conduct of an individual charged with acting as magistrate at Bow Street. It is surely easy enough to understand the feeling of extreme pressure Fielding had come under after two days of sustained rioting. Only a cynic would conclude that he had been unduly motivated by a wish to protect bawdy-houses bringing revenue to the Duke of Bedford.

Fielding brought his blind half-brother John to share his work at Bow Street, and as his health failed, more responsibility gradually passed to his half-brother. Interestingly, the connection between Fielding and the magistracy and Westminster was to last for a long time after the novelist's death. John Fielding, who was knighted in 1760, continued to serve as chief magistrate at Bow Street until his death in 1780.[11] (As he lay on his deathbed, many of his own and Henry's official papers were burned at Bow Street in the Gordon Riots, beside which the episode of 1749 pales into insignificance.) He saw to it, in true eighteenth-century fashion, that William Fielding, the novelist's son, was appointed a magistrate. Among documents recently published by M. C. Battestin is a letter from William, written in 1770, unsuccessfully applying to the Duke of Bedford for 'the same kind of favour which he so nobly conferred on my Father—namely a qualification to act as Magistrate for the County of Middlesex'.[12]

Less well known to students of Fielding, perhaps, is the record of William Fielding's 'evidence' to a Select Committee on the Police of the Metropolis in 1816. A Whig social reformer, Henry Grey Bennet, chaired the Select Committee, and on 6 June 1816 interviewed the crippled 68-year-old magistrate from Queen's-square police office. Part of the evidence reads as follows:

> How many years have you been in the Police?—My father, Henry Fielding, was an old Magistrate. God knows, I have seen a good deal of the Police of the Metropolis; I am a very old Magistrate for Westminster; I have been near fifty years standing in the commission. . . .

17

Do you not recollect that it was a complaint made in all the publications of the day, about 30 or 40 years ago, that in almost every eighth or tenth house in the Metropolis there were spirits found for sale?—I know, from my father's writings upon that particular subject, there did exist a vast number of spirituous liquor-houses.

Hogarth has attacked the subject in his drawings?—Yes, he has. In that treatise which my father wrote, namely, a consideration of the increase of robberies, which has been rather a popular little thing, though not so great a favourite as his Tom Jones, the idea of the gin-shop was terrible. He then acted as a Magistrate, and, I believe, was then the only Magistrate in London of any degree of consequence, and ought to know something of the subject.[13]

There is something touching in this glimpse of a physically incapacitated member of the Fielding family, himself a magistrate, with his best years behind him, talking proudly of Henry Fielding's views on the gin menace. The passage also serves as a reminder that Fielding's writings and example were cited many times in the debate about social control in the period between his death and the introduction of Peel's police. To cite two instances only: in 1785 Sir William Blizard wrote,

Let every magistrate read and well consider that excellent work of H. Fielding, Esq., *An Enquiry into the Causes of the late Increase of Robbers, etc.* This will afford them many admirable hints, and directions for their conduct.

In 1829, with a new era about to begin, Edwin Chadwick would 'fervently adopt' Fielding's views on preventive police.[14]

Of the tracts which Fielding wrote on matters relating to his work as a magistrate, *An Enquiry into the Causes of the late Increase of Robbers, etc.* (1751) did most to stimulate public concern. As will be shown, it contains a powerful and eloquent argument for seeking more effective checks over potential and actual lawlessness. The 1816 conversation quoted above between Henry Grey Bennet and William Fielding points to a key factor which helped to make this publication well known. Fielding's treatise lodged in the public mind along with Hogarth's famous prints of 'Beer Street' and 'Gin Lane'.[15] Pictures and words gave the same urgent warning. Luxury, and especially abuse of strong drink, threatened the very lifeblood of society.

Hogarth and Fielding were old friends, with considerable respect for each other's art. How exactly it came about that they made common cause in attacking 'Gin Lane' is unknown; they were, after all, responding to an obvious and much reported evil of the time. Yet Ronald Paulson's summing up, in *Hogarth: His Life, His Art, and Times*, carries authority:

> It is difficult to say whether Fielding had any influence on *Industry and Idleness* back in 1747 before he was a magistrate. The influence of Hogarth's prints, in their emphasis on "idle persons" and idleness as a source of crime, and even in some of their images, may, however, be felt in Fielding's writings. There was certainly no coincidence in the appearance, with almost synchronized precision, of major attacks in January and February 1750/1 by both Fielding and Hogarth.[16]

Hogarth's strategy, as always, was to contrast a good and a bad set of possibilities. 'Beer Street' shows scenes of health, pleasurable work, and social ease. In the more famous 'Gin Lane', on the other hand, there is not a single happy face. A gin-sodden mother wears a drunken smile—and not much else—while her child slips from her grasp over a dangerous-looking drop; the starving figure of 'Mr. Gin' sits in the right foreground; and a pawn-shop and street quarrels fill the background.

The scope of Fielding's *Enquiry* includes much more than the evils of drink; but on this topic he is at one with Hogarth, writing in 'Section II. Of Drunkenness, A Second Consequence of Luxury Among the Vulgar':

> The drunkenness I here intend is that acquired by the strongest intoxicating liquors, and particularly by that poison called *Gin*; which I have great reason to think is the principal sustenance (if it may be so called) of more than a hundred thousand people in this metropolis. Many of these wretches there are who swallow pints of this poison within the twenty-four hours; the dreadful effects of which I have the misfortune every day to see, and to smell too.[17]

He goes on to ask 'What must become of the infant who is conceived in Gin? with the poisonous distillations of which it is nourished both in the womb and at the breast?' Given that his treatise was published before 'Gin Lane', it seems very likely that this sentence helped to inspire the mother and child motif in Hogarth's satire.

Fielding's opening tactic in his *Enquiry* is to issue a blunt warning that the increase in the number of robberies poses a challenge to civilized life as it has been known. He writes,

> The great increase of robberies within these few years is an evil which to me appears to deserve some attention. . . . I make no doubt, but that the streets of this town, and the roads leading to it, will shortly be impassable without the utmost hazard; nor are we threatened with seeing less dangerous gangs of rogues among us, than those which the Italians call the Banditti.[18]

The main thrust of his subsequent argument concerns the alleged harmful effects of imitation of well-to-do people by the poor. In Fielding's view, emulation of 'the great' by persons equipped neither by wealth nor background to cope with temptation, lies at the root of a large number of social ills, including the 'flagrant evil' of street robbery. This may seem an unacceptably patrician attitude today; but Fielding makes it clear that he does not exempt the upper classes from their share of responsibility. The 'vast torrent of luxury' abroad in the nation has its source among the aristocracy; and this fact has implications:

> I am not here to satirise the great, among whom luxury is probably rather a moral than a political evil. But vices no more than diseases will stop with them; for bad habits are as infectious by example, as the plague itself by contact. In free countries, at least, it is a branch of liberty claimed by the people to be as wicked and profligate as their superiors. Thus while the nobleman will emulate the grandeur of a prince, and the gentleman will aspire to the proper state of the nobleman, the tradesman steps from behind his counter into the vacant place of the gentleman. Nor doth the confusion end here; it reaches the very dregs of the people, who aspiring still to a degree beyond that which belongs to them, and not being able by the fruits of honest labour to support the state which they affect, they disdain the wages to which their industry would entitle them; and abandoning themselves to idleness, the more simple and poor-minded betake themselves to a state of starving and

beggary, while those of more art and courage become thieves, sharpers, and robbers.[19]

Fielding then proceeds to illustrate his view that London offers too many opportunities for idleness and extravagant behaviour on the part of those who can least afford such a style of behaviour. Masquerades come in for particular criticism as 'temples of drunkenness, lewdness, and all sorts of debauchery', and he also comments severely on the degree to which the lower levels of society have learned to copy the habit of gambling which he takes to belong historically to the aristocracy. His main concern throughout is with the delinquent behaviour of the poor, but there is characteristic irony in his incidental strictures on young 'bucks':

> we may, I think, reasonably desire of these great personages, that they would keep their favourite vice to themselves, and not suffer others, whose birth or fortune gives them no title to be above the terror of the laws, or the censure of their betters, to share with them in the privilege.[20]

Fielding places considerable emphasis on the need to control vagrancy. He writes with the authority of someone who has seen for himself the pattern of urban crime, and who can moreover turn to highly experienced witnesses, his professional associates at Bow Street. He quotes at length from a chilling report by Saunders Welch, high-constable of Holborn, on conditions in one of the most notorious of all the 'rookeries', in the parish of St. Giles, and comments, 'This picture, which is taken from life, will appear strange to many; for the evil here described is, I am confident, very little known, especially to those of the better sort.'[21] Part of the value of the *Enquiry* was precisely its capacity to shock. Even Horace Walpole, no friend of Fielding or his work, was led to comment on it as an 'admirable treatise'.[22]

Fielding combines sympathy for the honest poor with a tough-minded determination to curb lawlessness on the part of criminals.[23] In the second half of the *Enquiry*, he lists a number of the factors which in his view make robbery easy, and proposes specific remedies. He is especially harsh on one major weakness of the time, the lax position relating to receivers. On this, as on other problems of the magistracy, he

21

shows a remarkable ability to put his central criticism simply
and directly:

> Why should not the receiving stolen goods, knowing them to be
> stolen, be made an original offence? by which means the thief,
> who is often a paltry offender in comparison of the receiver, and
> sometimes his pupil, might, in little felonies, be made a witness
> against him; for thus the trial of the receiver would in no case
> depend on the trial or conviction of the thief.[24]

A generation later, a keen admirer of Fielding, the Scottish
social reformer Patrick Colquhoun, would take up a very
similar position in his *Treatise on the Police of the Metropolis*
(1795), which was to prepare the way for Peel. But reform was
slow in coming. The extent to which Fielding was ahead of his
time on the question of receivers can be seen in extended
perspective when we recall Fagin in *Oliver Twist*.

In his *History of English Criminal Law*, Leon Radzinowicz
pays tribute to the *Enquiry*, and comments accurately that
Fielding's manner of presenting his case is 'pugnacious, vivid,
and humane'. Typical of Fielding's approach is this passage
from Section VI, in which he draws attention to the difficulty
of keeping track of wrong-doers in a rapidly expanding city:

> The other great encouragement to robbery, beside the certain
> means of finding a market for the booty, is the probability of
> escaping punishment.
>
> First, then, the robber hath great hopes of being undis-
> covered; and this is one principal reason why robberies are
> more frequent in this town, and in its neighbourhood, than in
> the remoter parts of the kingdom.
>
> Whoever indeed considers the cities of London and West-
> minster, with the late vast addition of their suburbs, the great
> irregularity of their buildings, the immense number of lanes,
> alleys, courts, and bye-places; must think, that, had they been
> intended for the very purpose of concealment, they could scarce
> have been better contrived. Upon such a view the whole appears
> as a vast wood or forest, in which a thief may harbour with as great
> security as wild beasts do in the deserts of Africa or Arabia; for, by
> *wandering* from one part to another, and often shifting his quarters,
> he may almost avoid the possibility of being discovered.[25]

Modern historians have pointed to the lack of effective
communication among those charged with law enforcement in

dozens of separately administered parishes as one of the chief contributory causes of crime. Colquhoun would argue with undeniable logic, 'A *Centre-point* is wanted to connect the whole together, so as to invigorate and strengthen every part.'[26] Fielding knew the sensitivity of his fellow countrymen on the subject of traditional parish liberty, which many people held to be compromised by the idea of any central organization. One clear implication of his argument in the *Enquiry*, however, is that to combat the exploitation of London's ever-expanding size by law-breakers, some co-ordination from the centre was required. It was this that his office in Bow Street sought to supply.

As this exemplifies in one sphere of his activity, perhaps the single quality about Fielding which stands out above all others is his positive attitude towards experience. His literary career is that of someone energetically seeking to entertain and persuade his contemporaries through every major prose medium—drama, journalism, and finally the novel. He has an exceptional appetite for life, and a robust tolerance to match. When describing people he is clearly in his element, almost indeed to the same degree as Chaucer, the English author whom he most closely resembles. Whether or not he happens to admire those he writes about, he communicates curiosity about each one. Similarly, in outlining where he stands in relation to particular issues in morality, fiction, or social thought, he conveys an impression that he cares greatly about the subject in hand, and loves nothing so much as a good argument.

Fielding's social experience was partly aristocratic and partly miscellaneous. He knew the real world of his time, respectable and otherwise. His cousin, Lady Mary Wortley Montagu, put her finger on an essential truth in stressing as his leading characteristic a capacity for enjoyment, whatever the company he was in:

> I am sorry for H. Fielding's death, not only as I shall read no more of his writings, but I believe he lost more than others, as no man enjoyed life more than he did, though few had less reason to do so, the highest of his preferment being raking in the lowest sinks of vice and misery. I should think it a nobler and less nauseous employment to be one of the staff-officers that

conduct the nocturnal weddings. His happy constitution (even
when he had, with great pains, half demolished it) made him
forget everything when he was before a venison pasty or over a
flask of champagne, and I am persuaded he had known more
happy moments than any prince upon earth. His natural spirits
gave him rapture with his cookmaid, and cheerfulness when he
was fluxing [undergoing medical treatment] in a garret. There
was a great similitude between his character and that of Sir
Richard Steele.

He had the advantage both in learning and, in my opinion,
genius. They both agreed in wanting money in spite of all
their friends, and would have wanted it if their hereditary
lands had been as extensive as their imagination, yet each of
them so formed for happiness, it is a pity they were not
immortal.[27]

This comment, from a letter to Lady Mary's daughter, seems
to confirm as accurate the kind of reading of Fielding's work
which places the main emphasis on sociability, *joie de vivre*, and
'good nature'. These qualities belonged to the man and the
author from his early high-spirited experiments in play-
writing until late in life.

As Lady Mary Wortley Montagu knew and regretted,
however, the cheerful hedonism which was part of her cousin's
nature had been over-shadowed before his death by his habit
of 'raking in the lowest sinks of vice and misery'. The reference
here is not to any gratuitous 'slumming' on Fielding's part,
but instead to the way in which he chose to discharge his
duties as 'first magistrate' of Bow Street. She was probably
recalling part of the Author's Introduction to the post-
humously published *Journal of a Voyage to Lisbon*. There,
Fielding writes:

by composing, instead of inflaming, the quarrels of porters and
beggars (which I blush when I say hath not been universally
practised), and by refusing to take a shilling from a man who
most undoubtedly would not have had another left, I had
reduced an income of about five hundred pounds a year of the
dirtiest money upon earth to little more than three hundred
pounds; a considerable proportion of which remained with my
clerk; and, indeed, if the whole had done so, as it ought, he
would be but ill paid for sitting almost sixteen hours in the
twenty-four in the most unwholesome, as well as nauseous air

in the universe, and which hath in his case corrupted a good constitution without contaminating his morals.[28]

The use of the word 'nauseous' in the private letter suggests a direct influence from Fielding's personal account of what it had been like to contend with the underworld from day to day. It is revealing that his clever, snobbish cousin had little real sympathy for such an undertaking, which she appears to have judged simply as a loss of happiness and waste of brilliant gifts.

Given other of Fielding's statements in the same Introduction, Lady Mary Wortley Montagu's attitude seems frivolous indeed—even although her concern for Fielding the individual human being remains to her credit. Fielding tells the story of how in 1753 he took great pains to meet the wishes of the Duke of Newcastle that he should put an end to 'those murders and robberies which were every day committed in the streets'. His plan for doing this was accepted and £600 were promised for the purpose. As a result,

> I had delayed my Bath journey for some time, contrary to the repeated advice of my physical acquaintance, and to the ardent desire of my warmest friends, though my distemper was now turned to a deep jaundice; in which case the Bath waters are generally reputed to be almost infallible. But I had the most eager desire of demolishing this gang of villains and cut-throats, which I was sure of accomplishing the moment I was enabled to pay a fellow who had undertaken, for a small sum, to betray them into the hands of a set of thief-takers whom I had enlisted into the service, all men of known and approved fidelity and intrepidity.
>
> After some weeks the money was paid at the treasury, and within a few days after two hundred pounds of it had come to my hands, the whole gang of cut-throats was entirely dispersed, seven of them were in actual custody, and the rest driven, some out of the town, and others out of the kingdom.
>
> Though my health was now reduced to the last extremity, I continued to act with the utmost vigour against these villains; in examining whom, and in taking the depositions against them, I have often spent whole days, nay, sometimes whole nights, especially when there was any difficulty in procuring sufficient evidence to convict them; which is a very common case in street-robberies, even when the guilt of the party is

25

sufficiently apparent to satisfy the most tender conscience. But courts of justice know nothing of a cause more than what is told them on oath by a witness; and the most flagitious villain upon earth is tried in the same manner as a man of the best character who is accused of the same crime.

Meanwhile, amidst all my fatigues and distresses, I had the satisfaction to find my endeavours had been attended with such success that this hellish society were almost utterly extirpated, and that, instead of reading of murders and street-robberies in the news every morning, there was, in the remaining part of the month of November, and in all December, not only no such thing as a murder, but not even a street-robbery committed. Some such, indeed, were mentioned in the public papers; but they were all found, on the strictest enquiry, to be false.

In this entire freedom from robberies, during the dark months, no man will, I believe, scruple to acknowledge that the winter of 1753 stands unrivalled, during a course of many years; and this may possibly appear the more extraordinary to those who recollect the outrages with which it began.

Having thus fully accomplished my undertaking, I went into the country, in a very weak and deplorable condition, with no fewer or less diseases than a jaundice, a dropsy, and an asthma, altogether uniting their forces in the destruction of a body so emaciated that it had lost all its muscular flesh.[29]

I have quoted at some length from the Introduction to the *Journal of a Voyage to Lisbon* because it supplies Fielding's fullest first-hand account of one specific episode in the struggle against serious crime on the streets of the capital, for which he sacrificed the health remaining to him in the years after publication of *Tom Jones* and his acceptance of the office of magistrate at Bow Street. Several points of interest belong to his typically frank description of the interaction of work pressure and declining health. The first of these concerns the nature of his work at Bow Street. Fielding interpreted his rôle as being much more than merely deciding levels of reward and punishment in petty disputes, although, as his remark about 'beggars and porters' indicates, plenty of these came his way. What he proudly describes here is the first real initiative taken by any Westminster or London magistrate to introduce a group of men with the special task of tracking down and bringing to justice hardened criminals. He does not call them 'police'; but his innovation on this occasion anticipates the use of what would later be called a 'specialised detective branch of the metropolitan police force'. This means that Fielding can be seen as someone who significantly contributed at the beginning of a long process of applying improved social control. There is popular propagandist documentation of his own and his thief-takers' reputation in such contemporary ballads as 'The Highwayman':

> I robbed Lord Edgumbe I do declare
> And Lady Templar of Melbourne Square . . .
> Till taken by such as I never knew,
> But I was informed they were Fielding's crew.
> The judge his mercy did extend,
> He pardoned my crime, bade me amend,
> But still I pursued a thriving trade . . .
> O now I'm judged and doomed to die.[30]

Secondly, there is his comment on the 'dirtiest money on earth'. Not only was Fielding an innovator in facing the challenge to combat organized crime with organized detection. He broke with a long and disreputable tradition, that of the 'trading justice' who levied a charge for every service he performed, whether it was in giving bail or in aiding prosecution. In 'composing' the minor quarrels of the streets, instead of looking for his own fee, Fielding set an example of magistracy as allied, where possible, to a spirit of recon- ciliation, rather than to mercenary interest and shabby compromise. His exceptional enterprise in helping to create a method of clearing the streets of serious crime went along with a steady personal integrity.

In a footnote to his remarks on the financial sacrifice he made at Bow Street, Fielding comments on the man he had followed, Sir Thomas de Veil:

> A predecessor of mine used to boast that he made one thousand pounds a year in his office; but how he did this (if indeed he did it) is to me a secret. His clerk, now mine, told me I had more business than he had ever known there; I am sure I had as much as any man could do. . . .[31]

De Veil had been in office over a long period, during which he had become known both for toughness in dealing with serious crime and for being a trading justice. Understandably, Fielding felt himself under an obligation to distance himself from de Veil's reputation. The position he occupied was an exposed one. Charges of corruption were commonplace. It is a measure of the authority he brought to his work at Bow Street that—despite hostile criticism in certain pamphlets and periodicals—few accusations of this kind were made against his own magistracy.

The Introduction to his *Journal of a Voyage to Lisbon* is by no means the only 'literary' piece of writing in which Fielding draws on his Bow Street experience. There is a sense in which the whole of his last novel, *Amelia*, is designed to communicate some of the main ideas he had formed through his work as a magistrate. *Amelia* appears at times to be the fiction of a man grown weary of mere fiction—it certainly lacks the resilient spirit of fun which characterizes *Tom Jones*—but from the biographical and historical point of view it is nevertheless a fascinating work. The opening pages of the novel offer a glimpse of a 'trading justice' at work. Fielding has just been describing the feeble efforts at law enforcement of the 'poor old decrepit' Watchmen 'in our Metropolis'. He continues:

> The higher we proceed among our public Officers and Magistrates, the less Defects of this kind will, perhaps, be observable. Mr. *Thrasher*, however, the Justice before whom the Prisoners above-mentioned were now brought, had some few Imperfections in his magisterial Capacity. I own, I have been sometimes inclined to think, that this Office of a Justice of Peace requires some Knowledge of the Law: for this simple Reason; because in every Case which comes before him, he is to judge and act according to Law. Again, as these Laws are contained in a great Variety of Books; the Statutes which relate to the Office of a Justice of Peace, making of themselves at least two large Volumes in Folio; and that Part of his Jurisdiction which is founded on the common Law being dispersed in above a hundred Volumes, I cannot conceive how this Knowledge should be acquired without reading; and yet certain it is Mr. *Thrasher* never read one Syllable of the Matter.
>
> This perhaps was a Defect; but this was not all: for where mere Ignorance is to decide a Point between two Litigants, it will always be an even Chance whether it decides right or wrong; but sorry am I to say, Right was often in a much worse

Situation than this, and Wrong hath often had Five hundred to
one on his Side before that Magistrate; who, if he was ignorant
of the Law of *England*, was yet well versed in the Laws of
Nature. He perfectly well understood that fundamental
Principle so strongly laid down in the Institutes of the learned
Rochefoucault; by which the Duty of Self-love is so strongly
enforced, and every Man is taught to consider himself as the
Centre of Gravity, and to attract all things thither. To speak the
Truth plainly, the Justice was never indifferent in a Cause, but
when he could get nothing on either side.[32]

Fielding's satirical purpose is clear, but the point has been well
made that 'Justice Thrasher is not a caricature, it is a portrait
(ironic but not exaggerated) of a type.'[33] The intention is to
shock any reader who blindly trusts in those by law established. Much more in similar vein is to follow, so that *Amelia*
becomes among other things a deliberately disillusioning
guide to life in London. It raises to the level of a dominant
concern what had been one motif only in the second half of
Tom Jones.

At once, for example, and this is characteristic of his
approach in *Amelia*, Fielding shows Justice Thrasher making
the misjudgements of lazy prejudice. The novelist's main
concern throughout is with his characters' lack of moral
imagination. In order to show what Thrasher's decision-
making amounts to, he creates comedy out of a type of
incident which he must have observed many times:

The first who came upon his Trial was as bloody a Spectre as
ever the Imagination of a Murderer or a Tragic Poet conceived.
This poor Wretch was charged with a Battery by a much
stouter Man than himself: indeed the accused Person bore
about him some Evidence that he had been in an Affray, his
Cloaths being very bloody; but certain open Sluices on his own
Head sufficiently shewed whence all the scarlet Stream had
issued; whereas the Accuser had not the least Mark or
Appearance of any Wound. The Justice asked the Defendant,
What he meant by breaking the King's Peace—To which he
answered,—'Upon my Shoul I do love the King very well, and
I have not been after breaking any Thing of his that I do know;
but upon my Shoul this Man hath brake my Head, and my
Head did brake his Stick; that is all, Gra.' He then offered to
produce several Witnesses against this improbable Accusation;

29

but the Justice presently interrupted him, saying, 'Sirrah, your Tongue betrays your Guilt. Your are an *Irishman*, and that is always sufficient Evidence with me.'

The second Criminal was a poor Woman, who was taken up by the Watch as a Street-walker. It was alledged against her that she was found walking the Streets after Twelve o'Clock, and the Watchman declared he believed her to be a common Strumpet. She pleaded in her Defence (as was really the Truth) that she was a Servant, and was sent by her Mistress, who was a little Shopkeeper, and upon the Point of Delivery, to fetch a Midwife; which she offered to prove by several of the Neighbours, if she was allowed to send them. The Justice asked her why she had not done it before. To which she answered, she had no Money, and could get no Messenger. The Justice then called her several scurrilous Names; and declaring she was guilty within the Statute of Street-walking, ordered her to *Bridewell* for a Month.[34]

Thrasher shows similar carelessness in dealing with a poorly dressed 'young Fellow, whose name was *Booth*', who has been wrongly accused of beating a Watchman. 'Had the Magistrate been endued with much Sagacity', writes Fielding,

> or had he been very moderately gifted with another Quality very necessary to all who are to adminster Justice, he would have employed some Labour in cross-examining the Watchmen; at least he would have given the Defendant the Time he desired to send for the other Persons who were present at the Affray; neither of which he did. In short, the Magistrate had too great an Honour for Truth to suspect that she ever appeared in sordid Apparel; nor did she ever sully his sublime Notions of that Virtue, by uniting them with the mean Ideas of Poverty and Distress.[35]

As a result of Thrasher's disinclination to look beyond appearances, Booth is committed to Newgate, from which much is to follow; for Fielding goes on to illustrate his belief that 'these (not improperly called infernal) Regions' offer far larger inducements to amorality than to reformation. In terms of social history M. C. Battestin is undoubtedly right to comment that, 'accurate and terrible' as it is, Fielding's representation of life in Newgate 'if anything mitigates the inhuman conditions that actually obtained there for the great majority of inmates who had no money to pay for better treatment'[36]. Fielding's main object in *Amelia*, though, is to probe into moral issues, rather than to create a documentary sociological surface. With a sometimes almost Bunyanesque reliance on parable, he conveys the point—already established through different means in *Jonathan Wild*—that Newgate *corrupts*. In Fielding's eyes, the lesson is one for a whole society, not only for magistrates.

NOTES

1. See Pat Rogers, *Henry Fielding: A Biography* (London: Elek, 1979), *passim*.
2. *The Covent-Garden Journal* is particularly valuable for the light it throws on the propagandist convergence of Fielding's interests as magistrate and journalist, reflected in such comments as this, in the issue of 1 February 1752: 'More shocking murders have been committed within this last year, than for many years. To what can this be so justly imputed, as to the manifest decline of religion among the lower people. A matter which, even in a civil sense, demands the attention of the Government.'
3. M. C. Battestin has stressed the degree to which *Tom Jones* reveals 'the pressure of [Fielding's] personal circumstances and the climate of life and thought in which he wrote', and offers 'a world in which fiction and actuality coalesce' (General Introduction, xxxiv, Wesleyan edition 1974).
4. For detailed 1749 chronology, see M. C. with R. R. Battestin, 'Fielding, Bedford, and the Westminster Election of 1749', *Eighteenth-Century Studies*, XI, 2 (Winter 1977–78), 143–85.
5. Cf. *A Charge to the Grand Jury* [1749]: 'Grand juries, gentlemen, are, in reality, the only censors of this nation. As such, the manners of the people are in your hands, and in yours only. You, therefore, are the only correctors of them. If you neglect your duty, the certain consequences to the public are too apparent; for, as in a garden, however well cultivated at first, if the weeder's care be omitted, the whole must in time be over-run with weeds, and will resemble the wildness and rudeness of a desert; so if these immoralities of the people, which will sprout up in the best constitution, be not from time to time corrected by the hand of justice, they will at length grow up to the most enormous vices, will overspread the whole nation, and, in the end, must produce a downright state of wild and savage barbarism.'
6. Rogers comments 'How improbable it would have seemed, only a decade earlier, that the roistering garret-writer should have arrived at the judicial bench' (*Henry Fielding: A Biography*, p. 164).

7. *Tom Jones*, ed. R. P. C. Mutter (Harmondsworth: Penguin Books, 1966), p. 35.
8. See M. C. with R. R. Battestin, 'Fielding, Bedford, and the Westminster Election of 1749'.
9. Ibid., p. 180.
10. See Peter Linebaugh, 'The Tyburn Riot against the Surgeons', in E. P. Thompson *et. al.*, *Albion's Fatal Tree: Crime and Society in Eighteenth-Century England* (London: Allen Lane, 1975).
11. On Sir John Fielding, see Leon Radzinowicz, *A History of English Criminal Law and its Administration from 1750* (London: Stevens & Sons, 1948 ff.), Vol. 3 (1956), pp. 13–62.
12. M. C. with R. R. Battestin, p. 184.
13. *Select Committee Report on the Police of the Metropolis*, Minutes of Evidence, 6 June 1816. On changes and continuity in the eighteenth and early nineteenth century debate about crime and the need for organized police, see Donald A. Low, *Thieves' Kitchen: The Regency Underworld* (London: Dent, 1982), Chapters 2 and 3.
14. Cited by Radzinowicz, pp. 11–12.
15. In 'Henry Fielding and the Criminal Legislation of 1751–52', *Philological Quarterly*, L (1971), 175–92, Hugh Amory rejects claims put forward by Radzinowicz and other scholars that Fielding directly influenced Parliamentary measures in 1751–52. The evidence is finely balanced; but it is clear at least that Hogarth and Fielding created a new level of public awareness of social problems in London.
16. Ronald Paulson, *Hogarth: His Life, Art, and Times* (New Haven and London: Yale U.P., 1971), Vol. II, p. 97.
17. *The Works of Henry Fielding Esq.*, ed. Leslie Stephen (London: Smith & Elder, 1882), Vol. VII, p. 176.
18. Ibid., p. 161.
19. Ibid., pp. 163–64.
20. Ibid., p. 180.
21. Ibid., p. 240.
22. Horace Walpole, *Memoirs of the Reign of George II* (London: H. Colburn, 1836), Vol. I, p. 44.
23. Cf. *A Proposal for Making an Effectual Provision for the Poor, for Amending their Morals, and for Rendering Them Useful Members of the Society* (1753). Malvin R. Zirker, Jr. discusses both this treatise and the *Enquiry* in *Fielding's Social Pamphlets* (Berkeley and Los Angeles: University of California Press, 1966).
24. *Works*, Vol. VII, p. 224.
25. Ibid., p. 225.
26. *Treatise on the Police of the Metropolis*, (6th edn., 1800), p. 520.
27. Quoted in Wilbur L. Cross, *The History of Henry Fielding* (New Haven: Yale U.P., 1918; reissue New York, 1963), Vol. III, pp. 109–10.
28. *Jonathan Wild* and *The Journal of a Voyage to Lisbon*, intro. A. R. Humphreys (London: Dent, 1973), pp. 193–94.
29. Ibid., pp. 192–93.
30. *The Penguin Book of Eighteenth-Century Verse*, ed. Dennis Davison

Mr. Fielding of Bow Street

(Harmondsworth: Penguin Books, 1973), p. 243.

31. *Jonathan Wild* and *The Journal of a Voyage to Lisbon*, p. 194.
32. *Amelia*, ed. M. C. Battestin (Oxford: O.U.P., 1983), p. 21.
33. Dorothy George, *London Life in the Eighteenth Century* (1925; Harmondsworth: Penguin Books, 1965), p. 19.
34. *Amelia*, pp. 21–2.
35. Ibid., pp. 24–5.
36. Ibid., p. 25, n. 1.

2

Fielding's Politics

by MORRIS GOLDEN

Fielding imagined in an atmosphere heavy with politics. It fed him as a writer, though as a man—mentally more at ease on the side of administration than in opposition—he would have preferred untroubled air. Of the major literary figures of his day he was the most deeply and extensively involved in the regular activities of politics, arguing partisan issues like taxes, wars and the conduct of elections, pursuing rewards, and mingling with dignitaries more routinely than Johnson, Smollett, Swift and Defoe. Fielding joked about politics in his early plays, wrote political farces and pamphlets, and conducted three partisan newspapers—to make the experience full, the first in opposition, the other two for an administration. After he assumed the magistracies of Middlesex and Westminster (through the patronage of the very political Duke of Bedford), everything he did and published was attacked by the opposition press, though his pamphlets on social problems and his fourth newspaper, the *Covent-Garden Journal* (where he defines 'PATRIOT. A Candidate for a Place at Court. POLITICS. The Art of getting such a Place'[1]), were intended to be non-partisan.

Whatever his temperamental or psychological orientation, Fielding was by family and social ties a Whig from the beginning. Whichever leaders he followed at particular times in his career, for whatever reasons, they were always Whig leaders, never Tories. But in Fielding's adulthood the Tories were merely a part of the Opposition, first to Sir Robert

Walpole, then to a Whig coalition, and finally to Henry Pelham. The question for most of Fielding's political contemporaries who were not shaped into Toryism by eccentricity (like Johnson) or family (like Smollett) was, what sort of Whig to be. For Walpole? For Pulteney and Carteret? For Argyll and Chesterfield? For one or the other of these at different times, possibly by way of the Prince of Wales's floating opposition?

During Fielding's initiation into adulthood and political London from 1728 (when he was 20) to the fall of Walpole in February 1742, Whigs and Tories both claimed to adhere to the Constitution and the principles of the Glorious Revolution of 1688. But Whigs, including Fielding, were generally identified with the Protestant succession; a limited monarchy, with its limits loosely agreed on; a due balance of influence among landowners (gentry and aristocrats) and merchants-craftsmen-labourers; liberty of the subject, again loosely agreed on, for there was always danger of a licentious explosion of power in one area or another; a parliament to represent these free subjects and keep the king's prerogative within proper bounds; and for the conduct of government a group of men, none pre-eminent, to act as agents of both king and parliament. Tories were presumed to be high-church Anglicans devoted to the church establishment, the king's prerogative (though not the Hanoverian incumbents themselves), and the privileges of the country landowners, with a 'reflexive dislike of central, as opposed to local, administration'.[2] On 13 September 1740 Job Vinegar, a Fielding persona in the *Champion*, described the TRYs and WHGs, the most prominent animals in a land to which he had voyaged, as pretty much the same. A Whig, he says, is slightly smaller than a Tory, whose love for ale has fattened him (and whose only ideological feature is an ultra-high-church orientation), but 'otherwise scarce distinguishable from him by the Eye'.[3]

In his influential *Dissertation upon Parties* (1735), Bolingbroke argued not only that parties were bad—the old view of opposition to the king's government as divisive faction, mordantly expressed at the infancy of the English party system in Dryden's *Absalom and Achitophel*—but that in fact the words Whig and Tory were now meaningless. Court party and Country party, he wrote, would accurately describe the current opponents.[4] Confounding further any attempts to make neat distinctions, in Fielding's time the City merchants, usually in opposition over taxes and insufficient protection on the high seas by Walpole's pacific government, were in fact sympathetic to Tory and off-centre Whig positions; and the financiers, the great merchants concerned in international companies and banking, approved of Walpole and his successor in the Whig mainstream, Henry Pelham. In general, the Tories, partly because their theories affirmed the king's prerogative to keep his ministers, were less inveterately against Walpole than their occasional allies in Opposition. It was the Whig Samuel Sandys who asserted a major Opposition charge in his famous Motion of 13 February 1741 for Walpole's removal: that by the very fact of being a prime minister he was disrupting the Constitution, which assumed only one monarch with a variety of servants. A number of Tories marched out before the vote on the Motion, and some others voted against it.[5]

Although Fielding took his political jokes where he could in his early farces, he had come to London from a distinctly Whig family and he early cultivated his famous relative Lady Mary Wortley Montagu, who was a Walpole supporter. To her Fielding dedicated the printed version of his first play, *Love in Several Masques*; he cited her as having approved his *Modern Husband*; and for her he wrote poems (possibly in her literary wars with Pope) in which he praised Walpole as the country's Protestant bulwark.[6] In the early 1730s a playwright for Drury Lane (the theatre licensed to the administration favourite Colley Cibber), dedicating *The Modern Husband* (1732) to Walpole and addressing two poems to him, Fielding would then have been seen as a supporter of Walpole, perhaps in return for money.[7] But as the elections of spring 1734 approached, he signalled a change, moving from Drury Lane to the Haymarket and dedicating to the Opposition leader Chesterfield his *Don Quixote in England*. In it, he exposed the corruptions of modern England (featuring election sequences in an advertisement for the printed version in the *Universal Spectator* of 20 April 1734), the charge *ad nauseam* against the 'Great Corrupter' Walpole. This move allowed him to stage a number of political farces, culminating in the immensely successful *Pasquin* (1736) and the pointedly anti-Walpole *Historical Register for 1736* (1737). The Licensing Act of 1737, chasing Fielding out of the play-writing business and into legal studies at the Middle Temple, confirmed his opposition to the prime minister.

At this time he entered the arena of political journalism, where he stayed, with one significant interruption, for over a decade. His school friends Lyttelton and Pitt, and their current ally Chesterfield—who had spoken memorably against the Licensing Act in the Lords—came to his rescue, supporting him in their new political organ *Common Sense* (named for his character in *Pasquin*) and presumably helping him initiate his own Opposition paper, the *Champion*, in November 1739, under the name of Captain Hercules Vinegar.[8] As director of this conspicuous paper, he also fought the related London battles. His accurate analogy of the Common Council with the House of Commons[9] implies the corollary, of the Alderman with the Lords; and as in the Lords Walpole was secure, so he kept a majority with the Aldermen—who elected the mayor. Fielding seems to have participated in the turbulence of the mayoral election of September–October 1740, both personally and as journalist. According to a taunting account in the 9 July 1740 *Daily Gazetteer*, for example, a meeting of the Half-Moon Club, of merchants influential in London, voted to give the needy author of the *Champion* a pair of shoes, two shirts, a coat, and a badge with the city arms on it. As the election, between the aldermen Heathcote (Walpole's candidate) and Godschall (the Opposition's) warmed up (see e.g. the Opposition *London Evening Post* of 27–30 September and *Daily Post* of 15 October), the *Daily Gazetteer* of 20 October repeated an earlier report that the Opposition merchant-poet Richard Glover had been in the chair of a noisy meeting in Vintner's Hall, made a speech, and given it for printing in the *Champion* to 'his good Friend Capt. *Vinegar*, who appeared there as one of the Liverymen of the City of London' amid a mob of rabble. On 12 November, it laughs at Fielding as a quixotic propagandist for mob rule.

As the parliamentary attacks on Walpole gathered momentum, a print on the February 1741 Motion to remove him gives a sense of Fielding's position: captioned 'The Political

Libertarians, or Motion upon Motion', it shows among others
'The Champion', holding 'Pasquin' and 'Common Sense', 'led
by the nose by [the chief Opposition leader] Pulteney'.[10] But
Fielding had never been able to maintain simple party loyalty,
at least in opposition. The perception of seediness on all sides
that he had dramatized in *Pasquin* tended to poke into his
official political writings. Since the quarrels were within the
Whig family, allegiances among its members did not seem as
morally definitive as Fielding at times argued in his partisan
papers. Indeed, even his most partisan, the *Jacobite's Journal* (of
26 March 1748) claims a political writer's right to change sides
on the same principle as the lawyer's right to work for whoever
hires him, at least in times of national calm. He was
ambivalent about motives, sometimes including his own. A
January 1740 piece on turncoats suggests Fielding's sense that
some opposition was merely a wish to be in rather than out:

> It must be granted [he writes] that no Man is so good a Judge of
> the true Merits of a Cause, as he who hath been on both sides of
> it. It is not sufficient to say, that this Knowledge may be
> acquired by a strict Examination into them: It is notorious,
> that, while a Man is attached to one Party, he is always partial
> in his Enquiry; nor is he indeed able to search to the Bottom,
> there being Secrets at the Bottom of all Parties, which no one
> discovers but to Men of the same Principles. So that,
> thoroughly to understand which Side of the Question hath the
> greatest Right, it is perfectly necessary for a Man to have
> declared himself on both. (*Champion*, I, 180)

It is dangerous, for example, to stay in one party when the
other is in power, as witness Charles I–Cromwell–Charles II–
James II–William III; one loses friends by being doctrinaire;
one may be mistreated by one's party, and that's a reason to
change, as is a good large offer of money from one's opponents
(*Champion*, I, 181–82). Although the irony was made overt in
the last few paragraphs, his mind had played sympathetically
with a number of persuasive arguments for change.

A letter from the persona Nehemiah Vinegar on 14 February
1740 most elaborately indicates the conflicting directions of
the arguments. His friends want him to 'apply myself to
Politics' instead of moral essays. Those against the administration say that now

Poverty like a Deluge seems breaking in on the whole Nation, when Trade is almost at a Stand, and our Manufactures at an End; when the Poor are a greater Burthen than the Land Tax was last Year on our Estate, and yet are but scantily provided for. When Luxury hath insinuated itself amongst all Ranks of People, and introduc'd her Daughter Corruption along with her. When the poor, slavish, racked Tenant, with all Industry and Success, can scarce pay his Rent, and waits but a Year of general Plenty or Dearth to be undone, when his Landlord Languishes for Quarter-Day, to pay his hungry Tradesman, who is as impatiently solicited by his Merchant; the two last of which live as much beyond their Gains, as the Gentleman beyond his Estate, when a prodigious Debt, a useless Army, an immense Fleet, and dreadful Taxes to support them, when a dilatory War, formidable Enemies, and suspicious Allies hover over us.

On the other hand, the pro-administration people say that it's a grand time, when

> we have as strong Fleets as heart could wish, and as fine an Army as a Man would desire to see on a Summer's Day, . . . that every Thing is in the most flourishing Condition, and never greater Plenty of all Kinds of Provision, both for Man and Beast, and all owing to those who have been abus'd by a set of infamous, base, false . . . Fellows. (*Champion*, I, 267–68)

The antis offer as rewards 'Reputation, Honour, Fame, and the like'; the pros 'ask me, if I have no Love for my Family, and talk of Vacancies, good Things, snug Places, &c' (I, 268–69). Fielding ends with a list of embarrassing questions for the ministry, but even the partisan weighting does not destroy the alternative view that he has provided.

Fielding had moved from Walpole to the Opposition in 1734, and now on the verge of the great election he was reconsidering. After the *Champion* and *Shamela*, when he was making headway on the *Miscellanies* and probably both *Jonathan Wild* and *Joseph Andrews*, the tumultuous events of late fall and winter of 1741–42 led him to write—possibly for Walpole's money—*The Opposition: a Vision*, an attack on the selfishness of the Opposition leaders that appeared on 15 December 1741.[11] Still dissatisfied with politics and political journalism, in the Preface to the *Miscellanies* he promised to publish nothing anonymously henceforth, but he withdrew the promise in the preface to his sister's *David Simple* (1744).

After other pieces for Pelham and the Broad Bottom coalition, he returned to the journalistic wars in the con-genially positive persona of *True Patriot* on 5 November 1745. Most of the early numbers, on the dangers posed by the Rebellion, constitute the least controversial of his political writings—for who was going to defend it? In keeping with the theory of a broad bottom, publicized by Bolingbroke in the 1730s, affirmed by Chesterfield early in the 1740s, and now practised by Pelham, Fielding professed non-partisanship. But as the danger from the Rebellion decreased, his praise of the ministry rose in frequency, as did his attacks on the opposition as faction. Selfish merchants (No. 11) and luxury lovers (No. 23), he says, resent the expense of money and energy for defeating the Rebels. Party spirit, which led the abhorred Carteret and Pulteney, now Earls Granville and Bath, to try their ignominious forty-eight-hour ministry (No. 16), corrupts even literary and dramatic criticism (No. 18). Now (No. 17), against an honourable, patriotic group of leaders, who 'have given . . . Proofs of their Integrity' by quitting rather than serve under Granville and Bath, it is clear that

> Opposition is really and truly Faction; that the Names of a Patriot and Courtier are not only compatible, but necessarily conjoined; and that none can be any longer Enemies to the Ministry, without being so to the Public.[12]

Pieces after Culloden offer gratitude to God and to his instruments the Duke of Cumberland and the wise admin-istration (Nos. 26 and 27) and point out Fielding's prominence in the 'String of Loyalists, who would have had the Honour of being hanged had the Rebellion succeeded', while praising the Duke and the King in raptures that were widely reprinted. After this non-partisan respite, the tone of the paper returns to querulous irritation with the nay-sayers in May and June.

About a year and a half after the *True Patriot*, and after writing other pieces for the Pelham administration to influence the election of 1747 against Prince Frederick's people, Fielding initiated the intensely partisan *Jacobite's Journal*, perhaps, as the 16–18 February *London Evening Post* sneered, primarily to answer that paper:

> Ass as thou art, Thou wouldst not have to *eat*,
> Did not the London Ev'ning give Thee Meat.

But he had a whole group of the opponents arrayed against him, some like *Old England* and his former colleague Ralph's *Remembrancer* developed for the current campaigns, and others like the *Westminster Journal* and the *Daily Post* long-term spokesmen for a variety of oppositions.

Particularly while Fielding maintained his Jacobite persona in the first sixteen numbers, he could pretend that his opponents were old-style Jacobites and thus flail away at their presumed mad absolutist principles. This helped him, for example, to destroy the Opposition objections to the ministry's war policies—the 'only important issue facing the Administration that year'[13]—by calling them the Jacobites' creed (No. 6, of 9 January 1748). Prominent among the delusions to which Jacobites were prone, he says (Nos. 1 and 33) is danger to the liberty of the press: always an opposition concern, that he himself had urged in the *Champion*. But one can expect no better of lunatic slanderers who (No. 15) seduce to Jacobitism the needy, the ignorant, and the uneducated country younger brothers who do not know about 'Athenian Liberty and old Rome'. To make his consistent point that Opposition was deviance, he could have sane letter writers to his crazy persona, as in No. 4, of 26 December 1747, where a liberally educated reader claims that against the French threat the vast majority of the English, including the greatest nobles, the wealthiest citizens, and the merchants of London, support the Ministry and the king.

But most of the papers defend the administration in less general terms, on specific issues. No. 9, of 30 January 1748, shows that only selfish merchants and booby Jacobite squires would oppose the administration decision on grain exports to France or on maintaining Hanover and the Hanoverian mercenaries. No. 11 exposes the evil that motivates attacks on an unpopular bill designed to encourage selective immigration by offering to naturalize some Protestants, at the same time dissociating Henry Pelham from it. In No. 24, of 14 May 1748,

Fielding calls a blessing on the Ministry of peacemakers, which in accepting the preliminaries of peace after the bad war it had inherited was reviving the nation. 'An Englishman's' letter in No. 43, of 24 September, rebukes the Opposition tumult over ceding Cape Breton in the peace treaty, pleased that

> in the Circle of this Administration are contained Men of the most known Abilities, of the longest Experience in Business, of the largest Property, and of the most confirmed Integrity that are to be found in the whole Kingdom.

After Fielding's magistracy, he was regularly abused by the Opposition, whether for publishing novels—*Tom Jones* in 1749 and *Amelia* in 1751—or for judicial actions. In 1749, for example, he remanded two young men for trial for leading a riot that pillaged and destroyed a brothel. The execution of one, Bosavern Penlez, became a political cause; when Fielding wrote a pamphlet arguing that he was guilty, he was called a murderer and tool of the brothel owners. In the acrimonious Trentham-Vandeput election for Westminster M.P. in 1749–50, the Opposition press accused Fielding of certifying illegal votes for Trentham to please his patron and Trentham's sponsor, the arrogant Duke of Bedford, and of attempting to intimidate a free citizenry with riot laws.[14] But even his enemies in the press printed the marvellously vivid releases on his court hearings, and one friendly response to his *Enquiry into the Causes of the Late Increase of Robbers* (1751) located an essential quality, literary as well as social, that Fielding had developed in his political immersion. In the pamphlet, the *Monthly Review* said, Fielding showed his unparalleled knowledge of

> that class which is the main subject of this performance, a class of all others the most necessary and useful to all, yet the most neglected and despised: we mean the labouring part of the people.[15]

To follow the main lines of Fielding's political thought through his career, we need to look past the arguments over bills and techniques of the moment, for or against taxes and military commanders, toward what sort of world he wanted. And then we find, I think, that he is a novelist and not a political philosopher, with no new theories but a vivid wish for national prosperity, safety, and order, so that the citizens—labouring class to landed gentry—could be prepared and permitted to fulfil their capabilities. In the Preface to the *Increase of Robbers*, his last, most ambitious conception of the commonwealth—which he had first elaborated in a 2 February 1740 *Champion* piece (I, 233)—he assumes that the constitution of a state, its ideal pattern, like the harmony of the soul or of a properly tuned musical instrument, derives from the proper relationship of its parts. If the customs and conditions change, the constitution inevitably changes even if it looks the same from outside. Since the best constitution was early in English history, the great changes of the past centuries have upset the desired balance. Although the flowering of trade yields many benefits, such as national greatness and advances in practical learning and in comfort, it has also led to the morally ambiguous increase in the independence of the common people and to the vicious, disproportionate increase in the power of money beyond the control of justice. The wealthy tradesman, not humanized by the kind of education that used to make gentlemen, laughs at law. Luxury seeps down, as nobles try to live like princes, gentlemen like nobles, tradesmen like gentlemen, and even 'the dregs of the people' want more than is their due, giving up jobs to become idlers, beggars, or thieves. Since the law is powerless to deal with high or rich offenders (as he had already said in the *Charge to the Grand Jury*, 1749), the civil power must control the lower social groups severely, for example limiting the right of the unemployed to wander.[16]

Fielding's desire for order in the state, underlying all of his attacks on Jacobitism and republicanism—neither of which had many followers—complicated by a fascination with the vitality of disorder, had formed the base for his anti-Walpole stand in the *Champion*. He stated it most fully in a leader of 8 May 1740, where he compares the functioning state to a

> grand Machine, which, like a piece of Clock-work in right Order, moves steadily and regularly by fixed and certain Laws.
>
> Now, as in the mechanical Machine, if any Body intervenes, which hath no Function assigned it by the Maker, it must necessarily disorder the Operation, and in Proportion to the

43

Weight and Power of this intervening Body, will be the Confusion and Disorder occasioned by it; the same must happen in the Political, whenever any Person intrudes into a Place, where, by the original Constitution of the Government, he ought not to be; for nothing can move by the Laws assigned it at its Creation, unless what preserves the same Form it had when those Laws were assigned.

But if the *Place to stand on* be found out, if a Man once discovers a Method of governing and setting this grand Machine in Motion, when and as he pleases, he may then turn round the Commonwealth at his Will, and . . . may play Tricks with it like the Master of a Raree-Shew, who sets Kings on their Heads, makes the Czar of *Muscovy*, the King of *France*, and all other great Personages dance at his Command in whatever Manner he pleases.

The Reader, I believe, already perceives that I point directly at a Prime Minister, a Magistrate, who, tho' not consistent with our Constitution, nor countenanc'd by our Laws, hath often found Means to insinuate himself into the Political Machine, and sometimes hath made a Handle of the Prerogative, by which he hath managed the whole according to his pleasure. . . .
(II, 188)

This great danger usually appeared to Fielding to rise from some ambiguous element, as much capable of good as of bad, going out of control by human and universal law; he had been formed in a world where Walpole appeared in caricatures as a colossus. Along with power went corruption, which—from Fielding's earliest understanding of the matter, and subverting his medieval vision of order—was exuded by the high and powerful and spread from them to poison the lower estates. His fiction is filled with figures wielding almost absolute power locally; and their deficiencies, usually tied to some form of sensuality in the bad and to delusion in the good, lead to the real or apparent corruption of those below. His most sinister early figure is Lord Richly of *The Modern Husband*, who corrupts whomever he touches; his worst late one, the Noble Lord of *Amelia*, the literal source of disease as well as the symbol of a corrupt society.

At the same time, Fielding conceives a world where vitality is shown by divergence, where order is as much in danger from the mechanical as from the impassioned. Freedom is as high a good as order in his world, and the two are sometimes incompatible, as he could best see when he wrote on the side of administration. For the opposition writer disorder follows excesses by authority; the government defender must always find room for liberty. The *Jacobite's Journal* No. 29, for example, affirms the liberty of the press even when slanders abounded:

> This is an Effect of that Licentiousness which will always, in some Degree, spring up in the same Soil where Liberty flourishes; nor can the nicest Hand of the Legislator totally pluck up and eradicate the former, without doing, at the same Time, some Injury to the tender Root of the latter.

Another unsettling element in the state was Party. As an Opposition writer he blamed party division on the minister, but consistently (even in the plays and fiction while he was an Opposition partisan) he conceived it as a mere cloak for selfishness. According to No. 42 of the *Jacobite's Journal*, in being subject to the party spirit people are inferior to animals:

> Party: A Word by which I would be understood to mean, a certain blind Instinct, that without any Foundation of Reason, or any Temptation of Interest, impells Men to act and to talk in the most absurd and unaccountable Manner; with the greatest Zeal and Fury to pursue their own Destruction, and with the utmost Inveteracy to fly in the Faces of all who would preserve them from it.

A Jacobite (or Opposition party man) is more like a machine, like 'a Ring of Bells', moved by non-rational impulses or the will of its owner, than an animal, which has at least the natural guidance of instinct.

Lacking the independence of liberal education, the multitude—of whatever social station—can be moulded by party, as it cannot check the passions or judge actions. Evil politicians, like those who mislead the young, he says in *Jacobite's Journal* No. 45, try to

> inflame the Minds of the People against their best and truest Friends; for before they can hope to accomplish their Ends, it is first necessary to draw them out of the Hands and Protection of an able and faithful Guardian.

Here is one of the clearest ties between his political positions and the themes of the novels. However he may have fashioned his journalism to suit his allegiances, his patrons, or his paymasters, his novels were all his own, and in them he is always concerned for the guidance of the young, the ignorant, and the weak.

In Fielding's general sense of the right commonwealth, as in *Jacobite's Journal* No. 15, education of the citizens is essential. Particularly liberal education, he insists in his newspapers and novels, alone can civilize us. Wrong education brutalizes and corrupts. Hence some of the violence of his attacks on Jacobites, for he sees extreme Tory clergymen as funnelling incivility into the ruling classes, the Thwackums as contributing to the viciousness of the Blifils and the oppression of the Toms; hence the *Jacobite's Journal* No. 22 argues that neither Catholicism nor Jacobitism should be permitted in the schools, because both, being false, endanger the nation. As Coley notes,[17] after decades of Whig appointment bishops were largely Whig; but country clergy were not, and they were the ones likely to educate the young. To some extent at least, Fielding's sense of the public importance of the teacher—amusingly but seriously presented by Parson Adams—reflected a view of his own worth. The highest human functions, as he defined them in *True Patriot* No. 8, are in essence educational. In His wisdom, he says, God varied human abilities so we can be useful to each other, especially so that the few with the right talents can raise the multitude:

> Indeed there are no Characters which are so seldom seen in their highest Perfection, as a great Poet, Lawgiver, and Statesman; as correcting the Morals, reforming the Laws, or regulating the Government of a Nation, are Works which as they demand the highest Talents, require but very few Persons.

By an easy extension *True Patriot* No. 14 applauds another leavening sort, even closer to home:

> those Gentlemen who, by their Writings, have either improved the Understanding, corrected the Will, or entertained the Imagination; such especially as have blended these Talents together, who have temper'd Instruction and Correction with Humour, and have led Men pleased and smiling thro' the Paths of Knowledge and Virtue.

To the journalist-novelist exercising an important educational function in society Fielding adds another rôle he had tried in his first newspaper and kept to his last: judge or censor of the nation. Even the mob, 'the fourth Estate' that terrorizes almost everyone, fears

> two Sorts of Persons. . . . These are a Justice of Peace, and a Soldier. To these two it is entirely owing that they have not long since rooted all the other Orders out of the Commonwealth.[18]

In *Covent-Garden Journal* No. 53, 'Counsellor England', speaking for the whole Town, begs the Censor-Fielding's persona as literary and social judge—not to end the paper, for

> It is you, Sir, who have so nobly stood in the Breach, and have alone defended the Cause of Wit, against the Incursion of an Army of Vandals, who still threaten the glorious Cause with Destruction, and who, had not you opposed them, had long since accomplished their fatal Purpose. (II, 54)

As a Westminster justice, Fielding helped regulate the machinery of government; as the literary Censor, he contributed to the right education of the citizens that alone could give life to the commonwealth. In both capacities, he was applying law to prevent chaos, as in all of his novels it is the law—and only the law—that provides the happy ending, the sense of providential concern as it glimmers in a fallen world.

Into the richer, more responsible conceptions of the novels Fielding brought the ideas and material of the political writings, but not always their allegiances. At times, indeed, the honest world of the imagination insists on exposing the absurdities and equivocations of his nominal party. In them, he portrays the contrast between the ideal and the practical reality of a world in which historical processes—like the problems of succession, foreign power, and trade—have eroded order; in which the borders between the parts of the polity are flexible, negotiable, always subject to change through living; and in which psychological processes contribute to current chaos. Even if the novels affirm the ideal under the surface of phenomena, he always allows for the possible, for life as it is more than as it may be; in art as in life, his politics take increasing account of an unsuccessful war, irreconcilable interests, and political groups united for selfish ends. And by the way, we can assume that the positions taken in the novels were in fact Fielding's and would have been so considered in his day. The narrative persona, the writer of all of Fielding's fiction after *Shamela*, was the public Henry Fielding, with a public record he could not have dodged if he had wanted to.

Since we know a good deal more about the deliberate contemporary allusions in *Joseph Andrews* and *Tom Jones* than we used to, we may at first sight be surprised at the tenor of the references—as for example to the satirized bellicose gentleman in *Joseph Andrews* or to the political affiliation of Bellarmine, the villain of the inserted Leonora story; for Bellarmine's opposition Country party, which had urged war on the unwilling Walpole, had also been Fielding's (as Battestin notes in his edition). In *Tom Jones*, which frequently alludes to the current foreign war and uses the Rebellion to move the central section of the plot, his scorn of minds fed on party clichés of whatever side leads him to make the political talkers the blindest of all: Partridge, Squire Western, and even Mrs. Western, whose clichés are on Fielding's side. *Amelia* alludes scornfully to the popular Opposition cries of Liberty, but is otherwise non-partisan, or even—lamenting corruptive politics and great men—subversive of the administration of Fielding's patrons.

Insofar as the novels recreate the world, Fielding cannot help imagining them with political context and connection. Some of this conception is surely conscious, such as the association of *Shamela*'s Parson Williams (the squire's treacherous appointee) with Walpole[19]; some, like Squire Booby's parallels with George II, would be denied by author and printer; and the hint of Walpole in Shamela herself—raised from a dunghill, deceiving her master, ruling in his place, and so on—may be wholly unconscious. But Fielding's writing habits in the preceding few years, and contemporary political journalism generally, would have made such uses of narrative normal. The *Champion* leader of 12 February 1740, for example, ostensibly a letter complaining that the writer's freehold has been incompetently defended against a neighbouring lord by the steward of the lord of the manor, is a typical allegory about England (the manor), Walpole (the steward), Spain (the neighbouring lord), Jenkins's Ear, and the rest. Fielding was exposing the lies of Richardson's *Pamela*, as we all know, and of Walpole's political supporters Colley Cibber (in his *Apology*) and Conyers Middleton (in his *Life of Cicero*); but he was using a form that in the political journalism of both opposition (especially the *Craftsman*) and administration (*Daily Gazetteer*) often suited allegory. However we read *Shamela*, a book written and published on the verge of the critical election of 1741, it does conclude with the overthrow of a usurping 'young Politician' and the imminent reinstitution of order on the Booby estates.

For *Joseph Andrews* (as for *Jonathan Wild*) the context is the Walpole-Opposition struggle of 1741, the minister's fall in 1742, and the ensuing turmoil. Amidst a world of chaos, Joseph and Fanny have to discern the better world at the base, in the teachings of Adams and the example of the Wilsons. They must suffer the effects of the local absolute rule of Lady Booby, the Wilsons' neighbouring squire, and the Roasting Squire of Book III—the last sharing fox-hunting and a wild open house with Walpole as well as the cynical view of human nature attributed to him by his enemies. When their gentility is recognized, the lovers join the Wilsons in what Adams compares to the Garden of Eden. Insofar as they reflect the nation's best hope, however, the local squire reminds us of the Fall by killing their dog with impunity, and we remember a scattering of selfish powers (like Peter Pounce, the Roasting Squire, and Lady Booby) at large in the land.

In the novel directed at politics, *Jonathan Wild*, Fielding shows the same ambiguities, I think occasioned by Fielding's reflection on his own and his country's changes. As the great professional politician, Wild is scornful of party labels—a position that would be particularly encouraged by the jockeying for power among Walpole's followers, the differing opposition Whigs, and the differing opposition Tories after Walpole's fall. We cannot, however, read it as an allegory developing the events of 1741–42, with Wild, Roger Johnson, Bob Booty, Firebrand, Bagshot, Blueskin, or the 'very grave man' individually representing Walpole, Pulteney, Prince Frederick, Bolingbroke, the Tory leader Windham, Sandys, or any other one person. Wild is the greatest and most varied rascal, presumably most like Walpole, but he does things that at times fit other people more closely, and other gang figures have their Walpole analogies too. As Fielding says in the preface to the *Miscellanies*,

> To confess the Truth, my Narrative is rather of such Actions which he might have performed, or would, or should have performed, than what he really did; and may, in Reality, as well suit any other such great Man, as the Person himself whose Name it bears.[20]

Despite its doses of grimly realistic low life, the book is a sort of parable like Hogarth's Rake's and Harlot's Progresses. Disgusted with Party—the *sine qua non* of politics—Fielding paints politics as purely a struggle among manipulators, who are all dupes as well as exploiters.

Tom Jones shows the most elaborate effect of the various elements of Fielding's political attitudes, including education—where the force of example and humane rule, concentrated in Allworthy, overcomes the harm done by venal tutors (one an Anglican bigot like the Jacobite clergy of Fielding's newspapers) except when exercised on the intractably bad Blifil nature. Much suggests that Paradise Hall is the expression of the royal court; and in Tom and Sophia Fielding shows at least the prospects for England's best youth, perhaps by extension the benign union of epic hero-king and heroine-nation. By the end they are rulers of a great estate, willingly conceded by the heroine's Jacobite father, and they dispense bounty and even greater mercy than Squire Allworthy's. But their wealth has little effect in London, where other powers roam almost uncontrolled. Lady Bellaston continues as predatory as she was, and the Lord Fellamars will remain as arrogantly gullible; elsewhere Blifils lurk in the north, contemplating runs for Parliament. In Fielding's most hopeful period as novelist—after elimination of the Jacobite Rebellion's massive threat to order and the establishment of Pelham's just administration under the just George II—he creates the best polity as the impregnable manorial estate, abandoning the city where wealth and privilege ripen the seeds of evil in the human heart. He can conceive a better polity, he says in his picture of the gypsy king's devoted absolute rule—but he cannot think that such a creature would be found in the real world, or be reliable if found, or if reliable have a similar successor.

At a less exhilarating time for Fielding and the nation, *Amelia* brings its hero and heroine to even more qualified felicity, specifically conditioned on their avoiding London except on the most urgent occasions. As Harrison discovers when he consults his friendly acquaintance the political lord (a likely version of the Duke of Newcastle), the corrupt rich and aristocratic rule London, and through the party system the rest of the nation as well. Only the law functions, when it directly faces simple crimes like those revealed by Robinson. But Fielding does something in this novel special in his work, even more indicative of his sense of a changing national constitution than the contemporaneous *Increase of Robbers*. He creates an associate hero and heroine, practically (though not ideally) good, caught up in and sympathetically representing the social changes that he normally just deplores. Atkinson rises from the labouring class to move into the gentry, paying various social-psychological prices. Besides the pain of knowing he cannot achieve his lifelong ideal (Amelia) and a consequent tendency to despair, he undergoes marriage to a damaged woman who has sinned in ways Fielding does not elsewhere tolerate among the genteel. She has committed adultery, and though she had been drugged her susceptibility had been due to selfish plans for her first husband's rise; she cast her unspotted friend Amelia's good name in doubt to further selfish plans for her second husband; and under stress she drank and bullied her husband. Flawed as they are, the Atkinsons constitute the hope of active England. Friends and admirers of the idealized but retired Booths, these socially mobile people—alternatively, socially unstable, socially disruptive, as they might have appeared in Fielding's earlier fiction (*e.g.* Northerton in *Tom Jones*)—will cope with England's present and coming dangers.

As a political journalist, Fielding had considerable strategic talent, mainly by playing with what then appeared as quixotic buffoonery and contrasting gentility. He confused the Walpoleans (as witness a piece surveying his career in the 30 July 1740 *Daily Gazetteer*) and angered the Opposition to Pelham. However, he sneered at the genre, and if his reputation depended on it, only the dedicated antiquarians among us would know him in the mob. The *Champion* has its stretches of high spirits, the *True Patriot* a couple of vivid apocalyptic dreams, the *Jacobite's Journal* amusing experiments with irony, and all three his clear and vigorous prose. But though he was successful in stirring readers and enemies, he was too thin-skinned for the resulting bitterness, too self-conscious (and self-revealing), and too sensitive to his own compromises for the most powerful political journalism, such as Swift's or Paine's. Even in the newspapers he seemed to enjoy most the novelist's immediate understanding of life, not the theoretical far-off rewards of the politically committed. To judge by the responses of enemies like the *Daily Gazetteer* and *Old England*, his own delight in the irreverent absurdities of Captain Vinegar and John Trottplaid, his pictures of crazy Jacobite squires and mean-spirited merchants, broke the tedium of routinely sober or indignant polemics. In his writings over-all, his best effects came neither from fresh social or political understanding (like Defoe's or George Eliot's) nor (like Swift's and Paine's) from impassioned identification with the mistreated, but from imagining moral or psychological confusions—Lady Booby's attempted seduction of Joseph, Adams's wanderings in the night, Square's embarrassment behind the blanket, Tom and Sophia's discovery of love, the chaotic dinner in *Tom Jones*'s Upton, the masquerade in *Amelia*.

Since we have the novels, we can find additional interest in the journalism: for its definition of characteristic mid-century Whig stances; for its experiments with the complexities of plot, persona, style, tone, and lead essay (source for the famous first chapters of books); for its emphasis on discovering secrets and motives; above all for its forcing Fielding to look past literary convention, stock figures, current sensations, and pure disorder (the bases of his plays) to the actual operations of individuals and social groups in the world. Without the journalism and the experience as lawyer and judge, the novelist might not have developed his special appreciation of the human range and his sense of pattern (law that is not subject to selfish distortion) turning life into history.

Underneath the changing surface of allegiances, the

journalism and fiction express the same political vision of a
traditional ideal long subverted by the energies of selfishness.
Before he came to fiction, Fielding had been a Walpole Whig
at least from 1728 to 1734 and then an Opposition Whig
through spring 1741, when the crucial election loomed. At this
culminating point he wrote his first extended fiction, *Shamela*,
the celebration of an interloper's power, shamelessness, and
defeat by her own arrogance and the national sense of right. In
the next period of deliberate abstention from partisanship, a
political pamphlet (*The Opposition: a Vision* of December 1741)
repudiates the anti-Walpole leaders and two extended fictions
(*Joseph Andrews* and *Jonathan Wild*) picture the best elements in
the nation arriving at precarious havens in a world beset by
political self-interest and tenuously protected by law. After
defending the coalition Pelham administration through the
Rebellion and its only serious election campaign (in the *True
Patriot* and the *Jacobite's Journal*) Fielding completed in *Tom
Jones* a vision of a nation reconciled and flourishing, though
always in some danger from its divisive forces. And in *Amelia*
and the social pamphlets—notably the *Increase of Robbers* but
also the *Proposal for Making an Effectual Provision for the Poor*
(1753)—the sense of apocalypse that had amused him in
Captain Vinegar's buffooneries and frightened him with
visions of Rebel victory, obliged the responsible magistrate to
seek palliation or delay. The solution of the pamphlets—
fatherly restraint of the poor and resigned damnation for the
others—despite a show of practicality only laments the lost
vision of a commonwealth. In the Atkinsons of *Amelia*,
however, the mixture of mobile classes offers dim and
undefined hope for a future polity. After the lifelong espousal
of an unchanging, admittedly quixotic (impossible) order—
aristocratic, even feudal despite the Whigism—he was at last
accepting the legitimacy of opposing energies (which we might
call bourgeois), of worldly compromise without damnation:
the legitimacy, in short, of politics.

53

Henry Fielding: Justice Observed

NOTES

1. *Covent-Garden Journal*, ed. Gerard Edward Jensen (New Haven: Yale University Press, 1915), Vol. 1, p. 157.
2. W. B. Coley (ed.), *The Jacobite's Journal and Related Writings* (Oxford: Clarendon Press, 1974), p. xxviii. For a discussion of differences between Tories and Whigs, see Archibald S. Foord, *His Majesty's Opposition 1714–1830* (Oxford: Clarendon Press, 1964), esp. pp. 136–38.
3. Henry Fielding, *The Voyages of Mr. Job Vinegar* from *The Champion*, ed. S. J. Sackett, Augustan Reprint Society No. 67 (Los Angeles: Clark Library, 1958), p. 33.
4. Henry St. John, Viscount Bolingbroke, *A Dissertation upon Parties* (London, 1754), Vol. 2, p. 251.
5. Foord, p. 139, cogently gives their reasons.
6. See Isobel M. Grundy, 'New Verse by Henry Fielding', *P.M.L.A.*, LXXXVII (1972), 213–45.
7. 'Marforio', *An Historical View of the Principles, Characters, Persons, &c. of the Political Writers in Great Britain* (London: W. Webb, 1740), ed. Robert Haig, Augustan Reprint Society No. 69 (Los Angeles: Clark Library, 1958), pp. 49–50, says that Walpole sent Fielding 'a considerable Supply' to help him out of a country arrest. Sheridan Baker, 'Political Allusion in Fielding's *Author's Farce*, *Mock Doctor*, and *Tumble-Down Dick*', *P.M.L.A.*, LXXVII (1962), 221–31; W. B. Coley, 'Henry Fielding and the Two Walpoles', *Philological Quarterly*, XLV (1966), 157–78; Hugh Amory, 'Henry Fielding's Epistles to Walpole: A Reexamination', *P.Q.*, XLVI (1967), 236–47; and Bertrand A. Goldgar, *Walpole and the Wits: The Relation of Politics to Literature, 1727–1742* (Lincoln: University of Nebraska Press, 1976), pp. 100–15, discuss Fielding's probable relations with Walpole in the 1730s before the Licensing Act.
8. A piece by Tom Gentle, in the *Universal Spectator* of 10 February 1739, may have planted the seed of the persona. It comments on the profusion of current hack writers, including 'Poets that mend Molière, nay, Shakespeare himself'—and Fielding had been a notable Molière mender—and of satirists, 'Drawcansirs of the Grey-Goose-Quill', who have an easy time, for calling names is 'no Herculean Labour'. Fielding's persona is Captain Hercules Vinegar, who like later Fielding personae sometimes refers to himself as a Drawcansir (a character in Buckingham's *Rehearsal*).
9. I use the two-volume collection of *Champion* essays of 1741. *The Champion: Containing a Series of Papers, Humourous, Moral, Political, and Critical* (London: J. Hugginson, 1741), Vol. 1, p. 109.
10. *Catalogue of Prints and Drawings in the British Museum*, Division I, Political and Personal Satires, prepared by Frederic George Stephens and Edward Hawkins, Vol. 3, Part 1 (London 1877), p. 383.
11. G. M. Godden, *Henry Fielding: A Memoir* (London: Sampson Low, Marston & Co., 1910), p. 139, quotes 1 March 1742 minutes of a *Champion* meeting that say Fielding had not written for the paper 'for above Twelve Months past'. Valuable discussions of Fielding's political

positions at this time are in Martin C. Battestin's introduction to his edition of *Joseph Andrews* (Middletown, Conn.: Wesleyan University Press, 1967), xv–xxiv; Henry Knight Miller, introduction to his edition of the *Miscellanies, Vol. I* (Oxford: Clarendon Press, 1972); and Bertrand Goldgar, *Walpole and the Wits*. In general, Battestin and Goldgar believe that Fielding changed sides for Walpole's money, chiefly on the evidence of *The Opposition: a Vision*; I would, however, agree with Miller, and with Coley and Amory (see above, n. 7), that the evidence is significant but not conclusive. The pamphlet, advertised in two-line notices in the *London Daily Post and General Advertiser* for 14 December, *Daily Post* for 15 December, and *London Evening Post* for 12–15 December, apparently created no interest. No opponent brought it up against Fielding in any of the bitter attacks that marked the rest of his life.

12. *The True Patriot; and The History of Our Own Times*, ed. Miriam Austin Locke (University, Ala.: University of Alabama Press, 1964), 25 February 1746.
13. Coley, ed. *Jacobite's Journal*, p. xliii.
14. See M. C. and R. R. Battestin, 'Fielding, Bedford, and the Westminster Election of 1749', *Eighteenth-Century Studies*, XI (1977/78), 143–85; *Remembrancer* of 2 and 9 June 1750 for charges of threatening free assembly.
15. *Monthly Review*, IV (January 1751), 229.
16. Henry Fielding, Esq.; Barrister at Law, and One of His Majesty's Justices of the Peace for the County of *Middlesex*, and for the City and Liberty of *Westminster*, *An Enquiry Into the Causes of the late Increase of Robbers, &c* (London: A. Millar, 1751), pp. xiii–xiv.
17. Coley (ed.), *Jacobite's Journal*, p. lxviii.
18. *Covent-Garden Journal*, No. 49, 20 June 1752; in Jensen (ed.), Vol. II, p. 35.
19. For some Walpole analogies, see Charles B. Woods, 'Fielding and the Authorship of *Shamela*', *P.Q.*, XXV (1946), 248–72 and Hugh Amory, '*Shamela* as Aesopic Satire', *E.L.H.*, XXXVIII (1971), 250.
20. Henry Fielding, Esq.; *Miscellanies*. In Three Volumes (London. Printed for the Author: And sold by A. Millar, opposite to Catharine-Street, in the Strand), Vol. I, p. xviii. For the relation of the politics of the time to *Jonathan Wild*, see William Robert Irwin, *The Making of Jonathan Wild: A Study in the Literary Method of Henry Fielding* (New York: Columbia University Press, 1941) and the articles and editions by Battestin, Miller, and Amory, n. 11 above.

3

Fielding and Shaftesbury Reconsidered: The Case of *Tom Jones*

by LANCE ST. JOHN BUTLER

When reading Shaftesbury's *Inquiry Concerning Virtue, or Merit*, and the other 'treatises' in his principal work, the *Characteristics of Men, Manners, Opinion, Times, Etc.*[1] of 1711, one is struck by a deeper affinity with Fielding than is commonly allowed for. Fielding and Shaftesbury seem to coexist in a wider stretch of moral territory than discussions of the influence of the philosopher on the novelist usually comprehend. The assumption is now current, however, since Martin Battestin's *Moral Basis of Fielding's Art*[2] of 1959, that Shaftesbury is really irrelevant to Fielding and that the notorious opinion of Sir John Hawkins that Fielding's morality is 'that of Lord Shaftesbury vulgarised' is simply inadequate. Battestin makes a convincing case for tracing certain central moral issues in Fielding to their sources in the Latitudinarian divines, Barrow, Clarke, Hoadly, Tillotson and others, with whose sermons and other writings Fielding was clearly familiar. This rather pushes Shaftesbury to one side and he is pressed further into the wings in the discussions of John Preston ('*Tom Jones* and the "Pursuit of True Judgement"'[3] of 1966) and Bernard Harrison (*Henry Fielding's 'Tom Jones': The Novelist as Moral Philosopher*[4] of 1975). It is the contention of this essay that, without prejudice to Battestin's main thesis, there may be a case for reinstating Shaftesbury somewhere near the centre of Fielding's moral world.

Fielding's strategy is to command an easy assent and, in *Tom Jones* particularly, he so organizes his material that the reader concurs with the narrator's moral judgements simply as a matter of common sense. Shaftesbury, too, makes this kind of appeal, going so far as to give the title *Sensus Communis* to the second 'Treatise' of the *Characteristics*. He is not a satirist or a comic writer, of course, and he avoids the creation of strongly marked characters and the irony that are Fielding's hallmark, but he does employ a Fieldingesque strategy often enough. In the fifth and last 'Miscellany' of the *Miscellaneous Reflections* (Treatise VI of *Characteristics*) for instance, he sets up a roomful of religious disputants one of whom is a man of considerable sense who has the best of the argument. The 'passionate reproaches' of his 'zealot auditors' naturally incline the reader to side with this 'Gentleman of some rank' who has been provoked by a 'violent bigoted party'. When his opinions turn out to be moderate, liberal and sensible we find ourselves concurring with them as freely as we concur with Fielding's judgement of Tom when that young man is surrounded by the bigots and monsters of Paradise Hall.

It is not, however, in such matters of technique that the serious comparison between Fielding and Shaftesbury is to be made. The question here has correctly been posed as one of moral content rather than aesthetic form, and this is what must be pursued, but it is worth observing that there is an aesthetic consequence for Fielding of this similarity of content. Both Fielding and Shaftesbury are *moralists*. Fielding is a writer of moralities, even of Moralities; *A Journey from this World to the Next* is nothing but a series of quasi-picaresque moral fables, *Jonathan Wild* exists explicitly and exclusively in a moral dimension and, like *Shamela*, has the economy of a fable in which all considerations extraneous to the central moral point are suppressed. The three main novels, of course, go beyond this, but it is significant that *Joseph Andrews* in part relies on the simple moral equations that can be made between the names of the heroes (Joseph, Abraham) and their biblical prototypes. *Tom Jones*, too, is the fable of Everyman (the hero's names being about as empty of meaning as they could be, he is left a sort of naked Adam or Everyman) who travels through a series of moral parables towards Wisdom (Sophia) and the Heaven of Paradise Hall.[5] These fables are about how to live, not about how to please God (directly at any rate) and that is exactly what we find in the *Characteristics* where each treatise recommends, without early reference to religion, how best to live. Shaftesbury does not tell stories or create fables, but he at least defends, *avant la lettre*, the right of such as Fielding to proceed in the comic way he does:

> Let the solemn reprovers of vice proceed in the manner most suitable to their genius and character. I am ready to congratulate with them on the success of their labours. . . . I know not, in the meanwhile, why others may not be allowed to ridicule folly, and recommend wisdom and virtue (if possibly they can) in a way of pleasantry and mirth. (*Sensus Communis*, Part IV, Sect ii)

Martin Battestin is surely right in his attribution of some of the moral basis of *Joseph Andrews* to the Latitudinarian theologians. But is he right to dismiss Shaftesbury as he does (after all, intellectual influence is a complex and overlapping business and one source need not exclude another) and, in particular, is his thesis adequate for *Tom Jones*? Early in his book, Battestin has this to say:

> The inadequacy of Square's speculative Shaftesburianism is clearly demonstrated by its inability to account for the reality of unmerited suffering (the occasion of Tom's broken arm) or to provide a reliable moral imperative (the encounter in Molly Seagrim's closet.)[6]

He then goes to point out that Square's eventual acceptance of Christianity bears witness to the inadequacy of his philosophy. The ground thus cleared, Battestin makes an admirable case for his Latitudinarians. Without diminishing this case, I think Shaftesbury needs saving from this abrupt dismissal (as it appears in this reference to Square and Tom's broken arm) and there are six arguments that seem to demand this saving which must be deployed before we can reconsider Fielding and Shaftesbury without a referee.

First, Square is no more a good Shaftesburian (even if we

take this term to mean no more than the Deism with which Shaftesbury is branded) than Thwackum is a good Christian. Shaftesbury does *not* maintain, as Square does, that 'such accidents as a broken bone [are] below the consideration of a wise man' or that pain is 'the most contemptible thing in the world' (*Tom Jones*, p. 204). On the contrary, he is careful in the *Inquiry Concerning Virtue, or Merit* to establish the existence of 'private Affections' in all creatures which, insofar as they preserve the creature, are good:

> For if a Creature be self-neglectful, and insensible of Danger; or if he want such a degree of Passion in any kind, as is useful to preserve, sustain or defend himself; this must certainly be esteem'd vitious . . . (*Inquiry*, Bk. II, Pt. I, Sect. III, p. 55)

Now pain is undoubtedly a 'Passion' the want of which will expose a human creature to harm and, as such, is not at all below a wise man's consideration. Furthermore it is the perfect Christian, Parson Adams, who, in the novel that is Battestin's own topic, *Joseph Andrews*, preaches a stoicism which he is then immediately unable to sustain in the episode where he is brought the (false) news that his favourite child has been drowned (*Joseph Andrews*, Bk. IV, Ch. 8). Insofar as Battestin finds sources for this sermonizing of Adams[7] in Clarke and Barrow, he must lay himself open to the charge that here it is the unrealistic injunctions of the Latitudinarian Christians, rather than the ideas of Shaftesbury, that Fielding is criticising. Besides all this *Thwackum* is not held, by any critic who has discussed the topic, to constitute evidence that Fielding was anti-Christian; by the same token Shaftesbury cannot be condemned on account of the behaviour of *Square*. On the occasion of this latter's visiting Tom when his arm is broken it is worth remembering that Fielding has him quote 'sentences, extracted out of the second book of Tully's *Tusculan Questions*, and from the great Lord Shaftesbury' (*Tom Jones*, p. 204). Nowhere does Fielding mock a classical source such as Cicero ('Tully') and, indeed, merely by putting Shaftesbury and Cicero in the same company, he adds lustre to the English moralist's name. In other words, both Shaftesbury and Cicero emerge unscathed from their adoption by Square and the overall impression is that he has simply misapplied their stoical ideas, as his subsequent absurd behaviour implies.

Second, Thwackum is a good deal worse than Square. The solidly built divine is more of a hypocrite and less easily forgivable than the slender stoic. Thwackum's Christianity sits uncomfortably close to the monstrous perversion of that religion by the Blifils *père et fils*. Square's hypocrisy at least has its basis in sexual appetite (Battestin's other example) and in Fielding this is the mark of a potentially good nature. For example, leaving aside the obvious application of this to Tom Jones himself, in *A Journey from this World to the Next* we read that sexual forwardness is 'more consistent with good-nature than with that virtue which women are obliged to preserve against every assailant'[8] and in the 'Essay on Conversation' we are told that sex is 'one of our highest and most serious pleasures' (*Miscellanies*, Vol. 1, p. 148)[9] It must be admitted that Fielding hopes to distribute the palms equally in the contest between Thwackum and Square when he says:

> Had not Thwackum too much neglected virtue, and Square religion, in the composition of their several systems; and had not both utterly discarded all natural goodness of heart, they had never been represented as the objects of derision in this history. (*Tom Jones*, p. 131)

But surely more readers would be prepared to befriend Square than Thwackum, and, if that is too personal a judgement, perhaps it has more force if we emphasize that, even on a crude reading of this summary of Fielding's, of the trio 'religion, virtue, goodness of heart', two of the three items are Shaftesburian. Furthermore, if 'goodness of heart' is the ultimate touchstone, it is more closely akin to the concept 'virtue' than it is to the idea of 'religion'.

Third, the general 'mixture' of moral ideas in Fielding resembles Shaftesbury more than Battestin allows for. He may be right to stress the Latitudinarian elements in Fielding but he is wrong, I think, to imply that Shaftesbury is to be excluded on account of his lack of interest in religion. In fact, whereas the Latitudinarians are orthodox Christians of a more than usually tolerant frame of mind, Fielding, like Shaftesbury, is a commonsense moralist and man of the world, interested in good nature and virtue, who regards religion as the crowning glory of a moral man rather than his deepest reality. It is as if we might say that in Latitudinarianism Fielding found a Christianity that matched up to his humane and human requirements (in which case his position is identical to that of Shaftesbury whose first published work was, after all, an edition of Whichcote's *Sermons*) whereas Battestin indicates a deeply Christian Fielding for whom religion came first and for whom it just happened to be the case that Latitudinarian Christianity was popularly available. For both Fielding and Shaftesbury, in my view, the priorities are aligned: Virtue first, Religion second. Both protest, vigorously if a little unconvincingly, that this is not an *ontological* priority but it does seem that it is a practical, realistic and *de facto* ordering. Tom Jones, as Everyman, starts with a good heart, and it comes as absolutely no surprise to us to learn that religion has to be added to this, as in Mr. Allworthy's well-known comment:

> I am convinced, my child, that you have much goodness, generosity and honour in your temper; if you will add prudence and religion to these, you must be happy: for the three former qualities, I admit, make you worthy of happiness, but they are the latter only which will put you in possession of it. (Bk. V, Ch. VII, p. 228)

This is the mixture as in Shaftesbury:

> And thus *religious Conscience* supposes *moral* or *natural* Conscience. (*Inquiry*, II, II, i, p. 75)

> We may easily conclude, how much our Happiness depends on *natural and good Affection*. (*Inquiry*, II, II, i, p. 78)

> HENCE we may determine justly the Relation which VIRTUE has to PIETY; the *first* being not compleat but in the *latter*. . . .
> AND thus the Perfection and Height of VIRTUE must be owing to the *Belief of a* GOD. (*Inquiry*, I, III, iii, p. 47)

The *order* of moral and religious priorities in Fielding is that of Shaftesbury, not of liberal theology.

Fourth, it seems that Battestin may be a little unfair in his chronological ordering of Shaftesbury and the Latitudinarians. 'In one important respect', he says[10] 'these clergymen differed from Shaftesbury, whose views of human nature they

anticipated' (my italics). This gives a somewhat false impression
in that it suggests that Shaftesbury is less likely to be an *original*
source for Fielding, or anybody else, because his ideas are
largely present in earlier writers. It also makes it seem possible
that Fielding knew of his work later than he knew of that of the
theologians. In fact Battestin makes a point in a lengthy
end-note[11] of attributing Fielding's first knowledge of Barrow
(and possibly of Tillotson, Clarke and Hoadly) to the period
1740–41 whereas it seems that Fielding was conversant with a
wide range of Shaftesbury's ideas at least contemporaneously
with this (the period of the composition of *Joseph Andrews*) and
most probably at an earlier date (the 1737 sixth edition of the
Characteristics is the latest possible one with which Fielding can
have been familiar, and let us not forget that Shaftesbury was
in print with this collection in 1711). Turning to the more
important point about Shaftesbury's originality, some hard
dates are needed to clear this matter up. Shaftesbury was born
in 1671 and the first, pirated, edition of his *Inquiry* appeared in
1699, with the complete *Characteristics* appearing, as we have
seen, in 1711. The first generation of Latitudinarians were
indeed old enough to have 'anticipated' Shaftesbury by a good
distance: Barrow lived from 1630 to 1677 and Tillotson from
1630 to 1694. But Clarke lived from 1675 to 1729, and his
influential Boyle Lectures of 1704 and 1705 were not
published until 1712, while Hoadly lived from 1676 to 1761.
Shaftesbury died in 1713. The Pelagianism of the Cambridge
Platonists (Whichcote died in 1683 and Cudworth in 1688)
and the earlier Latitudinarians may have 'anticipated'
Shaftesbury, but there is a case for seeing him as a contributor
to, rather than a legatee of, the theological debates of the
period. As early as the *Inquiry*, which was being written as
early as 1689[12], Shaftesbury is making his own distinctions
between styles of religion in what seems to be an original way.
Speaking of antidotes to 'ill-humour' he writes:

> If it be said perhaps, that . . . *Religious Affection* or *Devotion* is a
> sufficient and proper remedy [to 'ill-humour']; we answer, That
> 'tis according as the Kind may happily prove. For if it be of the
> pleasant and chearful sort, 'tis of the very kind of *natural*
> *Affection* it-self; if it be of the dismal or fearful sort; if it brings
> along with it any Affection opposite to Manhood, Generosity,

> Courage, or Free-Thought; there will be nothing gain'd by this
> Application: and the *Remedy* will, in the issue, be undoubtedly
> found *worse than the Disease*. (*Inquiry* II, II, i, p. 72)

Here, surely, the young Shaftesbury is putting something in
to the religious controversies of his time rather than reacting to
their outcome.

Fifth, we must deal with the assertion that Shaftesbury is a
prudentialist of the *Pamela* kind, and here we had better quote
Battestin *in extenso*:

> Of equal importance in supplementing natural compulsions to
> virtue were the 'rod and Sweetmeat' incentives of religion. Here,
> especially, Fielding's realistic estimate of the limitations of good
> nature as a universal moral imperative differs from Shaftesbury's
> speculative idealism. One of several reasons for Fielding's
> disapproval of *Pamela* was its mercenary moral of 'virtue
> rewarded' *in this life*.[13]

Battestin goes on to quote the well-known anti-Shaftesburian
dictum of Fielding's that the doctrine 'that virtue is the certain
road to happiness, and vice to misery, in this world' is one to
which he has 'but one objection, namely, that it is not true'
(*Tom Jones*, XV, 1, p. 695). Now there is a confusion in all this
which is pointed up by Fielding's earlier quite opposite
assertion, in the introduction to *A Journey from this World to the
Next* of 1743:

> The greatest and truest happiness which this world affords, is to
> be found only in the possession of goodness and virtue; a
> doctrine which, as it is undoubtedly true, so hath it so noble
> and practical a tendency, that it can never be too often or too
> strongly inculcated on the minds of men. (*A Journey*, p. 3)

With such a contradiction in view we had better make an
estimate of what Fielding seems to believe in practice, and
then of what Shaftesbury has to say on the matter.

In practice Fielding rewards virtue and punishes vice 'in
this life' if anything more neatly than Richardson. Joseph
Andrews and his Fanny come through their trials to the
perfect happiness that we have long known to be waiting for
them; Parson Adams' virtuous temperament makes him
happy under almost any circumstances and is rewarded at the

end of the novel ('a living of one hundred and thirty pounds a year'), while Tom Jones himself (a) is nearly always happy on account of his excellent nature, (b) is made unhappy the moment he behaves badly (Sophia's muff appearing immediately after his infidelity to her, for instance), and (c) is finally handsomely rewarded for his goodness with just about everything a man could want. Blifil, conversely, gets his comeuppance. Mr. Allworthy is contented with life, and with the prospect of death, in direct proportion to his virtue. In all this religion plays almost no part; how often, in *Tom Jones*, do people go to church, for instance? There is not space here to argue the matter in more detail, but it seems clear enough that in Fielding, at least before *Amelia*, there is a connection between happiness and virtue largely independent of the 'rod and sweetmeat' incentives of religion.

Shaftesbury adopts the same position, of course, but both he and Fielding take the matter a little further. They both insist on the 'beauty' of virtue, a point that carries with it an implication of pleasure. It is not merely a question of virtue *leading* to happiness (the question canvassed by Battestin) but of virtue *being* happiness. In the 'Dedication' of *Tom Jones* to George Lyttelton, Fielding talks of offering examples of virtue such that virtue itself can become an 'object of sight . . . and strike us with an idea of that loveliness, which Plato asserts there is in her naked charms'. He goes on to talk of his work 'displaying that beauty of virtue which may attract the admiration of mankind'. Only then does he claim that mankind's 'true interests' dictate a pursuit of virtue (*Tom Jones*, p. 37). This is pure Shaftesbury. The *Inquiry* concludes with the assertion that 'VIRTUE is *the Good*, and VICE *the Ill* of every-one', an assertion preceded by these observations, among others:

> 'VIRTUE, which of all Excellencys and Beautys is the chief . . .'.
> '*Every thing which is an Improvement of Virtue, or an Establishment of right Affection and Integrity, is an Advancement of Interest and leads to the greatest and most solid Happiness and Enjoyment.*' (*Inquiry*, Conclusion, pp. 109–10)

In 'The Moralists' we read 'that beauty and good are still the same'.

This, surely, is the real meaning of Fielding, in spite of his brief lapse into an inconsistent opinion at the start of Book XV of *Tom Jones*. His whole endeavour is to recommend the true happiness that can flow from virtuous behaviour for such beautiful people as Joseph, Fanny, Tom and Sophia. Their happiness, virtue and beauty, as in Shaftesbury, are quite inseparable and, to a well-judging mind, each equally obvious on first sight.[14]

The sixth and final point that should help reinstate Shaftesbury at least on the same level as the Latitudinarians in our understanding of Fielding is the simple one of the numbers of references made to the philosopher in comparison to the number made to the theologians. This may not amount to proof, but granted that the references are not satirical, as they are not, it cannot be entirely insignificant that, in *Tom Jones*, we come across two very slight references to the Latitudinarians (a *very* slight reference to Hoadly, in Bk. II, Ch. 7, and the story in Bk. III, Ch. 9 of Tillotson's sermons being stolen) against three substantial references to Shaftesbury by name (V, 2; VIII, 1; XIII, 12) in which his ideas are used to further the intellectual drift of Fielding's argument. If we turn to the *Miscellanies*, Volume 1, in Henry Knight Miller's 'Wesleyan' edition,[15] we find that Fielding quotes Shaftesbury twice, in ways showing considerable familiarity with his work, while he quotes Hoadly once and the other three divines not at all. Miller's extensive explanatory and comparative annotations call upon the four Latitudinarians seven times in all but bring up Shaftesbury no fewer than twelve times. Other works by Fielding would show a similar proportion and even in *Joseph Andrews*, Battestin's chosen topic, Shaftesbury is quoted, approvingly as always, in the Preface, while his Latitudinarians appear only once in the rest of the text.

In order to get what Shaftesbury would have called 'a right BALLANCE' in our estimate of this matter it seems necessary to see both Shaftesbury and Fielding as themselves intellectually balanced between Stoicism and Christianity, between Square and Thwackum. One might guy Shaftesbury by aligning him with Square, but only at the expense of guying

Christianity by aligning it with Thwackum. Fielding, like Shaftesbury, is convinced of the necessity of religion, but neither writer has very much to say on this topic and I have the impression that there is an element of lip-service in the rather ritualized bows to religion that both make. It is extremely hard to judge in these matters, but I would suggest that although Fielding and Shaftesbury are both serious in their beliefs in God, and genuinely respectful of an unhypo-critical Christianity, they had experienced rather too many of the evils of sham religion for this belief and this respect to sit easily on them. Their writing catches fire, not in praise of the Deity or in the loving exegesis of Christian texts and ideas, but in ridiculing the hypocrisies and 'enthusiasms' of their time. In the *Letter Concerning Enthusiasm* Shaftesbury, who is, as ever, arguing that religious fanatics should be laughed out of their absurdities, turns serious and even frightened when he contemplates the effects of mass hysteria:

> Popular fury may be called panic when the rage of the people, as we have sometimes known, has put them beyond themselves; especially where religion has had to do. And in this state their very looks are infectious. The fury flies from face to face; and the disease is no sooner seen than caught. They who in a better situation of mind have beheld a multitude under the power of this passion, have owned that they saw in the countenances of men something more ghastly and terrible than at other times is expressed on the most passionate occasion. (*Characteristics*, p. 13).

Against this we must set Shaftesbury's cool appeal, in the same letter, to treat religion with 'good manners' and to bring 'good humour' into our dealings with it.

In the same way Fielding devotes more energy and time to the exposure of the Parson Trullibers, the Blifils and the Thwackums than he does to the steady examination of any aspect of Christian doctrine. The whole thrust of *Tom Jones* may be to recommend Christian virtue, but *religion* hardly comes out of the novel very well. It is as if the deceits and evils of religion as generally practised have driven Fielding into the very Shaftesburian position of pleading for virtue (accom-panied by a polite wave to the Deity), while failing to recommend specific religious practice and while castigating most professions of religious faith.

Both Fielding and Shaftesbury have more than a sneaking sympathy with Julian the Apostate. This Emperor, reviled by a certain element in Christian thinking for choosing the older paganism of Rome in preference to the newer religion of Christ, appears as the hero of the *Journey from this World to the Next* where the narrator meets him in Elysium:

> This exceedingly amazed me; for I had concluded that no man ever had a better title to the bottomless pit than he. But I soon found that this same Julian the Apostate was also the very individual archbishop Latimer [via reincarnation]. He told me that several lies had been raised on him in his former capacity, nor was he so bad a man as he had been represented. (*A Journey*, Ch. 10, p. 44)

Thus Julian, for Fielding, is on a level with the great martyr of Protestant England, Latimer, and, after the many incarnations that form the bulk of this volume, gets to heaven. (Fielding's heaven, incidentally, is very nice but seems quite free of angels, saints, prophets and gods.)

Shaftesbury twice refers to Julian in the *Characteristics*. In the *Letter concerning Enthusiasm* he is praised for his tolerance and for his lack of religious zeal while in the second *Miscellany* there is a long footnote about him in which Shaftesbury calls him 'virtuous and gallant' and quotes extensively from an *Epistle* in which Julian argues for tolerance and against the murderous feuding of the Christian sects (*Characteristics*, Vol. 2, pp. 210–12). Julian for both men is a sort of test case; the question posed is whether his virtues outweighed his apostasy and in the case of Shaftesbury (whose *Inquiry* so triumphantly separates virtue and religion) the answer is clear; in the case of Fielding it is very interesting to find it just as clear: if Latimer is a saint, so is Julian.

Central to both Fielding and Shaftesbury is the notion of Good Nature. In Fielding we find many examples of this and many discussions of those examples (as, for instance, in *Tom Jones*, Bk. IV, Ch. 6) and perhaps the best definition of it appears in the poem 'Of Good-Nature' (*Miscellanies*, Vol. 1, p. 30 ff.):

> What by this Name, then, shall be understood?
> What? but the glorious Lust of doing Good?

The Heart that finds it Happiness to please,
Can feel another's Pain, and taste his Ease.
The Cheek that with another's Joy can glow,
Turn pale, and sicken with another's Woe. . . .[16]

This notion, as it appears in Fielding, is too well known to need further rehearsal; what needs stressing is how very close it is to Shaftesburian virtue. In Fielding Good Nature is *entirely* concerned with others; it is defined and measured by our sympathy, even empathy, with the feelings of others, and this sympathy is accompanied by a strong impulse to *do* 'Good'— that is, as we see in *Tom Jones*, to take practical action as a result of the sympathy. In Shaftesbury's *Inquiry*, we are clearly told that 'the publick Good, or Good of the Species' is the measure of goodness and that

> Nothing [is] properly either Goodness or Illness in a Creature, except what is from *Natural Temper*; 'A good Creature is such a one as by the natural Temper or Bent of his Affections is carry'd *primarily and immediately*, and not *secondarily and accidentally*, to Good, and against Ill:' And an *Ill Creature* is just the contrary; *viz.* 'One who is wanting in right Affections, of force enough to carry him *directly* towards Good'. (*Inquiry* I, II, ii, p. 15)

Here we have the same mixture as in Fielding. Goodness springs from a good nature or 'natural temper' which spontaneously sees the 'publick good' and desires it; that is, in less abstract language, which sympathizes with others and wants to help them. In both writers there is the implication of *action*: 'doing Good' in Fielding is represented in Shaftesbury by the vocabulary of action—'carry'd; immediately; force; directly towards' and so on.

This seems to me to dispose of Bernard Harrison's objection to Shaftesbury as a good parallel for Fielding. Harrison has it in *Henry Fielding's 'Tom Jones': The Novelist as Moral Philosopher*[17] that Shaftesbury provides another level above this level of the 'good Creature', a higher level on which man actually becomes *virtuous* first by reflecting on his own behaviour and then preferring, by a second 'affection', the good motions of his heart to the bad ones. This, Harrison maintains, is in contrast to Fielding for whom Tom's virtue resides in a 'somewhat' in his breast which immediately 'prompts' right and avoids wrong and whose use is 'not properly to *distinguish* right from wrong'. (Harrison quotes all this from *Tom Jones*, Bk. IV, Ch. 6 and intends to emphasize the word 'distinguish'.) For Harrison, in other words, Fielding's Good Nature is spontaneous and immediate, while Shaftesbury's is rationalized, abstracted, remote, a 'second order' affair, part of a 'curious category of second-order affections'. But this is no more than a quibble. Fielding's whole purpose in *Tom Jones* is to make a *rational* showcase for good nature, to '*recommend* goodness and innocence', to '*display*' the beauty of virtue and, above all, to '*convince*' mankind that 'their true interest directs them to a pursuit of [virtue]' (*Tom Jones*, Dedication, p. 37, my italics). As we have seen, in the poem 'Of Good-Nature', the first characteristic Fielding identifies is the 'glorious Lust of doing Good' which implies action of a sort for which *thought* must be essential. Besides this, Harrison has grievously and crucially misquoted Fielding. He quotes Fielding's opinion that the 'use' of the 'somewhat' in Tom's breast is 'not properly to distinguish right from wrong', a clause which he italicizes to emphasize the intellectual and rational 'distinguish' against the volitional 'prompt'. But Fielding actually wrote that the use of Tom's 'somewhat' is 'not *so* properly to distinguish . . .' In other words, it (the 'somewhat') *does* 'distinguish right from wrong' (although it also motivates the distinguisher). And, indeed, it distinguishes very nicely indeed, as Fielding goes on to demonstrate by comparing it first with a strongly-reacting critic at a theatre and then, significantly, with a judge:

> To give a higher idea of the principle I mean [the 'principle' in Tom's breast] . . . it may be considered as sitting on its throne in the mind, like the LORD HIGH CHANCELLOR of this kingdom in his court; where it presides, governs, directs, judges, acquits and condemns according to merit and justice; with a knowledge that nothing escapes, a penetration which nothing can Deceive. . . . (*Tom Jones*, Bk. IV, Ch. 6, p. 168)

This is *exactly* the Shaftesburian mixture: good nature 'prompts' us to the good of others and is also identical with the judgement we exercise over ourselves when deciding how to act. It is not 'curious' but only sensible of Shaftesbury to express this, in what is after all a philosophical work, by

establishing a double scheme of 'Affections' towards the good
and 'Affections' towards those affections.

We are on the threshold, here, of another central concept
linking our two writers—Moral Sense. If 'Good Nature' is
primarily thought of as belonging to Fielding, for our purposes
'Moral Sense' starts with Shaftesbury. His notion of this
faculty strikes a balance between immediate feeling and a
more rational 'distinguishing' capacity that is exactly like
Fielding's statements in Book IV, Chapter 6 of *Tom Jones* when
they are quoted accurately. For Shaftesbury the moral sense is
first a matter of immediate perception, just as it is for Tom:

> The Case is the same in the *mental* or *moral* subjects, as in the
> ordinary *Bodys*, or common Subjects of *Sense*. The Shapes,
> Motions, Colours, and Proportions of these latter being
> presented to our Eye; there necessarily results a Beauty or
> Deformity, according to the different Measure, Arrangement
> and Disposition of their several parts. So in *Behaviour* and
> *Actions*, when presented to our Understanding, there must be
> found, of necessity, an apparent Difference, according to the
> Regularity or Irregularity of the Subjects. (*Inquiry* II, II, iii,
> p. 16)

This is a very close equivalent of the first phase of Fielding's
Good Nature which spontaneously responds to moral
situations: Tom perceives an ill and is immediately distressed
by it; he can immediately see and feel the beauty or deformity
of an action from a moral point of view. Taking the example of
Tom's reluctance to court Sophia (which he sees in terms of
not wanting to 'repay' Squire Western's 'hospitality' by
'robbing' him of his daughter and his fortune), Fielding insists
that though Tom 'did not always act rightly, yet he never did
otherwise without feeling and suffering for it' (*Tom Jones*,
Bk. IV, Ch. 6, p. 168). In other words Tom has the first level
of moral sense: he feels there to be an imbalance, a debt that
needs to be repaid, in an immoral action—he perceives and
feels 'Difference' and 'Regularity'.

But Shaftesbury goes further than this. The human mind
'cannot be without its *Eye* and *Ear*; so as to discern Proportion,
distinguish Sound, and scan each Sentiment or Thought
which comes before it'. The mind operates as a censor and
virtue arises when the mind develops from its initial

impressions a 'Science of what is morally good or ill' (*Inquiry* I,
II, iii, p. 18). This is exactly the 'Lord High Chancellor'
judgement to which good natures such as Tom's attain so
easily and which others of us must attempt by reading such
moral tales as *Tom Jones*. For the two stages are really one and
the same 'motion' for the really good nature, and they only
become separated through blindness or evil. For Shaftesbury

> No sooner are actions viewed, no sooner the human affections
> and passions discerned ... than straight an inward eye
> distinguishes, and sees the fair and shapely, the amiable and
> admirable, apart from the deformed, the foolish, the odious, or
> the despicable. (*The Moralists*, Part III, Section 2, p. 137)

It is precisely Fielding's point that Mr. Allworthy does not
'view' the actions of those he judges (he does not really allow
Jenny Jones or Partridge or Tom to *explain what happened*, and
that is crucial to Fielding's meaning here) and he does not
discover the 'affections and passions' which enable us, the
readers, immediately and without difficulty to put very
different constructions on the behaviour of these people from
those adopted by Allworthy. Our strongest feeling on reading
of his misjudgements is 'Oh, if only he *knew!*' for we are certain
that he would then see things in a morally correct light as, of
course, he finally comes to do in Book XVIII.

John Preston, another anti-Shaftesbury critic, in his essay
'*Tom Jones* and the "Pursuit of True Judgement" '[18] of 1966,
makes a very interesting case for the proposition that
'Allworthy *should* have seen through Blifil'. He quotes Mrs.
Miller who, at the end of the novel, has only to see Blifil's face
change to pronounce him guilty ('Guilty, upon my honour!')
as an example of really good judgement. There is a difficulty
here, and it is the old difficulty many readers have had with
Mr. Allworthy and the judgement we are supposed to make of
him. In discussing this question we shall find, contrary to
Preston, that Fielding emerges more rather than less Shaftesburian and that, perhaps, the right way of seeing Mr.
Allworthy is to be discovered in Shaftesbury.

Preston maintains that the fact that Tom 'was never an
indifferent spectator of the misery or happiness of anyone' (Bk.
XV, Ch. 8) gives an un-Shaftesburian emphasis to Fielding's

hero. But, as we have seen, it is precisely Shaftesbury's conception of moral sense that indifferent spectating is impossible in the moral world: the mind cannot withhold '*Admiration* and *Extasy* . . . *Aversion* and *Scorn*' as it 'censures . . . other minds' and their actions (*Inquiry* I, II, iii, p. 17). Mrs. Miller shares with Tom the ability to empathize with others, and with Tom and Shaftesbury an unavoidable insight into the minds of others (here, Blifil's) together with a spontaneous emotion (here, scorn). Of course, mistakes are possible, hypocrisy and concealment can make judgement difficult, but here, too, Shaftesbury comes to our assistance. For him virtue depends on the conscious preference for the right over the wrong; he allows that we may be mistaken about what the facts of a particular case are, but he insists that we cannot claim to be virtuous if we make a mistake about what 'right' actually *is*. Only a perverted moral sense will prefer things that are actually evil. Thus:

> A MISTAKE therefore *in Fact* being no Cause or Sign of ill Affection, can be no Cause of Vice. But a Mistake *of Right* being the cause of an unequal Affection, must of necessity be the cause of vitious action, in every intelligent or rational Being. (*Inquiry*, I, ii, iii, p. 20)

Shaftesbury goes on to admit that there will be doubtful cases as to what is right and claims that, because of this doubt, a slight mistake as to what is right cannot 'destroy the Character of *A virtuous or Worthy man*'. It seems to me that Fielding pleads this amendment in the case of Allworthy. Tom, Sophia and Mrs. Miller have the immediate good nature of the simple creatures of the early pages of Shaftesbury's *Inquiry*. They see the good and the bad at once and exercise judgement accordingly. Mr. Allworthy is like the character who emerges a little later in Shaftesbury's work who is simply mistaken as to fact, who has more complex judgements to make but who can remain 'all-worthy' because his moral sense only requires a rather better pair of spectacles to function efficiently.[19]

What all this amounts to is a case for reinstating Shaftesbury in our battery of intellectual approaches to Fielding, particularly the Fielding of *Tom Jones*. Both men were highly critical of certain trends within contemporary Christianity; both took an optimistic view of human nature and preferred to discuss virtue in terms of goodness of heart rather than in terms of religious belief or practice. In this they were both, confessedly, partial adherents of a liberal tradition in Anglican theology, but they were very alike in the tentative nature of this adherence and, in the end, their mixture of Christian and non-Christian elements is almost identical. Fielding was less of a Christian than the Battestin school allows for (witness the triumphant conclusion of *Tom Jones* in which religion makes no appearance whatever), and Shaftesbury was more of a Christian than is generally admitted, as witness the following from near the end of the *Characteristics* 'As for ourselves [we are . . .] fully assured of our own steady orthodoxy, resignation, and entire submission to the truly Christian and catholic doctrines of our holy church as by law established' (p. 352, *Miscellany* V, Ch. III). If this smacks to some extent of lip-service perhaps we should look more closely at *Tom Jones* and ask whether the Christianity of that novel is not a little formal, too.

NOTES

1. In this essay I have used David Walford's edition of the *Inquiry* (Manchester University Press, 1977). All *other* references to Shaftesbury are to the *Characteristics*, ed. John M. Robertson (1900), reprinted by Peter Smith in Gloucester, Massachusetts, U.S.A., 1963.
2. Martin C. Battestin, *The Moral Basis of Fielding's Art* (Wesleyan University Press, 1959).
3. In Claude Rawson (ed.), *Henry Fielding: A Critical Anthology* (Harmondsworth Penguin Education, 1973).
4. Bernard Harrison, *Henry Fielding's Tom Jones: The Novelist as Moral Philosopher* (Sussex University Press, 1975).
5. Cf. *Tom Jones*, Bk. VII, Ch. 2, where Tom becomes Adam: '*The World*, as Milton phrases it, *lay all before him*.' (p. 303 in R. P. C. Mutter's Penguin edition, subsequent page references are to this edition.)
6. Battestin, p. 13.
7. Cf. Battestin, pp. 50–1.
8. *A Journey from this World to the Next*, ed. Claude Rawson (London: Everyman's Library (Dent Dutton), 1973), p. 45.

9. Shaftesbury took a similar view, and expressed it in terms that apply particularly well to Joseph Andrews: 'The honest man indeed can judge of *Sensual Pleasure*, and knows its utmost Force' (Inquiry, II, II, i, p. 64).

10. Battestin, p. 17.

11. Battestin, p. 159.

12. Cf. Introduction to David Walford's edition of *Inquiry*, p. ix.

13. Battestin, p. 63.

14. And, conversely, vice is its own punishment. See the results of avarice and extravagance (misery in both cases) in *A Journey from this World to the Next*, pp. 52–6 and 59.

15. Henry Knight Miller (ed.), *Miscellanies, Volume One* (Oxford: Clarendon Press, 1972).

16. Cf. also *An essay on the Knowledge of the Characters of Men* (*Miscellanies, Vol. 1*, p. 153 ff.) where this same idea is expressed in prose (p. 158).

17. Harrison, pp. 113–26.

18. In Rawson, pp. 537–53.

19. Interestingly, the very last reference to God in *Tom Jones* (p. 865) is to judgement. Sophia, countering Tom's plea that he is repentant, points out that repentance 'will obtain the pardon of a sinner, but it is from one who is a perfect judge of that sincerity [God]. A *human* mind may be imposed on' (my italics).

4

Fielding's Magisterial Art

by PATRICK REILLY

Not the standard alignment with Richardson but the contrast
with Swift is the more fruitful way to begin assessing Fielding.
The difference between the two satirists is revealed in the very
diverse ways they treat their readers, even to the contrasting
modes of address. Where Gulliver speaks placatingly to the
gentle, Fielding's narrator appeals directly to the judicious,
reader. Swift sets a trap for his prime enemy, the reader, who,
perhaps complacently, certainly with no prior knowledge of
the threat to himself, innocently turns the pages of the *Voyage to
the Houyhnhnms* or the *Modest Proposal* or the *Argument Against
Abolishing Christianity*. We stroll into Swift's courtroom serenely
unaware of the charges against us; we exit condemned, vainly
protesting that we are not Yahoos but victims of some chill
miscarriage of justice, some desperate case of mistaken
identity.

With Fielding we find ourselves in a very different courtroom with a very different judge. There is no trap, no hidden
malice towards the reader as there so frighteningly, finally is in
Swift. Instead there is a challenge, sincere and direct. If
Fielding's novels, like Swift's satires, read us rather than we
them, it is nevertheless in a radically different, much less
demoralizing way. Swift seeks to humiliate, to drive us from
our intolerable pride towards admission of guilt—the only
fitting response to the accusation 'thou art the man'. Fielding,
by contrast, undeviously invites us to act as jurors; there is a
case to be settled, a problem solved, and he genuinely seeks

75

the reader's support in directing him to the conclusion already arrived at by the magisterial author.

If we blunder in Swift and go incriminatingly astray, that is all according to the satiric plan, for it is we who are in the dock. Swift forever leads us on, tempting us into statements that will be damningly used against us. At certain points in this satire—the 'Digression on Madness', the climax of the fourth voyage, the disavowal of primitive Christianity as beyond any reasonable defence or recall—the reader is shockingly left treading air, seeking a toehold anywhere, bewilderingly aware that what he trusted has betrayed him. Betrayal is Swift's business; he is the master of literary entrapment. If we blunder in Fielding, we do so against his wishes, for he has no design to incriminate us. He wants us to share his view of Parson Adams and Tom Jones, of the transported postillion and 'the detestable doctrine of faith against good works',[1] and of all the other judicial problems that surface in his court. Swift despises the reader and contemptuously spurns his offer of alliance: 'I damn such fools, Go, go, you're bit.'[2] How dare we presume to agree. Hence the recurring problem throughout Swift of deciding the meaning—he deliberately frustrates agreement. Fielding, by contrast, tries to recruit the reader as friend and ally, so much so that from the beginning critics have objected to the author's intrusion into his fiction.

Lord Monboddo blames Fielding for gate-crashing his own novels, indiscreetly turning up where he has no right to be.[3] Sir Walter Scott begins by agreeing but changes his mind in pronouncing these chapters of authorial intervention the most entertaining in the book.[4] Today the narrator is generally recognized as being the most important character in Fielding's work. Clearly, those who resent the interventions are objecting to a vital element in Fielding's art. The narrator presides over the book like a judge over a court, always reserving the right to intervene in order to issue a fresh set of directions to the jury; to continue to call them misdirections is simply to advertise one's prejudice against Fielding's magisterial method. The narrator tells us, for example, to apply the moral law impartially to men and women alike: either be harsher upon male sexual offenders or easier on female.[5] The latter alternative is, presumably, the preferred one, but, in any case, we must be just and consistent. As with men and women, so with rich and poor. Fielding knows how severe we are disposed to be on 'whores in rags',[6] how less punitive when the whores are wearing the latest Dior creations—he challenges us as to what really offends us, the whores or the rags. He invites us to agree that there are far worse sins than sexual lapses or drunkenness or swearing, to recognize that a chicken-thief may be the Good Samaritan, or that setting a bird at liberty may, in certain circumstances, be irrefutable proof of malevolence. Nevertheless, though Fielding is an intentionally less baffling interlocutor than Swift, it is not enough that his reader be simply well-meaning; he must also be judicious, able to emancipate the inner truth from the surface appearance.

Central to this quality of judiciousness for Fielding is the need to be able to separate act and motive, deed and doer, and once again the contrast with Swift is instructive. Swift insists upon deeds as being the only reliable indicator of moral worth: a man is what he does—there is no spurious essence to defend us against an inculpating existence, no inner, commendable self to which a man can legitimately appeal against the incriminating evidence of his actual behaviour. A man is the sum of his actions and that is all. Swift supplies a catalogue of sordid, vicious habits as a description of how Yahoos behave; if, under oath, you are forced to confess these habits as your own, then you, too, are a Yahoo and there is no more to be said: *causa finita*. Fielding is far less rigorous and accusatory, exhibiting the generosity of a benevolent judge rather than the implacable pursuit of a Swiftian prosecutor. Not what a man does but what, at bottom, he is—this consoling distinction between existence and essence is, as Coleridge notes, the defining characteristic of Fielding as moralist.[7] Fielding believes that a man may fail himself in his actions, may perform acts which are a libel on his true essence, a treason to his nature; a man may be far better than his actual deeds. Deeds may be a deception. Tom Jones gets drunk and this is reprehensible, but a wise judge will consider the extenuating circumstance, the ungovernable joy at Allworthy's recovery. Blifil frees a bird from a cage not because he loves freedom but because he hates Tom. Even had the bird escaped, Blifil would get no credit; that the poor creature is instantly devoured by a predator simply helps clarify the malice that freed it in the first place. For Swift doing is the mirror of being: the filthy acts of men reveal their rotten hearts. Fielding calls instead for a judicious largesse; a man may look guilty and be innocent. Fielding summons us to judge, Swift to be judged.

Despite Coleridge's insight, it would, nevertheless, be a blunder to attribute to Fielding an antinomian contempt for conduct. Far from upholding faith against works or slighting the importance of deeds, Fielding agrees with Tillotson that 'that man believes the gospel best who lives most according to it'[8]; good living is for him the heart of religion, with doctrinal purity coming a long way behind. Fielding's practical Christianity is in line with Christ's warning that not those who mouth the Father's name but those who do the Father's will shall inherit the kingdom; Fielding's secularized version of the kingdom belongs to those with good hearts, benevolent impulses and actions to match. Actions *are* all-important; we are saved by works, not faith. That this issue mattered to Fielding can be seen in its recurrence throughout his work, but perhaps most obviously by the way it is almost dragged into *Jonathan Wild.*[9] Heartfree outrages the Newgate ordinary by arguing that a good pagan is more pleasing to God than a Christian rogue. Apart from rounding off the set of Heartfree's virtues, this has little to do with the plot, but that only serves to emphasize how large the theme bulked in Fielding's thought.

Still, it would be hard to deny that, for Fielding, essence finally determines existence. Blifil, bad in mind and nature, is incapable of a good action; what seems like one in such a man must be perverted at its root. Hence the paradox in Fielding: actions are *not* all-important. Whatever he does, Blifil is a rogue, rotten at the core. When Fielding ostentatiously refuses to make windows into Blifil—'it would be an ill office in us to pay a visit to the inmost recesses of his mind'[10]—has not the visit, for all practical purposes, in the very moment of its renunciation, been devastatingly paid? Conversely, Tom Jones may commit blunders and worse, but, as a fundamentally good man, is never really wicked, is always superior to his deeds. Gide was troubled that Fielding had no notion of sanctity[11]—by which Gide meant the deliberate, conscious effort to become pure in heart; and it is true that Fielding tends to distrust such effort as the hallmark of the hypocrite, the spoor of Tartuffe. Tom Jones is a hero because he is born with good impulses. When he learns some sense and acquires maturity, this natural goodness will, so we are assured, preserve him from the indiscretions of his youth. Evil stems from the will; it follows that, overt actions notwithstanding, Blifil is wicked and Tom good. The good man, like the good poet, is born, not made. This is the judge's direction to the jury. If there are jurors who are still puzzled, who want to ask, for instance, how one can *become* a good man like Tom Jones and join this elect rather than be condemned with the Thwackums and Blifils, the court ignores the question as irrelevant. The direction has been given; not to comply is to be a juror who rejects the judge's advice.

Fielding's summons implies the confident conviction that the reader has it within him to be a good judge. To be judicious is not enough either; justice without generosity is no help to fallible man. Parson Adams, that *naïf* who 'never saw farther into people than they desired to let him',[12] would make a very unsatisfactory magistrate; to be so consistently, unteachably stunned at the revelation of wickedness is a disqualification in a profession that demands insight into human nature. Yet Adams possesses a quality without which judgement verges upon damnation: mercy for sinners. Told by ·a man, who turns out predictably to be himself a coward, that all cowards should be hanged, Adams rejects this as far too draconian, since 'men did not make themselves'.[13] Weakness should be pitied, not punished; clemency is the best way to help people overcome failings. We search Swift in vain for a comparable lenity. True, Fielding maintains the doctrine of individual responsibility against those who would make society the scapegoat for our sins,[14] but his insistence is always tempered by a readiness for compassion. The really unforgivable sins, for him, are vindictiveness and heartlessness, and these can as easily be found among the respectable as among the arraigned—are, indeed, all too often the occupational hazard, the industrial disease, of those who sit in judgement on their weaker brethren. Fielding the novelist treats his characters with a magistrate's expertise, using his discretionary powers to the limit, extenuating actions in the light of motives; he clearly expects his ideal, judicious reader to do likewise. What kind of judge are you? This is the most important challenge that the reader of Fielding encounters.

Judgement is inescapable. Reading *Joseph Andrews*, we become aware that this is a society with a lust for litigation; people are forever being advised to go to law, to take out actions for damages, to sue for wrongful arrest, by other people who seem happy, if not eager, to forsake their everyday business in order to appear as witnesses. It is a judicial equivalent to the hue-and-cry—just as everyone deserts what he is doing to join in the hunt, so everyone seems stimulated at the prospect of a legal pursuit. The letter of the law has supplanted Christian fellowship as the basis of English life— the lawyer warns his companions in the coach that if they leave Joseph to die they may be charged as accessories to murder.[15] How effective the argument would have been is uncertain because the blasphemous postillion explodes into their deliberations with his own exasperated Christian humanism; what is certain is that Joseph would be still lying naked and wounded in the ditch had he depended upon their Christian compassion.

The narrator of the tale is also in love with litigation, though in his case the passion is wholly laudable. He involves the reader in a series of judgements, with doctrines and people put on trial so that in judging them the reader judges himself. Some of these cases are straightforward as when Adams deplores the fact that money can set people above the law, for even the millionaires will not be so brazen as to dissent.[16] Others are more testing. When Betty, caught in the master's bed by her mistress, defends herself by saying that what she has done is wicked but not unnatural, this is not just a joke; the initially comic antithesis compels the reader to ponder anew the relationship between Christianity and nature or between evil and the particular set of moral rules prevailing in a society at any given moment.[17] The reflection is the more exigent because we know that the narrator-judge, the God of the novel who is made in Fielding's image, proposes a revaluation of values. There are, he suggests, worse sins than the sexual, and marriages that are worse than adultery. Mrs. Towwouse, harsh and unchristian, will have a harder time before this magistrate than the sexually lax but generous Betty; Mrs. Towwouse is a respectable married woman but without a shred of compassion.[18] Those who love much will have much forgiven them.

The book continually challenges us to define ourselves in judging others. Is Lady Booby a figure of tragic intensity, Phaedra in a farthingale, or is she, as the end suggests, a randy woman who quickly consoles herself for Joseph's loss in a young captain of dragoons?[19] Is Joseph, entrenched behind his embattled chastity, a figure of fun, too good to be true (hence dangerously akin to the Blifil breed) or is he really upright and admirable? To help us reach the correct verdict, Fielding prevents us from judging this chastity as too highfalutin by quickly supplying us with an additional piece of evidence: Joseph's resistance is not, as with his biblical namesake, strictly or solely moral—he has a perfectly plausible, natural reason in that he is already in love with another woman.[20]

The central problem of the novel is, of course, the proper assessment of Parson Adams, and here Fielding does not make our task easy. Adam's derivation from Don Quixote has often been remarked; both are naïve idealists in a hostile world. There is, however, one significant difference. Quixote is a fool because the world is not as he pictures it, i.e. full of chivalrous knights, distressed damsels and ogres to overcome. Adams is similarly a fool for a similar reason—the world is not full of people who take the Beatitudes literally and try to live according to them. But Cervantes wrote for a society which had explicitly and even derisively rejected the chivalric ideal as no longer (if it ever had been) viable. Fielding, by contrast, wrote for a society which still claimed to be Christian and which would have been insulted to hear that claim denied. Cervantes tells his contemporaries that they are not knights errant and they unoffendedly, laughingly agree; Fielding tells *his* contemporaries that they are not Christian and they inadvertently prove his case by laughing at the best Christian in the book. They laugh, however, to their own discomfiture, for, in treating Adams as another Quixote, they have been trapped into accepting Christianity as another species of romantic absurdity. The book challenges us not simply to see the goodness in Adams but the double-think in ourselves. The society that treats Adams's beliefs as safely outmoded (just as though they were the antique fictions of a Quixote) condemns itself.[21] The book exists to criticize the world and not its deluded dupe, Adams.

Empson intriguingly suggests an affinity between Fielding and Calvin in that both men had seriously puzzled their heads over the Gospel and tried to give its paradoxes their full weight.[22] Adams is the Gospel paradox incarnate, and it would be unwise to assume that in the case of the world versus Adams judgement is clearly in favour of the former. We realize this the more when we ask what is the heart of Adam's folly. This consists in carrying, admittedly to a comical extreme, a cardinal and, one hopes, an irrevocable principle of English law: a man is innocent until proven guilty. Adams treats every stranger as the sincere Christian he seems and claims to be; if Adams goes so laughably astray over Parson Trulliber, is that finally to his or to the pig-man's dicredit? Fielding tended to be soft on the gullible, on those who are taken in because they believe too much in human goodness. Amelia is not a comic figure as Adams is, and Fielding seriously warns the reader not to be harsh on her for allowing herself to be deceived by a wicked person, since 'to speak plainly and without allegory or figure, it is not want of sense, but want of suspicion, by which innocence is often betrayed.'[23] Perhaps people should be suspicious and wary, but take this to an extreme and you reach the totalitarian mentality of Camus's Jean-Baptiste Clamence or Penn Warren's Willie Stark; everyone, however ostensibly innocent, is guilty and all we need do is dig to find the dirt. 'There is always something'; so says Willy Stark with corrupt assurance, but this only because, like Jonathan Wild, he looks within to find the world.[24] Adams, too, looks within in judging the world, but with vastly different results. The reader must judge whether the world or Adams comes off the worse from their encounter.

The dramatic basis of Fielding's art is long since a commonplace of criticism; the machine perfection of the plots has often been ascribed to the fact that Fielding is the outstanding example of the dramatist turned novelist. Yet even more important for his art, informing every aspect of it, is the equally well-known fact that Fielding was a magistrate. The magisterial bench is a central element in Fielding's work; we enter his novels as though summoned to jury service, to judge action, assess character, scrutinize motive, and, finally, to acquit or condemn. The obligation to be himself a good magistrate presses upon the reader throughout Fielding, though the resolution of *Jonathan Wild* reveals the requirement in its clearest form.

The character without whom *Jonathan Wild* would miss its comic destination and career instead straight towards tragedy is, significantly, nameless, being presented as a function rather than a person. We first meet him as the magistrate who, quite properly, sends Heartfree to prison on the strength of Wild's plausibly concocted evidence. Anyone, not just an innocent like Adams, can be taken in. Fortunately, for Heartfree and comedy alike, this official deserves the adjective that Fielding finally bestows upon him: the *good* magistrate. Having passed judgement, he neither obstinately sticks to it nor dismisses it as a settled thing, a decision irrevocably given. Instead, when new evidence points to a frame-up, the good magistrate, his mind refreshingly open, more concerned to prevent a miscarriage of justice than muffle his own mistake, resolutely pursues the truth. As a result Wild is arrested, convicted and hanged (Fielding's promptness to forgive precludes any sentimental sell-out of public safety) while the virtuous man is released and reunited with his Penelope of a wife. And they lived happily after: it is the virtue of the good magistrate, not that of the Heartfrees, that secures the fairy-tale ending. No doubt they *deserve* their good fortune; Fielding's comic art ensures that they *get* it.

The fear of every good magistrate—that, through no fault of his own, judging simply, as he must, on the evidence presented, he may condemn an innocent man—is averted; the fear of every innocent accused—that he may, nevertheless, be condemned—is dispelled. Not every judge gets a second chance to redeem a mistake, but neither is every judge generous enough to grasp it. 'I am convinced my innocence will somewhere be rewarded.'[25] Heartfree sustains himself with the religious hope that was once the standard refuge of the unjustly condemned, and, certainly, without the good magistrate, he would have had to wait for a future world to amend the injustices of this one. Mrs. Heartfree predictably shares her husband's optimistic eschatology: 'Providence will sooner or later procure the felicity of the virtuous and innocent.'[26] The trouble is that such a confidence wanes in proportion as faith in the next world dissipates. In any case, the Heartfree trust in eternity, however commendable, is unnecessary, for, quite apart from the verdict of heaven, they are in safe hands here and now; there is always a good magistrate in Fielding's books, if not literally among the *dramatis personae*, then infallibly in the narrator himself. Justice is guaranteed now, with providence simply a pseudonym for Henry Fielding.

So it is misleading to be told, in a discussion of Fielding's London, that we are never left in doubt of the terrible fate which could quickly overwhelm not only the feckless and the wicked but also the innocent.[27] However true of the real world that Fielding surveyed, this is misguided when applied to the fictional world he created. Nothing demonstrates this better than *Jonathan Wild* itself. The book deals with a shocking world in a humorous way, taming its fearful contents—robberies, rapes, murders—to a comic form. Instead of Defoe's outrage at the spectacle of Wild's iniquities, there is an amused, superior disdain. This explains why Fielding's book has the same reassuring effect as Orwell's *Animal Farm*; both texts deploy material that dismayed their creators in real life (Fielding is as disturbed by London crime as Orwell by European dictatorship) but do so in fictions that place us securely above the horrors described—we control them and not they us. Heartfree and Boxer may be deluded but in each case the reader easily detects the villain's transparent shifts. An essential part of the comic strategy is that the reader should not be taken in, and in each case the narrative style underwrites this comic guarantee.

Fielding is, however, an authentic comedian where the Orwell of *Animal Farm* is a pretender. Disgusted by European history and with diminishing hopes for the future, Orwell takes refuge in a comic fable. What happens to the animals is, however, no laughing matter. Fielding, by contrast, is 'the great optimist',[28] and his comic guarantee includes the assurance that in the end all will be well; the good man, regardless of the evidence stacked against him, will be vindicated, the villain, temporary triumphs notwithstanding, undone. In the legacy inherited by liberalism from Christianity is the notion of a secularized providence: truth must prevail and good triumph, evil is self-destructive, love is stronger than hate, and the rest. So Winston Smith believes as he sets out to challenge Big Brother; the pessimism of Orwell's prophecy is in its demonstration that these are mere dogmas, at best aspirations, at worst delusions. Fielding's work, however, does verify the promise shared by liberalism and Christianity alike that the good heart is sacrosanct and that whoever means well and strives manfully will not be allowed to perish. Even at the nadir of *Jonathan Wild* comes the comic reassurance: tell your piteous heart there's no harm done.

We encounter here no eighteenth-century equivalent of Orwell's Boxer, no deluded, innocent victim, no painful miscarriage of justice. Even those hanged on Wild's perjured evidence have no real complaint, for they *are* criminals, guilty of other offences which, detected, would have brought them to the same gallows. The closest to a tragic death is the execution of Marybone for refusing to be as thoroughly reprobate as Wild requires. Fielding prefers to point up the irony of Marybone's end: he is neither sufficiently wicked to survive Wild's malice nor sufficiently virtuous to deserve to, is hanged not for the undoubted evil he has done but for the evil he declines to do. Still, he is scarcely an innocent, and Fielding supplies the explanatory gloss: 'you had better be an honest man than half a rogue.'[29] Marybone does not contradict the rule that in Fielding only the wicked are punished. Heartfree is the good man and he is exonerated. 'The righteous are guided and protected by the Lord, but the evil are on the way to their doom.'[30] Fielding guarantees, at least in his fiction, that we need not wait for eternity to obtain justice. His fictional world is a magistrate's dream in which the innocent are always cleared and the guilty always exposed. What the magistrate vainly aspires to, the novelist triumphantly achieves; Fielding is the magistrate as novelist, recruiting the genius of the second vocation to remedy the shortcomings of the first.

The comedy of *Animal Farm* is born of defeat while that of *Jonathan Wild* springs from a confidence in omnipotent goodness. Seconding the good magistrate eager for justice is a good-natured narrator whose easy tone assures us of his total control. Rape itself becomes an occasion for comedy.[31] Such confidence can come from only one of two things: fatuous complacency or comic supremacy; either the speaker is a fool and a moral cretin or he is master of the game. We soon discover the answer and the confidence becomes contagious. The fiction is so clearly insured against calamity, in tiny detail as in overall structure. When we read of the villain that 'his soliloquy and his punch concluded together',[32] the zeugma is a confirmation that this villain is to be comprehended within a circle of derision. Similarly, the burlesque description of Wild's marriage fiasco, with the boy Hymen expelling the boy Cupid,[33] makes it plain that we are dealing with a fool, a malefactor of the red-nosed variety rather than a member of Macbeth's tragic brotherhood. Wild exemplifies the point that 'a man may go to heaven with half the pains which it costs him to purchase hell.'[34]

The final act of theft in the instant before execution highlights the irrationality of Wild's behaviour, dramatizing the senseless, obsessive quality of evil which so bewildered the Houyhnhnm Master pondering the iniquities of Gulliver's fellows. Wild is shown as fool or addict, committing profitless crimes that serve only to stoke up his own torment. His 'triumph' in supplanting Johnson as Newgate supremo is made emblematic of the criminal life in general. Wild's acquisition of the coveted mantle is futile, for 'to speak sincerely, there was more bravado than real use or advantage in these trappings.'[35] The glittering garments neither fit nor keep warm, 'and the cap was so heavy that it made his head ache'. Crime does not pay. Even Macbeth's tragic status does not exclude the notion of the fool who gives away his eternal jewel for nothing; Fielding eschews tragedy to emphasize the imbecility of evil, exposing Wild as a comic Macbeth who, even at the height of his 'success', cannot enjoy it:

> He was under a continual alarm of frights and fears, and jealousies. He thought every man he beheld wore a knife for his throat and a pair of scissors for his purse.[36]

86

Quod sumus scimus: we can only comprehend what we, in essence, are. Allworthy believes that everyone is as charitable as himself, Adams that everyone is as Christian. Wild likewise sees the world as a reflection of himself, so it is small wonder that his life is an unremitting panic. In the preface Fielding repudiates the view that Newgate is simply human nature with the mask off[37]; the idea of a universal Yahoodom is for him a slander on man and Wild is one of the slanderers. Fielding's antipathy to the black legend of human nature emerges in Booth's reprimand to Miss Matthew for praising Mandeville.[38] Even the paragon Amelia is rebuked by Dr. Harrison when, in her despair, she makes a blanket condemnation of human beings in Gulliver's style.[39] Wild's final end is at once proof of the falsity of his outlook and the justification of Fielding's comic ethos.

The secret of this ethos is that it fuses miraculously the infallible and the generous; here is a judge never mistaken and never harsh, a world where merit and reward are perfectly matched. Comedy is always concerned with revelation, with stripping and unmasking, the individual secret made public property; identity is manifested in community, human beings revealed for what they truly are in terms of their relations to each other. In Dorothy Van Ghent's words, 'the curve of comedy is spun socially and gregariously, as the common product of men in society.'[40] It follows that the characters of comedy are under no artistic obligation to change since they exist, not in order to develop, but to be undraped in the presence of their peers: Square in Molly's room, the naked truth behind the opened curtain, Gulliver shivering naked in the Yahoo line-up, his real identity humiliatingly exposed. Tom Jones, mistakenly seen by all as a scamp, is finally shown as the good man he essentially is; Blifil, outwardly so respectable, is unmasked as a rogue.

Comedy is an epiphany and the publicity of the disclosure is the salient fact. Herein lies the difference, theologically speaking, between the individual judgement of the soul after death, the private confrontation between Creator and creature, and the Last Judegment when the souls of all who ever lived are assembled to be publicly assigned the kind of eternity each has merited. Hence the essentially *comic* appeal of the Last Judgement during the era of western faith: everything will be made open, all wrongs righted, all hitherto slippery malefactors

87

caught, all hitherto neglected deservers rewarded, an exact correlation between performance and assessment achieved. Fielding's appeal is that he provides this judicial comedy here and now, with no possibility of oversight or evasion. What a reassurance to anyone obliged to come to the judgement place in whatever capacity, judge, juror, defendant or plaintiff. The gospel may warn us not to judge lest we be judged, but how, practically speaking, can we live in the world and withdraw from judgement? We have to judge despite knowing that there is no infallible court, no unerring magistrate, no jury immune from misdirection. Mistakes are unavoidable; our best hope, that of the good magistrate in *Jonathan Wild*, is that they should at least be corrigible. Crucial in the campaign to abolish the death penalty was the admission that innocent men might have been hanged. Have fallible men the right to make irreparable mistakes? A hanged man is guilty forever; an Alps of subsequent evidence to the contrary cannot revoke this brutal fact. As faith in the next world wanes, the need to prevent irrevocable blunders in this becomes the more exigent. Perhaps any Last Judgement is indefensible; one pronounced by a creature conscious of his own fallibility seems outrageous. Fielding liberates us from our cognitive misgivings by conferring, within his fiction, the gift of infallibility upon mistake-prone men; his readers join him upon a bench secured against error.

Yet the idea of a Last Judgement can chill as well as console. It is all very well to hear that the guilty will be punished and the good rewarded, but what kind of judge waits us and what are his criteria for distinguishing these categories? What if it is a hanging judge like Swift's terrible joker in 'The Day of Judgement'? Here is the second source of Fielding's appeal: *his* Last Judgement will terrify only the incorrigibly vicious. This explains why Fielding, in certain aspects so clearly Swift's legatee, is finally so different a satirist. Swift would have scorned as a foolish concession to Yahoo man the lenity which informs Fielding's transactions with his characters. Swift's satire, at its most characteristic, teeters on the brink of explosive exasperation: 'I cannot but warn you once more of the manifest destruction before your eyes, if you do not behave yourselves as you ought.'[41] Jehovah is about to pulverize a besotted people. Swift will not go on prescribing a dose for the dead; Gulliver (here, at least, surely his creator's spokesman) tells cousin Sympson that Yahoo reform is a delusion which he has abandoned forever.[42] What reader is so fatuous as to dream himself exempt from the general condemnation? This is a hanging judge, unforgiving and remorseless.

Swift's advice to the woman whose daughter, anticipating Richardson's Clarissa, was set on marrying against her parents' wishes, makes his attitude admirably clear: the mother is to make one last attempt at dissuasion and then should this fail, never see or communicate with the rebel again.[43] Even one lapse is a trial to Swift's tolerance, and more than one is an outrage. *Fiat justitia et pereat mundus*: this sentiment, so thoroughly at home in Swift, is unthinkable in Fielding. He loves the world and its inhabitants too much to sacrifice them to any abstraction, however exalted; even the beloved Aeschylus burns unregarded in the grate until Adams is sure that no harm has come to Fanny.[44] Life always comes first. A woman may very reasonably object to a naked man in a coach but not when excluding him means death or injury; *then* such scruples must be exposed as the pernicious hypocrisies they are, for nakedness, like Aeschylus, does not count when life is at risk.[45] And so Fielding never sees the world and justice as opposed choices; he wants justice so that the world will *not* perish. The court over which he presides is marked by generosity, even indulgence; those condemned there would be hard pressed to find defenders anywhere. When we hear that 'Thwackum was for doing justice, and leaving mercy to heaven',[46] we know that he has just been irretrievably rejected as a candidate for Fielding's bench.

Fielding himself, in turn, has been disowned as a responsible magistrate on the ground that he is too slack a scrutineer of human behaviour. This is not simply a matter of alleged individual laxities, as in the case of Mrs. Fitzpatrick in *Tom Jones*, but of his whole attitude to life which is rebuked as reprehensible. Swift would have given Mrs. Fitzpatrick short shrift as a she-Yahoo, but in Fielding's more genial view she is far from that. She does not, of course, evoke the admiration so deservedly given to Sophia, but neither, sexual indiscretions notwithstanding, is she a bad woman. Swift would have sent her to the Bridewell to be flayed and her appearance changed for the worse; Christ would have stopped the flaying but told her to sin no more. Fielding is happy to leave her 'at the polite end of town' where she 'is so good an economist, that she spends three times the income of her fortune, without running into debt'.[47]

The easy solution is to say that Fielding can joke about Mrs. Fitzpatrick's economic miracle because he is himself a carelessly immoral man, condoning the depravity he shares. The correct answer is that he is easy on her precisely because he *is* a moralist, though of a very different school from Richardson. Fielding's target is not the sins that are seen, the obvious and glaring offences like drunkenness and fornication, but the unseen and far worse sins that sometimes fester behind fastidious facades: pride, envy, spite, malice; not the sins that go sprawling flagrant in the gutters, but the prim sins that have the astonishing facility to disguise themselves as virtues. Mrs. Fitzpatrick's sexual laxity is more than balanced by her instinctive generosity, just as the public scapegrace, Tom, is an infinitely better man than the decorous Blifil. If the likes of Thwackum and Square cannot see this, so much the worse for them. Fielding *is* a morally subversive writer, though not in Dr. Johnson's sense[48]; he does not repudiate values but calls, rather, for their revaluation. 'How is it possible for young people to read such a book and to look upon orderliness, sobriety, obedience, and frugality, as *virtues*?'[49] Cobbett's complaint misses the point. Young people are always exhorted to regard these not only as virtues, but often as the most important, indeed the only, virtues there are. Fielding never denies that they are virtues—he simply reiterates, in his own terms and for his own times, St. Paul's insistence that without charity all these are futile. Being an artist, he puts the Pauline message in his own dramatically rhetorical way, but who will say that the message was, or is, redundant? The mean, the hypocritical and the spiteful do well to fear arraignment in Fielding's court; in every other case, he is happy to utter a *nolle prosequi*.

But the attack upon him transcends his alleged laxity towards individual sinners to become a denunciation of his attitude to life and of the artistic form he devised to dramatize this. Lady Mary Wortley Montagu rebuked him for encouraging an optimistic recklessness in young people, a foolish assurance that they could launch into love without thought of the consequences or prudent provision for the future, a charge repeated more than a century later by Ford Madox Ford.[50] Dr. Johnson likewise complained that Fielding's rogue-heroes were a bad model for the young, much as some people today deplore the behaviour of pop-stars as likely to lead their idolatrously imitative followers astray.[51] What most angers Lady Mary is that Fielding fosters improvidence in the young, inciting them to marry for love with no heed to the testing future and the indispensable income. Despite Fielding's repeated claim that his work champions nature against romance, Lady Mary attacks him for subordinating nature to fairy-tale and its happy-ever-after mentality.

In fact, Fielding's work exhibits a secularized Christian hope, a trust in providence rather than a predilection for fairy-tale. Jesus himself occasionally encourages a similar heedlessness as in his words about the unreflecting lilies of the field that, without striving or fretting, are nevertheless more splendid than Solomon. Worry, on this view, is an offence against God, a disbelief in his promise, for, if not even a sparrow falls without his consent, it is a sin to fear calamity. If God is for us, who can be against? So Jesus tells man not to worry since God loves him. However bad things look, all will be well. Fielding's work provides a secularized version of this assurance, 'a kind of comic analogue of the true believer's reliance on a benign providence in real life'.[52] Tom Jones, despite his thoughtlessness, will not be lost because he is in Fielding's keeping. Even when the narrator speculates that Tom may end on the gallows, the very mention of this possible fate has precisely the opposite effect in guaranteeing that it will not happen; we now know that, whatever else, Tom will not be hanged.[53] The reader trusts the narrator as the Christian trusts God and unhesitatingly confides the resolution to him: for each the world is a comedy in which all will be well.

Moreover, Fielding loves Tom Jones for the very qualities that Lady Mary finds reprehensible. Tom, like the lilies of the field, is thoughtless and uncalculating—the complete opposite of the villainous Blifil, precise and scheming, forever taking thought of the morrow. It is precisely because Tom does not clinically seek a reward that Fielding makes sure he gets one. Those who do not care will be cared for, those who care overmuch will lose both the prize and themselves. Again, the secret is related to the secularization of a religious idea: seek ye first the kingdom and all things shall be added unto you. The good will be happy but only because they put goodness before happiness, whereas those who thought only of their own happiness will miss that and everything else. This is the central Christian paradox. It is, of course, true that Fielding's kingdom is completely of this world; his values are, at bottom, thoroughly and autonomously humanist—friendship, good-nature, compassion, love, and so on. If the terminus of *The Pilgrim's Progress* is the Celestial City, that of *Tom Jones* is the marriage-bed, with Sophia the supreme felicity in Fielding's perspective. Tom is not preparing for heaven, he is there already. Far from plotting with chill, Blifil precision, how to obtain it, he has come recklessly close to throwing it away—but only he who loses his life will save it. Improbable though it seems at first glance, the drunken womanizer who outraged Dr. Johnson, 'the fellow that sells himself',[54] in Thackeray's scornful dismissal, Lady Bellaston's gigolo, the Augustan Midnight Cowboy, is the secularized embodiment of this key Christian belief. Blifil, by contrast, is a loser at last *because* he is obsessed with winning. Fielding's humanism will not properly be appreciated by those who miss how rooted it is in Christianity.

Fielding's own paradox makes sense only in the context of its Christian derivation, for otherwise there would be an irreconcilable clash between competing impulses: the wish to show goodness as its own reward, hence to criticize any form of egotistic calculation, and the even stronger compulsion to create comic masterpieces. Tragedy suggests itself as the more appropriate medium for the first impulse; clearly, the goodness of Cordelia *is* its own reward because it is so bleakly its only one—no other reward is given her. Fielding is, however, a comedian; all of his heroes end up united or reunited in marital bliss with the women they love—nothing is here for tears. The calculators will fail while the spontaneously virtuous will get the reward; generosity is the best policy but only when it is not a policy—this is Fielding's paradox. The young hero in the fairy-tale wins the golden girl and the golden mountain because he treats the old crone, in reality the queen of the fairies, with respect and kindness; his competitors are discomfited because they are rude and selfish to an apparently insignificant old woman. Nobody, of course, knows at the time her true identity; it is just that the good man is instinctively, naturally good, while the bad man has to be bribed to act decently—no bribe, no decency.

But it would be perverse to say that the moral is that we should treat kindly the next old crone we meet on the long shot that she might be queen of the fairies; that would be to degrade a gratuitous, altruistic act into a piece of strategic calculation. Every old woman should be treated as if she were the queen of the fairies because, in the Christian sense, every old woman is. Jesus makes this clear when he answers his puzzled interlocutors: when you do this to the least of all my brethren, you do it to me. Those who go sharp-eyed to help the important and the influential, while leaving the helpless to rot, are not good men but good strategists. Tom Jones is no strategist at all. His blessings come to him as a consequence of his impulsive generosity. His urge to make amends to Molly for, as he mistakenly thinks, letting her down, sends him to her room where he finds her with Square and then learns about Will Barnes as her original seducer.[55] Doing the generous thing gets him off the hook, but his release is the felicitous by-product of his magnanimity, not its deliberate object. He owes his ultimate success to two factors: his own natural goodness and his situation within a Fielding comedy. The Lord was with Joseph and he was a lucky fellow. Fielding's Joseph is a lucky fellow too, and Tom Jones, Heartfree and Booth share his good fortune in having Fielding as their progenitor. Nowhere else in literature is the reader so conscious of the author as benevolent deity, of the narrator as the god of the novel, forever overseeing the action. The narrator is the most important character, the ultimate source of the comic warranty. The good characters are his instruments but could not by themselves achieve the comic resolution. Despite being a good man Allworthy goes consistently wrong. Allworthy is not all-wise and his cry of self-reproach at the novel's end—'Oh, my child, to what goodness have I been so long blind!'[56]—alerts us to the tragedy which might have occurred had the omniscient, benevolent narrator not been at his post.

Lady Mary is really asking Fielding to be Richardson when she complains that his young lovers are not prudent and forethoughtful, in a word, not Pamela. Fielding, however, had not written *Shamela* in order to end up celebrating what he had originally ridiculed. The irony is that all of Fielding's books could equally lay claim to Richardson's sub-title of *Virtue Rewarded*; Richardson at least wrote *Clarissa*, but where in all Fielding does virtue not reap its reward in this world? The quarrel with Richardson is over means, not ends. Pamela is a strategist, Tom the happy-go-lucky beneficiary of his creator's benevolence, but each is a success story. In both writers providence, moving in its own mysterious ways, seeks out and bestows its blessings upon the virtuous, though Pamela, the attentive pupil of providence, meets her benefactor halfway. The difference is not that one character is rewarded and the other not, nor is it even in the kind of reward given; it is that each is rewarded by very different moralists employing radically opposed criteria. Fielding contemptuously denies that Pamela is a good woman; she is merely a shrewd accountant, and that puts her, if anywhere, in Blifil's camp rather than Tom's. Richardson, for his part, sees in Tom not a good man but a drunken libertine, in Lady Mary's phrase, 'a sorry scoundrel' who is rescued from his just deserts by his complaisant accomplice, Fielding.[57]

Neither writer ascetically restricts virtue to its own reward. Fielding, indeed, despite ridiculing the belief that happiness always accompanies virtue in this world, is even more determined than his rival to reward virtue here and now, and this because he is finally more humanist and more materialist than Richardson. Richardson can dispense with earthly happiness because he holds heaven in reserve for Clarissa, but Fielding, at least in his fiction, is not much interested in heaven. Empson correctly discovers Fielding's 'secret' in his celebration of this world's values[58]—for example, Tom's supreme felicity in possessing Sophia transcends his pleasure with Mrs. Waters, but the difference is in degree rather than kind—but it is surely a very ill-kept secret to any attentive reader of Fielding. In *Joseph Andrews* punch is preferable to prayers, shirts are more serviceable than sermons, and the book's moment of supreme joy is when Adams's son is restored to life; all the copy-book maxims of religious consolation are dross in comparison with the living human being.[59] *This* Abraham rebels against his son's sacrifice and will not be comforted at the thought of reunion in heaven. Heaven, for Fielding, is where we want to go when we have to go, but who wants to rush there? He celebrates the life we have. Joseph may compare himself to the tragic hero of *The London Merchant* but Fielding is not auditioning for that rôle.[60] Unlike Richardson in *Clarissa*, he will not depend on heaven to recompense virtue, but provides without fail the terrestrial happy ending. 'Secret' is a curious word to use for something so glaringly obvious.

It does, however, make his attack upon *Pamela* the more puzzling:

> There are a set of religious, or rather moral writers, who teach that virtue is the certain road to happiness, and vice to misery, in this world. A very wholesome and comfortable doctrine, and to which we have but one objection, namely, that it is not true.[61]

One is reminded of Hardy's onslaught upon Wordsworthian optimism in *Tess of the d'Urbervilles*.[62] But Hardy is consistent in matching tale to doctrine: if you mean to demolish the superstition that goodness always triumphs in this world, how better to do it than through the tragic story of the betrayed maiden who, unlike Tom Jones, does end up on the gallows? The appropriate response to shallow optimism is tragedy; when the world is misrepresented through rose-coloured glasses, darker lenses must be substituted. Hardy, outrageously for some readers, conspires with coincidence to arrange Tess's destruction. Fielding, curiously for a man who has just blasted the optimists, uses coincidence in an equally obtrusive way to bring about the happy ending; coincidence is really another device of benevolent providence. For Hardy there is no justice, here or anywhere else: 'The President of the Immortals had finished his sport with Tess.' For Fielding there is always justice, frequently in the world, unfailingly in his fiction—a curious stance for a man who sometimes speaks as though he were the scourge of the optimists. In *Tom Jones* he ridicules a particular set of writers and then joins their company.

The extra irony is that one of Fielding's major themes is the comic discrepancy between word and deed, profession and practice. He repeatedly insists that the deeds of men are a more reliable testimony to their true natures than the words they speak—which makes it the more piquant to detect the same divergence in Fielding himself. The rebuttal of the optimistic view that virtue must harvest happiness in this world is not, of course, intended as an argument for vice. He wants men to continue virtuous but to abandon the delusion that they must profit thereby; virtue is always its own reward and often its only one.

But if this is what he *says*, it is clearly not what his books *do*, for in them happiness and virtue are indivisible. The good characters can be careless of their own interests in texts whose author is vigilantly safeguarding them. Hardy says that Wordsworth is wrong and tries to show it too; Fielding derides optimism while creating a masterpiece of optimistic comedy. All of his books are triumphs of juridical optimism. Even *Amelia*, his most sombre production, so different in tone from its predecessors, does not surrender to despondency, though the temptation was never greater. Described as 'a criminal pamphlet expanded into a novel',[63] it opens with the hero's arrest and unjust imprisonment at the hands of a vicious judge: Booth is jailed when he ought to be thanked as a public benefactor; merit and recompense are totally out of kilter, not surprisingly when instead of the good magistrate of *Jonathan Wild* we have the intolerable Justice Thrasher. Nor is Booth's an isolated case, for it anticipates a major theme of the book: the failure of contemporary England to reward merit. The reader accompanies Booth on a shocking fact-finding tour of courts and prisons, learning about English justice and its alarming shortcomings. It is a magistrate's novel, packed with 'documentary' interest, revealing an insider's expertise, and much more seriously reformist in aim than its picaresque forerunners. Scenes and incidents that Fielding would formerly have exploited with comic gusto are now imbued with a certain earnest, even evangelical air; Dr. Harrison faces the abuses of England in a way very different from Parson Adams. So dark are these abuses that some readers object to the happy ending as a violation of the story. Others find the description of English life so pessimistic that they unearth, albeit unintentionally on Fielding's part, a revolutionary impulse in the book; Amelia, on this view, undermines respect for the aristocracy to which Fielding claimed kinship: why should we go on tolerating such 'noble' lords?

There is, unquestionably, something especially contrived in the way Fielding produces his happy ending; the recovery of Amelia's fortune through Robinson's confession is a device too uncomfortably reminiscent of the *deus ex machina* or of the sensational *dénouements* of Hollywood B-movie courtroom dramas. Those who fault *Pamela* as a piece of wish-fulfilment will scarcely find the comic resolution of *Amelia* any more convincing. But if the means surprise, the end surely does not. Who, reading Fielding, really expects tragedy? Amelia is a pearl among women, Booth, lapses notwithstanding, a fundamentally good man. How could a good magistrate like Fielding allow such characters to come to grief? Ratify the benevolence of the magistrate with the genius of the comic artist and the happy ending is the expected verdict. If the plot eventually rescues Booth from the consequences of his acts, it is because, finally, in the plotter's generous view, Booth deserves rescue. Though his sins are graver than those of Tom Jones, they are similarly attributable to weakness rather than wickedness, and Fielding is never vengeful towards weakness. How many times should we forgive our erring brother? Fielding seriously accepts the gospel injunction—not seven but seventy times seven, always provided he repents and asks forgiveness. Otherwise Fielding can be as harsh as the hardest hardliner could desire. There is no softness towards the noble peer and Mrs. Ellison, for each is destroyed, the woman by alcohol, the lord through his amours, 'by which he was at last become so rotten that he stunk above-ground'.[64] Even Swift would have been taxed to surpass the ferocity of this.

But for the deservers (a majority of his fellows for Fielding) there is always a second chance. Trust the tale rather than the teller. For all his *talk* of virtue being its own reward, Fielding is careful to make Booth and Amelia both virtuous *and* happy. Dr. Harrison pronounces the orthodox sentiments of stoical Christianity: 'A true Christian can never be disappointed if he doth not receive his reward in this world; the labourer might as well complain that he is not paid his hire in the middle of the day.'[65] This is irrefutably Christian and Fielding the Christian presumably concurs. It is Fielding the novelist who thinks and does otherwise. It is the same Harrison who brings Booth the splendid news of his earthly windfall: 'Your sufferings are all at an end, and Providence hath done you the justice at last which it will, one day or other, render to all men.'[66] However orthodox Harrison's earlier stoicism, one must conclude that it has nothing to do with the plot and that Harrison has redundantly been preparing Booth for a calamity that Fielding has no intention of permitting. For, even in this world, tribulations are temporary; there is no postponement of wages in Fielding, no moratorium while earthly injustice awaits heaven's reversal. To continue with Harrison's metaphor, Tom Jones, Joseph Andrews, Heartfree and Booth *do* receive their wages in the middle of the day, i.e. in the present world. And *Amelia* is the acid test, for, if there is a pay-off for virtue here, where in all Fielding could it possibly be refused? The beginning of this dark text is presided over by the disgraceful Justice Thrasher who treats an Irish accent as proof of guilt and poverty as proof of prostitution, but by the end Justice Fielding is in control, ensuring that the good people, even in so fallen a world, get their deserts, and that the wicked who evade the law do not thereby also evade punishment. A world barren of justice is a nightmare beyond Fielding's consent. Brecht erupts in irritated irony at the convention of happy-ever-after: 'So the whole thing has a happy ending! How calm and peaceful would our life be always if a messenger came from the king whenever we wanted!'[67] But Fielding in his fiction is the most obliging of kings and his readers can always count upon a royal pardon or a timely reprieve. Kafka is the place to go if we want to read about unattainable justice and frustrated plaintiffs; in Fielding, by contrast, we witness the comedy of justice—his trial is always an exoneration and his castle always a refuge. That is why his work is the perfect secular embodiment of the good news that Christianity brings.

Fielding's Magisterial Art

NOTES

1. *Joseph Andrews*, ed. R. F. Brissenden (Harmondsworth: Penguin Books, 1977), p. 93.
2. 'The Day of Judgement', *The Poems of Jonathan Swift*, ed. Harold Williams (Oxford: O.U.P., 1937), Vol. 11, p. 579.
3. Quoted in *Henry Fielding: Tom Jones, A Casebook*, ed. Neil Compton (London: Macmillan, 1970), p. 29.
4. Quoted in *Henry Fielding: Tom Jones, A Casebook*, p. 39.
5. *Jonathan Wild*, ed. David Nokes (Harmondsworth: Penguin Books, 1982), p. 159.
6. *Tom Jones*, ed. R. P. C. Mutter (Harmondsworth: Penguin Books, 1966), p. 145.
7. Quoted in *Henry Fielding: Tom Jones, A Casebook*, p. 34.
8. Quoted in *Henry Fielding: A Critical Anthology*, ed. Claude Rawson (Harmondsworth: Penguin Books, 1973), p. 397.
9. *Jonathan Wild*, p. 165.
10. *Tom Jones*, p. 157.
11. Quoted in *Fielding: A Collection of Critical Essays*, ed. Ronald Paulson (Englewood Cliffs, N.J.: Prentice-Hall, Inc., 1962), p. 81.
12. *Joseph Andrews*, p. 148.
13. Ibid., p. 140.
14. George Sherburn, 'Fielding's Social Outlook', in *Eighteenth Century English Literature: Modern Essays in Criticism*, ed. James L. Clifford (New York: A Galaxy Book, O.U.P., 1959), p. 265.
15. *Joseph Andrews*, p. 69.
16. Ibid., p. 106.
17. Ibid., p. 95.
18. Ibid., p. 72.
19. Ibid., p. 323.
20. Ibid., p. 65.
21. Pat Rogers, *Henry Fielding: A Biography* (London: Paul Elek, 1979), p. 124.
22. In *Henry Fielding: Tom Jones, A Casebook*, p. 148.
23. *Amelia* (London: Dent, Everyman's Library, 1978), Vol. VIII, p. 97.
24. Robert Penn Warren, *All the King's Men* (London: Secker and Warburg, New English Library, 1974), p. 67.
25. *Jonathan Wild*, p. 157.
26. Ibid., p. 203.
27. J. H. Plumb's Foreword to *Jonathan Wild* (New York: Signet Classics, New American Library, 1962), p. xvi.
28. Rebecca West, quoted in *Henry Fielding: A Critical Anthology*, p. 388.
29. *Jonathan Wild*, p. 131.
30. Psalms in *Good News Bible* (London: Collins, 1979), pp. 539–40.
31. *Jonathan Wild*, p. 114.
32. Ibid., p. 97.
33. Ibid., p. 148.
34. Ibid., p. 220.

35. Ibid., p. 175.
36. Ibid., p. 160.
37. Ibid., p. 30.
38. *Amelia*, pp. 111, 114.
39. Ibid., Vol. IX, p. 131.
40. Dorothy Van Ghent, 'On Tom Jones', in *Henry Fielding: Tom Jones, A Casebook*, p. 62.
41. *Prose Works of Jonathan Swift*, ed. Herbert Davis (Oxford: Basil Blackwell & Mott, 1939–68), Vol. X, p. 4.
42. *The Correspondence of Jonathan Swift*, ed. Harold Williams (Oxford: O.U.P., 1963–65), Vol. III, p. 501; *Prose Works*, Vol. XI, p. xxxvi.
43. *Correspondence*, Vol. IV, p. 178.
44. *Joseph Andrews*, p. 157.
45. Ibid., p. 68.
46. Tom Jones, p. 147.
47. Ibid., p. 872.
48. Quoted in *Henry Fielding: Tom Jones, A Casebook*, p. 32.
49. Quoted in *Henry Fielding: A Critical Anthology*, p. 400.
50. Quoted in *Henry Fielding: Tom Jones, A Casebook*, pp. 25–26; 129.
51. Quoted in *Henry Fielding: A Critical Anthology*, pp. 115–16.
52. Wayne Booth, quoted in *Henry Fielding: Tom Jones, A Casebook*, p. 235.
53. *Tom Jones*, p. 778.
54. Quoted in *Henry Fielding: Tom Jones, A Casebook*, p. 45.
55. *Tom Jones*, pp. 209, 215.
56. Ibid., p. 859.
57. Quoted in *Henry Fielding: Tom Jones, A Casebook*, p. 25.
58. Ibid., p. 144.
59. *Joseph Andrews*, pp. 75, 101, 290–91.
60. Ibid., p. 50.
61. *Tom Jones*, p. 695.
62. *Tess of the d'Urbervilles*, ed. David Skilton (Harmondsworth: Penguin Books, 1978), pp. 61–2.
63. Wilbur Cross, *The History of Henry Fielding* (New Haven: Yale University Press, 1918), Vol. II, p. 312.
64. *Amelia*, Vol. XII, p. 310.
65. Ibid., Vol. IX, p. 147.
66. Ibid., Vol. XII, p. 299.
67. Quoted in *Henry Fielding: A Critical Anthology*, p. 472.

5

The Innocence of *Joseph Andrews*

by NEIL RHODES

Like Polonius's 'tragical—comical—historical—pastoral', Fielding's first novel (1742) is something of a hybrid. Fielding himself described it in the Preface as 'a comic epic-poem in prose',[1] by which he meant a kind of 'comic romance', but even this capacious definition fails to account for its excursions into literary criticism, moral fable and parody. This last element tends to be played down nowadays, as critics have sought to show that *Joseph Andrews* is a purposefully structured work which does not merely start out as a burlesque of *Pamela* and then wander off on a course of its own. Such a case can be, and has been, well made.[2] But it is also clearly the case that Fielding's antagonistic relationship with Richardson's novel gives us our most direct point of entry into *Joseph Andrews*. *Pamela* is a subtler novel—certainly a psychologically subtler novel—than Fielding allowed, but it is easy to understand his hostility to what he saw as the hypocrisy of its heroine, the smug, middle-class morality of its author, and the claustrophobic atmosphere of the novel itself. Coleridge impressionistically summed up the difference between the two writers when he commented: 'How charming, how wholesome, Fielding always is! To take him up after Richardson, is like emerging from a sick room heated by stoves, into an open lawn, on a breezy day in May.'[3] In a comic vein this is just the contrast we find within *Joseph Andrews* itself, as Joseph

101

proceeds from the steamy bedchamber of Lady Booby's town
house to his strenuous adventures in the English countryside
with fellow innocents abroad, Fanny Goodwill and Parson
Abraham Adams. It is true that explicit parody of *Pamela* plays
a relatively small part in the novel, but it provides a starting
point for an exploration of what true innocence comprises.
The spirit of *Joseph Andrews* is consistently and deliberately at
odds with the unwholesome and self-regarding purity of
Pamela and with the moral assumptions of her creator.

The chief difficulty we have in finding Pamela's innocence
convincing is the fact that she is so knowing. Her letter-writing
activities reveal considerable practical cunning, and she is
quick-witted enough in conversation to seem pertly teasing to
her somewhat bumbling pursuer:

> 'Why, then,' said I, 'if your honour must know, I said, that my
> good lady did not desire your care to extend to the *summer-house*
> and her *dressing room.*'
>   Well, this was a little saucy, you'll say—And he flew into
> such a passion, that I was forced to run for it. . . .[4]

(Pamela is referring, of course, to the scenes of B.'s abortive
attempts to seduce her.) It is hardly surprising, then, that B.
should judge her to be 'artful' rather than 'innocent', and, as if
to forestall similar doubts in his readers, Richardson raises the
issue of art and innocence as early as letters 14 and 15 in the
conversation between B. and Mrs. Jervis: '*Innocent!* again; and
virtuous, I warrant! Well, Mrs. Jervis, you abound with your
epithets; but I take her to be an artful young baggage . . .'; and
again, after a clever riposte from Pamela: 'Well said, pretty
innocent and *artless!* as Mrs. Jervis calls you' (pp. 16, 18).
Despite Richardson's attempts to show us that B. is mis-
judging her, the impression Pamela gives is hardly one of
ingenuousness. Her replies are too neat, too calculated. As the
novel progresses, then, the sceptical reader comes to feel that
Pamela's 'innocence' is not so much a matter of simplicity, or
transparent good nature, as a commodity; her 'virtue' has a
price on it and the price is marriage. This is admittedly a
one-sided reading of the novel, but the relevant point is that
this is how Fielding read *Pamela*, and his reading is deliciously
summed up in the burlesque *Shamela* (1741), where his heroine

observes brazenly: 'I thought once of making a little fortune by my person. I now intend to make a great one by my vartue.'[5] What Fielding does in *Joseph Andrews* is deliberately to reject the notion of virtue as an artfully preserved sexual purity, and to look instead for his ideal of innocence in a combination of simplicity and open-heartedness.

But it would be wrong to see the moral themes of *Joseph Andrews* as deriving solely from Fielding's combative attitude towards *Pamela*. Similar concerns appear in his earlier writings, and the nature of virtue is, anyway, part of a more general debate in Augustan literature; as Pope put it at the end of one of his bitterest poems:

> Stranger to Civil and Religious Rage,
> The good man walk'd innoxious thro' his Age . . .
> Unlearn'd, he knew no Schoolman's subtle Art,
> No Language, but the Language of the Heart.
> (*Epistle to Dr. Arbuthnot*, 11, 394–95, 398–99)

('Innoxious' here is a variant of the word 'innocent'.) Fielding had begun his literary career as an admirer of Pope and as an aspirant Scriblerian, and many of his plays of the 1730s are part of that opposition to the ruthless and venal politics of the Walpole era. Disgusted by the fact that 'greatness' in public life (Walpole was called 'the great man') depended entirely on the corrupt manipulation of political power, Fielding tried to create characters in his plays and fiction whose 'goodness' consisted, as in Pope's lines, in the quite opposite quality of unworldly benevolence.[6] One such character is the pusillanimous Mr. Boncour in his last play, *The Good Natur'd Man* (1737). Boncour's passivity and indulgence towards his family have resulted in a selfish, domineering wife and a wastrel son, and he is on the point of being duped by a neighbour over a marriage settlement when his more cynical brother rescues him: 'You, brother, to obtain the character of a good-natur'd man, are content to be the bubble of all the world' (III, i). By the end of the play, with his good nature tempered by his brother's worldly wisdom, Boncour manages both to avoid impoverishment and to bring his family to heel. I do not wish to recommend the play any further, but it clearly illustrates that Fielding was aware, before he began his career as a novelist, of the insufficiency of mere complaisance as a practical guide to conduct.

A rather more searching discussion of good nature is to be found in *Jonathan Wild* (1743), which Fielding may have begun writing before *Joseph Andrews*, though it was published later.[7] Here a quite explicit distinction between 'greatness' and 'goodness' provides the central ironic motif of the novel, as the values of the gang-leader, Wild (who is also to be identified with Walpole) are pitted against those of his victim, Heartfree. While the latter is by no means as insipid as Boncour, he is a somewhat one-dimensional figure, since his function is largely to provide a corrective to Wild's inverted moral code. Further, there are rather too many scenes of tawdry domestic pathos for us to feel that Fielding is entirely at ease with his alternative hero. The problem is that Heartfree is not exactly a very spirited fellow. He is introduced to us as a schoolfriend of Wild's, and, 'whereas Wild was rapacious and intrepid, the other had always more regard for his skin than his money',[8] with the result that Heartfree would pay Wild to take a beating on his own account. Fielding never really manages to inject Heartfree with enough vitality to counteract this impression of feebleness, though he does on one occasion have him hit out at a sergeant who threatens his child. In the preface to his *Miscellanies* (1743) Fielding noted, 'I do not conceive my Good Man to be absolutely a Fool or a Coward.'[9] Boncour, insofar as he is a character at all, is both these things, and while the same cannot fairly be said of Heartfree, his sheer limpness means that he falls a fair way short of Fielding's ideal.

What Fielding set out to do in *Joseph Andrews*, then, was in the first place to write a different kind of novel from Richardson's and in the second place to put forward an ideal of virtue which could resist a variety of charges: in particular, those of sanctimoniousness, faint-heartedness and mere gullibility. What he was after was a kind of innocence. I choose the term, rather than the more usual 'good nature', because for us the range of meanings it covers indicates more fully both the themes and character of the novel. It suggests the healthy, open-air quality which Coleridge saw in Fielding, as well as Pope's 'Language of the Heart'. Innocence as distinct from

'purity' is the basis for a sexual ethic rather more humane than
Richardson's. Innocence as simplicity, or lack of worldly
wisdom, provides an alternative ideal to that of 'getting on in
the world', though at the same time it must be distinguished
from naïvety, gullibility, or mere ignorance. Finally, true
innocence for Fielding is always accompanied by a spirit of
open-heartedness and benevolence; the innocent man has a
spontaneous interest in the lives of his fellow human beings.

I do not wish to extend the preamble much further, but
before turning to *Joseph Andrews* itself, I would like to suggest
one unfamiliar point of comparison which may help to
illuminate Fielding's concerns. The work I have in mind—
and I am certainly not arguing for 'influence'—is *The Winter's
Tale*. That play begins on a note of soured pastoral. Polixenes
describes his boyhood friendship with Leontes thus:

> We were as twinn'd lambs that did frisk i' th' sun,
> And bleat the one at th' other: what we chang'd
> Was innocence for innocence: we knew not
> The doctrine of ill-doing, nor dream'd
> That any did.

(I, ii, 67–71)

Naïvety and ignorance (as opposed to innocence) are
inevitable in childhood, dangerous in a young husband, and it
is Leontes's closed mind and closed heart which lead him to
doubt Hermione and so create the poisonous emotional and
sexual atmosphere of the first part of the play. Act IV takes us
into the open air and offers us renewed pastoral, renewed
innocence. Perdita's blending of nobility and the natural life is
accompanied by an emotional openness and spontaneity
which is directly contrasted with her father's warped naïvety.
At the end of the play, she and Florizel return to Sicilia to
make 'old hearts fresh'; the lost child is restored to her parents,
and the families are reconciled. I do not wish to press the
comparison very far, as the structure and tone of the two works
are quite different, but certain similarities will be apparent
from this brief synopsis.

Fielding's story begins with Joseph leaving the country seat
of the Boobys to accompany them in the less salubrious

105

atmosphere of the town, with our hero fortified by Parson Adams's exhortations concerning 'his perseverance in innocence and industry' (p. 46). The former virtue is soon tested by Lady Booby in the chapter where we learn of 'the great Purity of Joseph Andrews', as Joseph gets his chance to emulate the stalwart qualities of sister Pamela:

> 'La!' says (Lady Booby), in an affected surprize, 'What am I doing? I have trusted myself with a man alone, naked in bed; suppose you should have any wicked intentions upon my honour, how should I defend myself?' (p. 49)

Fielding controls the rôle-reversal beautifully; Joseph's wriggling evasions make him seem gauche rather than artful, yet Lady Booby's mounting frustration finally results in the same accusation that B. makes to Pamela—'your pretended innocence'! Fielding's second thrust comes with Lady Booby's own renewed advances. With blushing dignity Joseph now claims that he would not allow his passions 'to get the better of [his] virtue', and the thunderstruck Lady Booby takes two minutes to recover her power of speech. At last:

> 'I am out of patience,' cries the lady: 'Did ever mortal hear of a man's virtue . . . can a boy, a stripling, have the confidence to talk of his virtue?' 'Madam,' says Joseph, 'that boy is the brother of Pamela. . . .' (pp. 58–9)

There is no doubting Fielding's arch tone here as Joseph adopts his self-consciously heroic posture, which is not to say that Fielding is laughing at the footman's failure to satisfy his mistress, but rather at the manner of his reluctance. Joseph's awkwardness in fending off Lady Booby's advances, together with his pompous concern for his purity, make him a slightly ludicrous figure—not so much an ideal of innocence as a little bit of a booby himself.

The point that Joseph's chastity is, in a sense, unbecoming is reinforced by the events at the Tow-wouses' inn. Joseph has been stripped of his livery and sent on his way back to the country by an irate Lady Booby, when he is attacked by robbers and left in a ditch 'as naked as ever he was born' (p. 68). A passing coach, after some haughty objections by its occupants to Joseph's condition, takes him to an inn where he is immediately tucked up in bed by the kindly and 'less squeamish' chamber-maid, Betty. A melodramatic interlude follows in which Joseph bewails his predicament: 'O most adorable Pamela! Most virtuous sister, whose example could alone enable me to withstand all the temptations of riches and beauty. . . .' (Joseph is forgetting what he owes to the moral tonic of Adams's sermons.) 'What but innocence and virtue could give any comfort to such a miserable wretch as I am?' (p. 74). There is an answer to this rhetorical question. Betty has all Fielding's most cherished virtues:

> good nature, generosity and compassion, but unfortunately her constitution was composed of those warm ingredients, which, though the purity of courts or nunneries might have happily controuled them, were by no means able to endure the ticklish situation of a chamber-maid at an inn. . . . (p. 96)

As she ministers to her comely patient, Betty's constitution soon begins to overheat, and, when Joseph is unresponsive to her hints, she desperately flings herself upon him, only to find herself carried forcibly out of the room and the door locked upon her. 'How ought man to rejoice, that his chastity is always in his own power', Fielding comments with mock sententiousness. The point here is not just that Joseph's behaviour is *unnatural*—and comically so—but that it is *uncharitable*. We inevitably contrast the spontaneous warmth with which Betty first receives the injured Joseph with his brusque rejection of the spontaneous warmth which she expresses rather differently.

This episode brings the first book to a close, and insofar as this book is chiefly concerned with the Pamelaic notion of innocence as purity, it is surely designed to expose the limitations of a morality which cannot accept the idea of innocent sensuality—not, of course, what Lady Booby likes to call 'innocent freedoms', but a sensuality which is predominantly the expression of a frank and generous nature. Such an ideal is close to the centre of *The Winter's Tale*. Both Hermione and the 'fresh princess' Perdita speak a language of the heart which is both emotionally and sensually free; it is a language which Leontes can only translate into his own cramped and rancid terms, unaware, as Paulina points out, that Hermione is 'a gracious innocent soul,/ More free than he is jealous' (II, iii, 29–30). It is also a pastoral ideal, and as such comes to flourish in the Bohemian countryside where Perdita is 'a gentler scion [married] to the wildest stock' (IV, iv, 93). It has frequently been pointed out that the story of *Joseph Andrews* is a journey back to the countryside and its redemptive values, and it is certainly true that the pastoral ideal is important in Fielding's writing (Tom Jones, for instance, finally returns from the corruptions of the town to Paradise Hall in the country). I would not, however, wish to make too much of the symbolic aspects of the plot here, because, while *Joseph Andrews* is in some ways a romance like *The Winter's Tale*, Fielding was also aiming to write a realistic novel. And this is part of the problem. Perdita represents the perfect marriage of nobility and nature; as pastoral requires, we are never in any doubt that she is a lady. Pastoral is about rusticity, but its central figures are never rustic in the pejorative sense which Fielding would have understood, and which *O.E.D.* defines as follows: '1. Lack of breeding, culture or refinement; clownishness, awkwardness. 2. Lack of intellectual culture, ignorance.' I have already suggested that Joseph is a little awkward and unrefined. What of Fanny, the girl for whom he has been saving his virtue? For one thing, she is completely illiterate (p. 66); for another, her person has some minor blemishes which suggest that she is not exactly out of the top drawer:

> She was so plump, that she seemed bursting through her tight stays, especially in the part which confined her swelling breasts. Nor did her hips want the assistance of a hoop to extend them. The exact shape of her arms, denoted the form of those limbs which she concealed; and tho' they were a little redden'd by her labour, yet if her sleeve slipt above her elbow, or her handkerchief discovered any part of her neck, a whiteness appeared which the finest Italian paint would be unable to reach ... Her teeth were white, but not exactly even. The small-pox had left one only mark on her chin, which was so large, it might have been mistaken for a dimple. . . . Her complexion was fair, a little injured by the sun, but overspread with such a bloom, that the finest ladies would have exchanged all their white for it. . . . To conclude all, she had a natural gentility, superior to the acquisition of art, and which surprized all who beheld her. (pp. 154–55)

The description is not mocking (though there seems to be some confusion about her whiteness), but 'natural gentility' is deliberately wide of the mark. Fanny is no Perdita, but a comely peasant girl, and the pastoral serenade which follows ('Say, *Chloe*, where must the swain stray') is delivered with Fielding's tongue in his cheek. He is too much of a realist to allow us to forget that his hero and heroine are peasants indeed, and not the more refined figures of pastoral. In attacking the middle-class morality of *Pamela* from a patrician vantage-point Fielding lands himself with two genuine rustics.

If innocence in *Joseph Andrews* is neither sexual purity nor mere rusticity, we must turn elsewhere for Fielding's ideal, and from Book II onwards a very different character comes to dominate the novel. Parson Abraham Adams, as his patriarchal name suggests, is a surrogate father to Joseph and Fanny—indeed, much to his wife's alarm he declares that all the parish are his children (p. 302); at the same time he is 'as entirely ignorant of the ways of this world, as an infant just entered into it could possibly be' (p. 43). All three travellers are in a sense babes in the wood, easy game for the predators they meet between London and Booby Hall. But Adams's innocence is of a different kind from that of his two protégés, and he is essentially a more robust reworking of the simple and good-natured Heartfree, who is himself a reworking of the even paler Boncour. With Adams, Fielding has tackled the familiar literary problem of how virtue can escape seeming passive and insipid by making his parson quite formidably energetic. Throughout the novel Adams is both the source and butt of violent physical activity; tattered, beaten, drenched and mud-stained, this clerical dynamo will caper with joy at the settlement of a debt, stamp about the room in a frenzy of distress, or hurl his Aeschylus into the fire to assist a fainting maiden. He is as ready to wade into a fight as he is to rap out 'a hundred Greek verses, and with such a voice, emphasis and action, that he almost frighten'd the women' (p. 194). Hostile contemporary readers of the novel claimed that Adams's dishevelled ebullience was an instance of the ridiculous which did not, *pace* Fielding's Preface, proceed from affectation, and it was even asserted that he had 'ridiculed all the inferior Clergy in the dry, unnatural Character of Parson *Adams*'.[10] Sarah Fielding, however, who had herself published *The Adventures of David Simple* two years after her brother's novel, disagreed warmly with those who 'think proper to overlook the noble simplicity of [Adam's] mind' and added,

> That the ridiculers of parson *Adams* are designed to be the proper objects of ridicule (and not that innocent man himself) is a truth which the author hath in many places set in the most glaring light.[11]

And she is surely correct. If Fielding is gently mocking in his treatment of the young lovers, he is whole-hearted in his enthusiasm for the irrepressible idealism of Abraham Adams.

Adams's innocence combines utter impracticality in a worldly sense with a fervent belief in the importance of practical charity as the central duty of a Christian; indeed, it is a measure of his impracticality that he is so constantly incredulous at the lack of charity in others. Book II opens with his discovery that the nine volumes of sermons which he confidently intends to offer to a London bookseller have not, after all, been packed in his saddlebags. It transpires that his wife has considered him more likely to be in need of clean shirts than sermons on his journey, which is sensible enough in view of the various states of undress he is reduced to in the course of his adventures, though it rather removes the point of the trip. While Adams's belief that his words of wisdom have a market value is a little optimistic, there is no doubt that they are words of wisdom. Impractical though he is, his religion centres on the importance of good deeds—acts of charity—as the means by which heavenly rewards may be won, rather than on a nominal acceptance of the articles of faith. It is the worldly parsons Barnabas and Trulliber whose religion is merely theoretical. Hence we have a neat dichotomy in which the Christian practice of Adams is sneered at by Barnabas and Trulliber as foolishly impractical, while their own indifference to good works is regarded by Adams as almost unbelievably self-destructive. To Barnabas and the bookseller, then, he exclaims:

> Can any doctrine have a more pernicious influence on society than a persuasion, that it will be a good plea for the villain at the

last day; *Lord, it is true I never obeyed one of thy commandments, yet punish me not, for I believe them all?* (p. 94)

And to the porcine Trulliber, who asks in outrage after refusing Adams a 'loan' of fourteen shillings, 'Do you disbelieve the scriptures?':

> 'No, but you do,' answered Adams, 'if I may reason from your practice: for their commands are so explicit, and their rewards and punishments so immense, that it is impossible a man should steadfastly believe without obeying.' (p. 168)

The first enjoinder is followed by Adams's claim that the virtuous heathen may be saved (a claim which Heartfree also makes to his disgusted fellow prisoners in Newgate) and the second by his insistence on the absolute priority of charity for the true Christian, which he repeats throughout the novel. The fact that Adams's unworldliness is often highly comic does not, of course, imply that Fielding is any less earnest than his parson in subscribing to such beliefs. Our laughter is not satirical.

The moral and religious issues raised in *Joseph Andrews* have been amply and ably discussed by M. C. Battestin, so we need not pursue them much further here. It has to be said, though, that Parson Adams is really too bizarre a figure to be comfortably aligned with the mid-eighteenth century Latitudinarian preachers such as Barrow and Hoadly.[12] The central question seems to be whether Adams's innocence is merely ludicrous, or whether it represents an ideal of virtue which the other characters in the novel fail to attain. As we have seen, Fielding's good man cannot be 'absolutely a fool or a coward', and he notes elsewhere that 'it is impossible for a fool, who hath no distinguishing faculty, to be good-natured.'[13] What Fielding presumably means by folly in these instances is mere stupidity, whereas Adams is both highly literate, and intelligent enough to justify his lack of worldly wisdom on religious grounds; he is scarcely the abject dupe of Jonsonian comedy. He is, however, a fool in a profounder sense. The most famous biblical passage on the excellence of charity appears in St. Paul's first epistle to the Corinthians, and it is here too that we find the scriptural authority for Adams's 'holy folly': 'If any man among you seemeth to be wise in this world, let him be a fool, that he may be wise. For the wisdom of this world is foolishness with God' (III, 18–19).[14] Adams's innocence is essentially Paul's Christian folly, and he is, albeit in a minor way, part of a literary tradition which extends from Erasmus's *Encomium Moriae* to Dostoevsky's *The Idiot* and the novels of William Golding. It is in a sense foolish for Adams to assume that Trulliber will lend him fourteen shillings with no prospect of repayment, but behind this episode are Christ's words in the Sermon on the Mount, 'Ask and it shall be given unto you, seek and ye shall find' (*Matthew* VII, 7)—words which Adams understands all too literally. It is true that he himself is so impecunious that his own resources of charity are rarely tested, but he is prepared at one point to sacrifice his entire livelihood rather than let Lady Booby thwart the marriage of Joseph and Fanny. Threatened with dismissal from his curacy, he replies:

> I know not what your ladyship means by the terms master and service. I am in the service of a master who will never discard me for doing my duty: and if the doctor (for indeed I have never been able to pay for a licence) thinks proper to turn me out from my cure, G—will provide me, I hope, another. (p. 267)

This absolute rejection of worldly self-interest has considerable dignity, and there is no hint here of the irony which accompanies Joseph's haughty retorts to the same lady in Book I. It is perhaps the most serious confrontation in the novel, and when Lady Booby later accuses Adams of being a fool, she does so on grounds which Fielding himself sharply exposed in his *Modern Glossary*, where, according to the definitions of the world, a fool is 'A Complex Idea, compounded of Poverty, Honesty, Piety and Simplicity'.[15] The definition is a perfect epitome both of the character of Adams and of St. Paul's ideal of the Christian fool.

Fielding's other proviso that his good man cannot be 'absolutely a coward' scarcely needs elaboration in the case of the pugilistic Adams, who is, we are told, 'brave to an excess' (p. 43) and who has wrists 'which Hercules would not have been ashamed of' (p. 95). But although he is always prepared for fisticuffs, he is more often than not on the receiving end of violence, and the journey back to Booby Hall in Books II and

III is managed with about as much comfort as an army assault course. It is entirely typical that after wading up to his middle through a pond (unnecessarily, as it turns out), Adams should transfer to a stage-coach, only to end up being drenched from head to toe with a pan of hog's blood at the first inn. The climactic scenes of violence occur in Book III, where the various indignities to which Adams is subjected by the squire and his cronies take on the nature of ritual torment and humiliation. After being savaged by a pack of hounds, he, Joseph and Fanny are invited back to dinner by the owner. What follows is well indicated by two of the subsequent chapter titles, '*A Scene of Roasting very nicely adapted to the present Taste and Times*' and '*Containing as surprizing and bloody Adventures as can be found in this, or perhaps any other authentic History*'. Adams has his chair pulled from under him, soup poured into his breeches, and gin poured into his beer; his wig is removed, he is lampooned and mimicked, has fire-crackers attached to his cassock, and is finally set upon a 'throne' which deposits him in a tub of water. This systematic baiting of an unworldly parson is echoed more sombrely in William Golding's novel *Rites of Passage*, where the Reverend Colley, similarly wigless, is put through a punishing series of 'rites', made to kneel before a 'throne' in a state of undress, force-fed with nauseous liquids, and doused in a 'paunch' of filthy water.[16] In both cases the victim is chosen for his innocence; he is mocked and brutalized *because* he is an unworldly oddity; his cloth, 'the ornaments of the Spiritual Man', as Colley calls it, and the symbol of his unworldliness, is torn and desecrated. By the end of his own ordeal Adams's garments have taken on the appearance of fool's motley:

> he had on neither breeches nor stockings; nor had he taken from his head a red spotted handkerchief, which by night bound his wig, that was turned inside out, around his head. He had on his torn cassock, and his great-coat; but as the remainder of his cassock hung down below his great-coat; so did a small strip of white, or rather whitish linnen appear below that; to which we may add the several colours which appeared on his face, where a long piss-burnt beard, served to return the liquor of the stone pot, and that of a blacker hue which distilled from the mop. (p. 255)

The ordeals of Adams and Colley are comic and tragic versions of the ritual vilification of the holy fool—a rite which has its origins in the tormenting of Christ himself. The difference between the two fictional characters is that, while Adams has no sense of shame, Colley dies of it. While Colley lies inertly in his cabin clutching a ringbolt, Adams capers on undaunted, ludicrous yet saintly, the battered but resilient victim of the world's abuse.

If the first book of *Joseph Andrews* is largely concerned with the theme of sexual innocence, Books II and III present innocence as Christian folly, a mixture of charity and simplicity which is ridiculed by the world at large. So do we have in Abraham Adams Fielding's ideal of the good man? The answer, I think, is that Adams is in a quite literal sense too much a figure of fun to fill this rôle adequately, and that Fielding is too much of a realist to imagine that a world peopled entirely by holy fools would be anything other than bedlam. There is also a more serious charge. Adams's ignorance of the ways of the world is accompanied by an ignorance of the wickedness of the world. To know not the meaning of ill-doing, nor dream that any did, is dangerously insufficient as a basis for moral conduct. When Adams tells Joseph that 'knowledge of men is only to be learnt from books' (p. 176), we know that he is wrong—isn't this how Pamela acquired her preternatural sagacity? Similarly, in their debate on education, Adams's preference for 'a private school, where boys may be kept in innocence and ignorance' (p. 221) may remind us of Blake's dictum, 'Innocence dwells with Wisdom, but never with Ignorance.'[17] What Blake meant by that is probably rather different from anything that Fielding would readily have understood, but it may serve as an introduction to the two interpolated tales in Books II and III, to which we must now turn.

Leonora's story and Wilson's story complement each other. One is about a fall, the other about a fall followed by a retrieval of innocence. One point of the stories is that they provide a more sophisticated perspective on the country world of booby squires, piggish clergymen and grasping innkeepers, a perspective which opens on to the worlds of Pope and

Hogarth. Fielding's own experience was, after all, hardly limited to his native Somerset, nor was his knowledge of men acquired solely from books or from the company of rustics. The characters in the interpolated tales are of Fielding's own class, and their lives are likely, therefore, to be of some relevance to the overall purpose of the novel. Leonora's world of balls and beaus is akin to that of *The Rape of the Lock*— though she is not, of course, moving in fashionable London society—and as with Pope, Fielding's targets are female vanity, caprice and fickleness, 'the moving Toyshop of their heart'. In fact, there seem to be deliberate allusions to Pope's work: 'Beaus banish Beaus, and Coaches Coaches drive' (I, 102) is illustrated by the arrival of the foppish Bellarmine, whose splendid coach and six is responsible for his supplanting Horatio in Leonora's affections. She declares it 'to be the completest, genteelest, prettiest equipage she ever saw; adding these remarkable words, *O I am in love with that equipage!*' When the fop himself appears, 'Her little heart began to flutter within her' (pp. 115, 116), reminding us of Pope's lines,

> Teach Infant-Cheeks a bidden Blush to know,
> And little Hearts to flutter at a *Beau*. (I, 89–90)

The result of her fickleness is that she ends up without either lover. There is also, perhaps, a hint of mock-epic here, as the two stages of Leonora's downfall are accompanied by Miltonic groans from Adams ('Here Adams groaned a second time', p. 117), echoing those of Earth in *Paradise Lost* ('. . . and nature gave a second groan', IX, 1001) when first Eve and then Adam eat the apple.[18] This tale, however, is a moral fable on the dangers of worldly vanity, rather than a story of paradise lost. It is in the second of the interpolated tales that Eden is more directly evoked.

Wilson's story, as has often been observed, owes a good deal to Hogarth's *The Rake's Progress*, though unlike that rake the end of his squalid adventures in town is not the confinement of a mad-house but idyllic retirement in the countryside. Further, Wilson's retirement is the precise opposite of Leonora's morose and companionless seclusion; it is paradise regained, Fielding's pastoral ideal, 'the manner in which people had lived in the golden age', as Adams exclaims on leaving the Wilsons' rural retreat. Their Eden is a garden without ornament: 'No parterres, no fountains, no statues', but with a great abundance of 'fruit, and every thing useful for the kitchin'. Wilson cultivates it himself:

> Hither I generally repair at the dawn, and exercise myself whilst my wife dresses her children, and prepares our breakfast, after which we are seldom asunder during the residue of the day; for when the weather will not permit them to accompany me here, I am usually within with them. . . . And sure as this friendship is sweetened with more delicacy and tenderness, so is it confirmed by dearer pledges than can attend the closest male alliance: for what union can be so fast, as our common interest in the fruits of our embraces? (pp. 216–17)

Where Leonora is punished in her retreat from the vanity of the world with sterile isolation, Wilson's retreat is noticeably fruitful, both horticulturally and sexually. And his retrieval of innocence also reaffirms Adams's belief in the priority of charity, for he owes his domestic idyll to the most significant act of charity in the novel, which is Harriet Hearty's generous decision first to give Wilson enough money to pay off his debts, and then to share her fortune with him in marriage. What this marriage represents is a combination of the sexual ideal which is pursued in Book I and the Christian ideal of charity which is pursued in Books II and III. Fielding is indulgent towards Betty the chambermaid earlier, as he is not to Leonora, because her sexuality is an expression of a generous nature, but his response to the Pamelaic hoarding of virginity is not therefore to advocate promiscuity, which is why we are treated to the tale of Wilson's gruesome philandering. Wilson is redeemed only by another's spontaneous act of charity.

Is Wilson's story then 'the philosophic, as well as structural, center of the novel', as Battestin has suggested?[19] It is conceivable that Fielding intended it to be, but even if we allow the possibility of a 'philosophical center' to such a light-hearted novel, the story still seems too oblique to the main action to be a centre of any kind. Wilson is introduced because unlike Joseph he is a gentleman, and unlike Adams he is very far from being 'entirely ignorant of the ways of this world'. What Fielding is now struggling for in his pursuit of innocence is a touch of class. Innocence must not be ignorance. Retirement must not be rusticity (in the sense defined above). Arcadia was not peopled by country bumpkins (indeed, in Sidney's *Arcadia* the rebellious country bumpkins have various parts of their anatomy playfully lopped off by the aristocrats). But Wilson is also introduced so that Joseph may be refurbished as hero in the last book by the addition of some gentle blood, for Wilson turns out, of course, to be Joseph's father, and Joseph therefore turns out not to be the mere rustic we had imagined him to be. Like Perdita the lost child is restored to its parents, but it is not the case, as it is with Perdita, that we have been aware all along that the country lad is in fact high-born. In fact it is in the last book that Joseph and Fanny appear at their most waif-like, when they are threatened with committal to Bridewell for the alleged theft of a twig worth three halfpence; the episode makes them look pathetic without giving Joseph any opportunity to reveal his latent gentility. It can be argued that he grows in maturity in the course of the novel and is in the end its rightful hero, but as Fielding himself remarked in the Preface, Abraham Adams is its most 'glaring' character, while Fielding's class sympathies undoubtedly lie with the one true gentleman, Mr. Wilson. The different characters present different versions of 'innocence', but none acquires exemplary status.

This may seem to be making heavy weather of what is essentially a comic novel, albeit one with strong moral themes. Certainly the ending of *Joseph Andrews* is splendidly light-hearted with its mixture of romance—the fanciful discovery of lost parents and children—and hectic bedroom farce. The comic resolution has been well described by Mark Spilka, who writes of Adams: 'by sending his beloved parson from bed to bed, Fielding has put a kind of comic blessing on the novel.'[20] But even Adams cannot be allowed to have the last word. The 'resolution' is an escape into fantasy because Fielding has not yet solved his problem, which is to find a hero who combines the various aspects of 'innocence' we have been exploring: simplicity, charity, natural gentility, a generous sensuality, and 'innocence—with—experience'. He discovered that hero in his masterpiece, *Tom Jones*.

NOTES

1. *Joseph Andrews*, ed. R. F. Brissenden (Harmondsworth: Penguin, 1977), p. 25. All references are to this edition.
2. See M. C. Battestin, *The Moral Basis of Fielding's Art: A Study of Joseph Andrews* (Middletown, Conn.: Wesleyan University Press, 1959) and the essay by Bryan Burns in the present volume.
3. S. T. Coleridge, *Table Talk and Omniana*, ed. T. Ashe (London, 1884), p. 295.
4. Samuel Richardson, *Pamela*, introd. M. Kinkead-Weekes (London: Dent, 1965).
5. *Joseph Andrews and Shamela*, ed. M. C. Battestin (London: Methuen, 1965), p. 325.
6. See the Preface to *Miscellanies*, Vol. 1, ed. H. K. Miller (Oxford: Clarendon Press, 1972), p. 11, on the distinction between greatness and goodness.
7. C. J. Rawson argues this point in *Henry Fielding and the Augustan Ideal under Stress* (London: Routledge, 1972), p. 234 and note, in the course of a penetrating discussion of 'The problem of Heartfree and other "good" characters in Fielding'.
8. *Jonathan Wild*, ed. David Nokes (Harmondsworth: Penguin, 1982), p. 83.
9. *Miscellanies*, p. 12; quoted as the epigraph to Chapter 7 in Rawson, p. 228.
10. 'Porcupinus Pelagius' in *Old England*, No. 266 (5 March 1748), quoted in Battestin, p. 142.
11. Ronald Paulson and Thomas Lockwood (eds.), *Henry Fielding: The Critical Heritage* (London: Routledge, 1969), p. 369.
12. See Battestin, Chapters 2 and 3.
13. *The Champion*, 27 March 1740; in W. E. Henley (ed.), *The Complete Works of Henry Fielding* (New York, 1903), XV, 258.
14. A similar point is made by James E. Evans in 'The World According to Paul: Comedy and Theology in *Joseph Andrews*', *Ariel*, XV (1984), 45–56. This article came to my attention as the present essay was going to press.
15. *The Covent Garden Journal*, 14 January 1752; reprinted in Ioan Williams (ed.), *The Criticism of Henry Fielding* (London: Routledge, 1970), p. 92.
16. William Golding, *Rites of Passage* (London: Faber, 1980), pp. 235–39.
17. Geoffrey Keynes (ed.), *Blake: Complete Writings* (London: Oxford University Press, rept. 1974), p. 380 ('Notes Written on the Pages of *The Four Zoas*').
18. Fielding alludes to *Paradise Lost* elsewhere in the novel, e.g. 'Beyond the realm of chaos and old night' (p. 184) and 'darkness visible' (p. 187).
19. Battestin, p. 119.
20. Mark Spilka, 'Comic Resolution in Fielding's *Joseph Andrews*', rept. in *Fielding: A Collection of Critical Essays*, ed. Ronald Paulson (Englewood Cliffs, N.J.: Prentice-Hall, 1962), p. 67.

6

The Story-telling in *Joseph Andrews*

by BRYAN BURNS

Joseph Andrews is one of the freshest and most vital works of fiction of the English eighteenth century. On the whole, modern criticism of the book has attributed its success to the linking patterns of its organization, and has seen it entire, as a work of consistent and connected design, rather than as a pleasingly random assemblage of the literary elements which Fielding had to hand.[1] In part, this is due to a correct perception of the themes and repeated circumstances and the witty devices of rhetoric and stage-management which thread themselves throughout the novel, and a sense of the hidden shapeliness of Joseph's endeavours, after he has been angrily cast out by Lady Booby, to make his way back to the 'rural paradise'[2] which he had earlier shared with the beautiful and innocent Fanny. It also arises from a desire, much fostered by Fielding himself in his 'Preface' and in the introductory essays to each book of *Joseph Andrews*, to acknowledge the work as establishing a well-considered new genre in English fiction, and one properly equipped with both definition and purpose. A third and crucial impetus to these correlating endeavours has been given by the undoubted and extraordinary unity of *Tom Jones*, the big brother which followed *Joseph Andrews* after an interval of seven years, and whose plot has been an object of admiration at least since the time of Coleridge. It seems fair to think that the complexity of *Tom Jones* has encouraged critics to seek its origins, and at times to see it already formed, in the earlier book from which many of its materials are evidently quarried. Given these inducements, it is unsurprising that so much effort has been spent in the tracing of correspondences within *Joseph Andrews*, the explanation of apparent inconsistencies and the elaborate vindication of the novel's status as a considered, mature work of art.[3] But it does not seem to me that it is desirable to try to tidy away all of the novel's roughnesses, repetitions and alterations of stance. Indeed, as I shall argue, the aesthetic appeal and comic vivacity of *Joseph Andrews* are dependent not on an impression of smoothness, assimilation and mastery, but rather on a sense of the unexpected and incongruous. It is, in fact, a book whose success rests largely on its closeness to the often disorderly realities of the everyday world of Fielding's time.[4]

Fielding's famous 'Preface' to *Joseph Andrews*, in which he sets out to describe and also to justify the new form he is attempting, has always seemed an appropriate starting-point for any estimate of his fiction. And, as a witty and well-substantiated essay on the 'comic epic-poem in prose' (p. 25),[5] complete with the authentication of a classical ancestry and suitability to a present-day need, it is a brilliant achievement. But it is not an entirely accurate account of the novel we have before us; there is an air of special pleading to the whole virtuosic enterprise. Fielding appears to be aiming firstly for inclusiveness, variety and energy, for a work which will accommodate an 'extended and comprehensive' (p. 25) action, much incident and a large cast of characters, and even a slight acquaintance with the book would certainly give one a sense of its agreeable heterogeneity and vividness. Yet a second purpose of the 'Preface' seems to be to subordinate this impression to a more sternly pointed view of the generic homogeneity of the novel and of its uniformly moral use of its materials in attacking the affectation which springs from 'vanity, or hypocrisy' (p. 28). The concern of any preface or afterword may be the same, to excuse deficiencies, to indicate charms and to cast a perhaps factitiously concordant gloss over the body of the work itself, and Fielding is not immune to these lures. Throughout *Joseph Andrews*, in fact, there is a conflict, never entirely resolved, between the desire to open the reader to a rich, free narrative of the often wayward doings of a life on the road and the desire to produce a highly patterned novel with a didactic core. This is the dilemma at the root of the book: its ambiguousness as to formal art, on the one hand, its urgent intimacy with experience, but at the same time its attempt to transcend this naturalistic attentiveness in the interests of symmetry of structure and thematic (in the end, ethical) control.

The vigour of this doubleness seems confirmed as we proceed through the text itself. *Joseph Andrews* offers itself as a quite different kind of novel from the uninterrupted flux of *Moll Flanders* or of other works which aim to immerse the reader in the particular details of a random experience of the world. Its divisions are noted with an emphasis which it is impossible to disregard, and which repeatedly calls attention both to the separateness of the various incidents, and simultaneously to the writer's urge to present a coherent, evolving whole. There is an extreme, almost a nervous, artistic self-consciousness in the prefacing of each of the four books of *Joseph Andrews* with a general critical essay, and the breezy explicatory titles given to even the briefest of the chapters.[6] Of course, Fielding is often jokey in these matters, and often intends us to smile at his paternal fussiness and the niceness of his care for his reader's understanding. But, in practice, the proliferation of chapters and books, all individually headed and excusingly signalled by Fielding's narrator, suggest a parody of thoroughgoingness and consistency rather than a genuine striving after them. Certainly this complex splitting up and separating out of the stories that form the novel prevents a smooth flow of material or easy transitions from one action, character or style to another. Thus, partly by design, but partly also by over-anxiousness, the reader comes increasingly to perceive the narrative in discrete, rather than unified, terms, and so to feel quizzical about the relationship between Fielding's wish to impute some general interpretation to his work, and his often contradictory delight in the vagary and singularity of human behaviour.

This problem is a matter of the texture of *Joseph Andrews* as well as of Fielding's arrangement of its parts. As the novel moves out of the rather rigid and awkward parody of

Richardson's *Pamela* which provides the rationale for its early London scenes, the reader becomes aware of another gap in the book's format, that between its arresting foreground and its usually more prosaic or strident background of moral purpose, of a didacticism which sometimes seems at odds with, or only loosely derived from, the incidents of which it is the supposed residuum.[7] Fielding's purpose was to combine vivid circumstantial detail, whether of Parson Trulliber, with 'a stateliness in his gate, when he walked, not unlike that of a goose, only he stalked slower' (p. 163), or of innumerable richly-cast scenes of inns and innkeepers, with the moral warnings and recommendations which he lays out for us in his 'Preface', and to relate naturalistic description in a securely causal way to a more pedagogic view of behaviour. But there is a tendency in *Joseph Andrews* for these two elements of Fielding's enterprise to separate out, and for his moral commentary to exist uneasily apart from his evocation of eighteenth-century road-life. There are frequent, teasing movements, especially at the beginnings of chapters and after rapidly paced set-piece incidents of comic action, between generality and particularity. Fielding's commentary is some-times gently ironic, sometimes ruminative, and sometimes firmly pointed, but it is not often embodied in the narrative itself. Instead, it is voiced *a posteriori* by the narrator, often in spruce, elegant paragraphs whose different tone and mode do nothing to assuage their statuesque detachment from the episodes whose significance they indicate. Some of the instances in which this seems not the case are those passages of combat in which Fielding burlesques the heroic manner in his rendition of the comically humdrum conflicts of his own day. In principle, however, Fielding is regularly pulled towards engrossedness in the immediate moment in this novel, and it is sometimes difficult to feel any intrinsic connection between his wonderfully free and varied response to the moment and the more stolid commentary by which it is surrounded.[8]

Many of these difficulties take their origin from the two forms of writing to which Fielding is most indebted in *Joseph Andrews*, the picaresque fiction and the drama. The picaresque is inherently predisposed towards the working through of a series of adventures linked mainly by the presence of a lively protagonist and issuing more naturally in minutely detailed scenes of low life than in convincing exhortations to virtue. We may see from the novels of Fielding's contemporary, Smollett, how seductive was the urge, in fiction of this kind, to give up almost everything except the flux that environs a figure like Roderick Random or Peregrine Pickle. At least *Joseph Andrews* is not so random and encyclopaedic as the early novels of Smollett; there is rhythm to its narrative, the twinning of the good but impractical Parson Adams with the good but increasingly worldly-wise Joseph Andrews is pointed and nice, and there is a satisfying completeness in the book's movement from the hypocrisies of London and servitude to Lady Booby to the love and liberty achieved by Joseph and Fanny in the countryside and under the aegis of Mr. Wilson. Nevertheless, in both authors there remains the considerable problem of coercing an untrammelled, slippery form like the picaresque into overall structural control and directed moral substance— this being fully achieved by each not in his first attempts, but by Fielding in *Tom Jones* and by Smollett, more obliquely, in *Humphry Clinker*. Both also, in all their writings, fortunately maintain the picaresque's entertaining primacy of well-rendered scenes, much action, robustness and a profusion of sharply observed detail. In the drama, which was Fielding's first choice as a writer, the closeness to experience which we feel in the picaresque is taken to extremes; it is only indirectly, if at all, that any sustained commentary on the action, or any continued drawing of a moral, may be obtained. Plays, particularly those by Fielding himself, are very much of the moment; everything depends on the sustaining of a circum-stance crisply in the audience's attention, undistracted by conspicuous nudgings as to thematic or ethical significance. And much of what Fielding learned in the theatre proves brilliantly apropos in his fiction. Despite all of Fielding's efforts at accommodation, and his evident awareness of what his intentions for *Joseph Andrews* will require, in technique as well as in content, despite all his ingenious ploys and narratorial bonhomie, it is his histrionic skills which provide the most energetic impetus to his prose. The fluency and ease of his dramatization are inexhaustible; given almost any scene between two characters at loggerheads, and especially when this involves some social nuance or unavoidable clash between propriety and individual impulse, Fielding produces the most intimately involved, precisely viewed, *theatrical* writing of his time. So, for instance, while his comments on the contrary impulses which are driving Lady Booby both towards and away from the satisfaction of her understandable lust for her handsome young servant are neat and engaging, they cannot compare with the superbly intense and *present* quality of his realization of the interviews between Lady Booby and the bemused Joseph himself, or between Lady Booby and the flouncing, well-informed Mrs. Slipslop. In the circumstances of explication, we are aware of a degree of effort, of conscious contrivance; in those of direct presentation, of a rightness that seems to come effortlessly to Fielding's pen. His instinct for drama and realism is evident in his handling not just of the life of the road, but, even more, of the world of women. *Joseph Andrews* is very much about the behaviour of women, slyly and finely observed, and given point by the new sexual freedom which its *donnée* permits them all. Thus, although Mrs. Slipslop may be given to us first as a caricature, 'not at this time remarkably handsome; being very short, and rather too corpulent in body, and somewhat red, with the addition of pimples in the face' (p. 51), and Fanny may promise little more than an orthodox virginal prettiness, both rapidly acquire substance as the novel progresses. In fact, every woman in the book, from the chambermaid Betty through to Lady Booby herself, is enlivened by exact and passionate speech, vigour and an acute penetration as to motive and social circumstance. These are the qualities of social comedy, and in Fielding they show themselves best in bright scenes, impressive by their precision and lucidity. These scenes are often presented to the reader with some brusqueness, and there are many of them, but Fielding has a theatrical assurance and a keen eye for subtleties of language and gesture which always brings them off.

But Fielding has difficulty in the connecting together of his scenes, and this is signalled by the many indecisions in the early, principally parodic part of the novel, before Joseph is freed into his risky and exciting life on the road. In Chapter 1, with its arch insinuations and uneasy tone, there is little sense of the convincing establishment of a unified or encompassing mode. Although individual paragraphs, sentences and satirical vignettes are well formed, one cannot avoid an impression of stiltedness in the presentation of material and of some doubt as to the kind of story the author has embarked upon. From the start, then, we must accustom ourselves to some degree of heterogeneity, and accept that discontinuousness and surprise will be of the essence of Fielding's disposition of his materials in *Joseph Andrews*. Pace and newness are central to the appeal of this work; something fresh and unexpected is constantly appearing before the reader, its drama heightened by the crisp movements from one topic to another and the vivacity of the changes of subject, tone and perspective as between one chapter and the next. Especially when it embarks on Joseph's pilgrimage from London to his home village, the book derives great emotional capital from its heady rapidity of tempo and avoidance of directness or orderliness in its presentation of story and event. There is a nice eschewing of monotony and an equally nice arrangement of differing pleasures: with the generality of the first chapter of Book II, for example, set off by the vivid, uncommented comedy of the second. We have an almost cinematic sense of zigzagging among styles of writing, direct and indirect, abstract and concrete, as well as a wide range of characters, places and circumstances, and respond more warmly to the novel's attractive busyness of surface, its colourful, action-packed foreground, than to the larger ethical purposes which lie beneath this surface. Fielding's essay on divisions in authors, at the beginning of Book II, seems an admission of his practice in this respect, and a sufficient explanation of its usefulness; it pays little attention to the notion that a book should be consistently patterned to a moral end, and instead encourages the reader to choose what appeals to him or her from among the rich assemblage of delights separately offered by separate chapters.

Fielding's major problem is the giving of an overall moral vision and sense of structure to diverse materials which both his own instincts and talents, and the aptitudes of the fictional form he has chosen, encourage him to leave in freedom. Hence the variety of means he adopts to generalize, and comment on, the adventures in which his characters are embroiled: the

views on behaviour both openly expressed and more covertly
infiltrated into the action, the discussions of literary
methodology, the ironic allusiveness of the prose, the attempts
to give opinions on many different human circumstances, the
parodies, the letters—above all, the interpolated tales.[9] In
fact, *Joseph Andrews* is almost entirely composed of stories
formally or informally arising as the travellers move on their
way, and this necessarily offers a broadening out of the
narrative. Most of these stories are told directly by or of
characters to whom we have already been introduced, and
give us a fuller sense of their lives and a deeper awareness of
their motives; others are properly separate from the main line
of action, such as the tale of Leonora, and function as
alternative or additional fictions within the enveloping fiction
of *Joseph Andrews* itself. Thus the foreground of the book is
composed of incident and immediate explanation; the background, of critical and interpretative material supplied in a
variety of ways, not least by complementary narratives like
that of Leonora. In general, these narratives reflect in both
literary and moral respects on the lessons to be learned from
the surface of Fielding's story, though they do not do so in any
evident way; all of them have at various times been attacked
for their apparent irrelevance. Their separateness cannot be
denied, but it seems to me that it is necessary to Fielding's
purposes, as I shall try to show. The main point of the
interpolations is precisely to interrupt, to tumble the reader
disturbingly from one manner and perspective into another—
to provoke Fielding's audience into wider and more general
views than they might otherwise obtain. This seems entirely of
a piece with the reliance on surprise and heterogeneousness
which we find throughout *Joseph Andrews*. But it has an
obliqueness and charm, and an impersonal appositeness, that
elevate it beyond the usual means by which we are controlled
and led to conclusions in a novel. The interpolated tales,
therefore, require a special sort of attention; they are
suggestive, spreading notions more broadly in time and space,
and indicating a surprisingly fuller conspectus than that
issuing summarily from the narrative. In essence, though they
are moral rather than literary-critical, they are like the
introductory chapters to each of the books of *Joseph Andrews*;

they move us away from the present situation, and encourage us teasingly to reconsider the implications of what we have seen, and the moral position of the work as a whole. Thus, as Hunter has said, the interpolations are 'places of rest and refreshment',[10] but they are also important and necessary devices by which Fielding strives to remedy the fissure in the technique of his novel and effectively to relate the didactic and the picaresque elements of his purpose.

The first of Fielding's interpolated tales in *Joseph Andrews* is 'The History of Leonora, or the Unfortunate Jilt' (p. 34), which is told to the travellers, during two separate coach trips interrupted by an action-packed stop at an inn, as Chapters 4 and 6 of Book II. Leonora's is a sardonic story of feminine greed and hypocrisy, and gives a pointedly ironic picture of the pretty, empty-headed Leonora, engaged to Horatio until the arrival of the affected, richer, Frenchified Bellarmine causes a sudden reversal of her feelings; Horatio is coolly disposed of, with the connivance of her unprincipled aunt, and Leonora's so-called devotion transferred to her new beau until her canny father, pleading poverty, scuttles the entire crass *amour*. And so Leonora is left, as we may think she deserves, to a 'disconsolate life' (p. 134), an object of ridicule, and without either of her lovers. Even given the discreteness of *Joseph Andrews*, one cannot fail to be puzzled by the length and prominence of the tale of Leonora and its apparently total distinctness from the rest of the novel; from the courtliness of its names, the formality of its style, right through to the derivative nature of its story, it could hardly present a greater contrast to the rough-and-tumble of highway travel as experienced by Joseph, Parson Adams and Fanny. The world of the Leonora story is self-consciously literary; it is governed by the standards of romantic fiction, and is expressed in a fulsome and redundant language which lifts it away from naturalism and towards the flaccid orthodoxies of some bookish, courtly cloud-cuckoo-land. Even communication between Leonora and her suitors often takes place not directly, but by means of hyperbolic letters whose every elaborate compliment is undercut by mercenary self-regard: as, most strikingly, when Bellarmine, finding his ' "*Adorable* and *charmante*" ' (p. 134) to be coming to him without any certain dowry, abruptly decides that ' "I am not the *heureux* person destined for your divine arms" ' and hurriedly returns to France. Coupled with the linguistic tawdriness of the characters, their inability ever to manage the direct acknowledgement of honest feelings, is the prime feature of their society, its frivolous attention to matters of show rather than of substance. Bellarmine, the 'French-English' (p. 117) man of the world, is characterized by his love of finery and his constant concern for his appearance, and his dedication to French at the expense of English styles (' "I would rather see the dirty island at the bottom of the sea, rather than wear a single rag of English work about me" ', p. 119). For Leonora, also, the lure of creating a stir, of distinguishing oneself from one's friends and competitors, is too strong to resist: ' "How vast is the difference between being the wife of a poor counsellor, and the wife of one of Bellarmine's fortune" ' (p. 118). One of the strengths of *Joseph Andrews* is its precise, full and unillusioned view of the social and sexual behaviour of women, and the tale of Leonora powerfully emphasizes this element of the novel. In the larger world beyond the confines of Leonora's disposal of herself in marriage, there seems a conspiracy of women drawn irresistibly by Joseph's well-detailed charms of person; within these confines, the conspiracy is to gain not sexual but financial advantage. Leonora's aunt, perceiving her niece's true inclinations, and remarking that ' "The world is always on the side of prudence" ' (p. 118), perfectly plays her Mephistophelean rôle—the two women together showing up the hegemony that wealth and status may have in a society like their own, dedicated to material advancement at the cost of emotional truth. So, by the end of the first chapter of the story of Leonora, we have been transported into a disagreeably new environment, and can hardly have failed to note the ironic implications of its presentation. Even the alteration from the colloquialism and comedy of the coach-journey on which the tale is told, with the humorous malice of Mrs. Slipslop and the coarseness of coachmen and innkeepers, to the insipid formalities of Leonora's polite existence, would be enough to alert us to Fielding's critical purposes in this interpolation. Equally, we cannot escape some sense of a comparison between the genuine, unpretentious love of Joseph and Fanny and the factitious relationships between Leonora, Horatio and Bellarmine. In the one case, we have warmth and directness, compounded by the unletteredness of Fanny; in the other, an interest only in the opinions of others, and the regard of others. Lending added force to these comparative suggestions are the repeated interjections of the reliably goodhearted Parson Adams himself, providing variety and recalling the reader to decency and common sense, and the pragmatic comments of the narrator, in a trustworthily cool and deliberative way, which keenly expose the folly of Leonora's behaviour. At this point, then, like Parson Adams, we are curious about the conclusion of the story, though we have assimilated its unfavourable evocation of worldliness and its sharpness as to the error of trusting to social considerations rather than to the intuitions of one's heart.

The next chapter in the novel, the brief interlude at the inn which suspends the outcome of Leonora's story and draws out our concern as to its development, is strikingly different. It begins with the resumption of the real world, where selfishness and hypocrisy are of course to be found, just as in the tale of Leonora, but with a freshness and immediacy which seem ironically remote from the literary indirection controlling her existence and that of her circle. Almost immediately we have Parson Adams and the innkeeper, far from the elegant ill-nature we have just encountered, fighting sturdily together until both are covered in blood (though the former is merely drenched by the contents of a convenient pan of hog's blood, wielded by the innkeeper's wife), and Mrs. Slipslop rewarding this woman with 'several hearty cuffs in the face' (p. 126). The comedy and earthiness of this violence, accepted in a good spirit by all participants, reflects sardonically on the hidden emotional violence we have recently witnessed in the story of Leonora, and the entire chapter compares critically with the courtly double-dealing which precedes it; at least at the inn, things are out in the open, and a conflict may be expressed and the air cleared in a straightforward and manly way. Fielding's recommendations are made plain in the ensuing discussions between two interfering guests who advise legal action to each disputant, but with no success; Parson Adams says, ' "do you take me for a villain, who would prosecute revenge in cold blood, and use unjustifiable means to obtain it?" ' (p. 128), and the innkeeper is much too grieved by the loss of his hog's blood, destined for blood puddings, to consent to any sort of legal wrangling. The chapter continues with the refusal by the snobbish Miss Grave-airs to countenance a mere footman like Joseph in the coach with her, resolved when she is taken off by her father, and concludes with a satisfying attack by the remaining ladies on the character of such a ' "*Myhummetman*" ' (p. 130) as she has shown herself to be. The effectiveness of this chapter separating the two halves of Leonora's story derives from its remarkable use of contrast; in subject-matter, in tone, in style, it gives us the robust comic obverse of bookish romance, and reminds us powerfully of the ordinary lives on which Leonora turns her back at her peril. But, neatly subsumed within this contrast, there are also quiet continuities, pointers which might lead us to consider the links between Leonora's world and the cruder world of the highway to which it is set in opposition. In both worlds, the cosmopolitanism of the traveller who prefers French or Italian to English is mocked; in both, Christian virtues are inconspicuously upheld; in both, 'society', which judges by appearance rather than by true worth, is condemned. This seems an excellent particular instance of Fielding's general method: a surface of rapid movement, change and drama, and beneath it a number of joint concerns, not over-stressed or highly structured, having principally to do with the definition of a sort of goodness which is practically useful in the real world.

After this interlude, we return expectantly to Leonora to discover the sad conclusion of her opportunism, in the forfeiture of both her lovers, universal mockery, and retirement from the *beau monde*. This is the ending we anticipate, but it achieves a greater emotional force for its retardation and produces even a kind of pathos, finally, in spite of its ironies, from the plight of Leonora and of the now rich and still unmarried Horatio. We have just been refreshed by the openness with which struggles are resolved in a freer ambience, and to revert to this constraint, to this pervasive, if subdued, nastiness, is bound to lend a more sympathetic overtone to the lives of those caught in such a circumstance.

Immediately after the ending of Leonora's tale, with the expedition which usually characterizes Fielding's handling of transitions, the novel returns to the brisk freedoms of the life of the road, and we are left only briefly to attend to the lessons of social, moral and literary naturalness which this interpolation has displayed for us. The next story which we come upon occurs much later in the book, and has a monitory significance like Leonora's, though it is more particular and more personal in its effect, and it also makes stronger positive suggestions than in her case. It has the air of a summation, a paradigm of the novel's various warnings and encouragements[11]; it is placed towards the start of Book III, as Leonora's story was placed towards the start of Book II, and prefigures Joseph's marriage to Fanny and rustic settlement at the same time that it emphasizes the more optimistic elements of Fielding's purpose. It seems plain that a linkage between the tale of Leonora and this tale of Mr. Wilson is indicated; not only is their function similar and complementary, not only do they appear at roughly the same point in their respective Books, but even their use of Parson Adams as excited interrupter and moral sounding-board is the same. Bluntly, Mr. Wilson's story recounts his misguidance and debauchery by the seductions of fashionable London, until eventually, weakened by sickness, drunkenness and disappointment, and imprisoned for debt, he is rescued by the charity of the woman who later becomes his wife and with whom he retires to the country to raise a family and to live a life of sufficiency, probity and contentment which Parson Adams compares to 'the golden age' (p. 220). Mr. Wilson dwells especially on his younger days in the metropolis, and gives an extraordinary panorama, somewhat ironic in its fullness and relentlessness, of pretty well anything that might go wrong with any gentleman in such a situation. He offers much detail as to the many vicious trivialities (and worse) of his behaviour, but pays marked attention to his bouts of venereal disease, which seem a fit emblem of the existence he endures: deeply and recurrently infected, and above all in that area which ought to be richest in joy and ease (and which is, when Mr. Wilson devotes himself to family love rather than to dissipation). The importance of this matter is additionally accentuated by the relations between Mr. Wilson's tale and Leonora's, as indications to the listening Joseph (and so, in the end, to Fanny) both of what to avoid and of the sort of circumstance—marital, unpretending and rustic—from which happiness is most likely to come. Also, the misadventures of Mr. Wilson in the fashionable world, mostly at the hands of the mercenary and hypocritical, parallel the similar but more comical and realistically textured misadventures on the road of Joseph and Fanny; and the serene connubiality of the Wilsons heralds a hopeful outcome too for the love between the younger couple. The continuation of Mr. Wilson's story, which emphasizes the durability of happiness under pastoral conditions, is evidently a setting forth of a model for the present day and for Joseph and Fanny, as well as an indication to them and to the reader that miracles may happen, and that ' "Fortune" ' (p. 214) and ' "Providence" ' (p. 215) may ultimately work to man's advantage. But, in order to prevent any impression of remoteness or absoluteness, Mr. Wilson himself points the moral of his tale, in his eulogy of naturalness and denunciation of artifice at the beginning of Chapter 4 of Book III. And, as we see neatly from the callous shooting of his daughter's spaniel which follows, the power of the great and the rich has not vanished, and even a life as fine as Mr. Wilson's cannot quite be insulated from injustice.

I have already shown some ways in which Mr. Wilson's story is like Leonora's, but the contrasts are more striking than the similarities. Although it communicates some ethical lessons, the tale of Leonora operates mainly as a literary critique, poking fun at the conventions of romance writing even more than at the falsities of romance behaviour. But from the start Mr. Wilson's autobiography has an edge of immediacy and particularity; its realistic detailing and lucid psychological truth give it a poignancy which could not come from an ironic pastiche like the story of Leonora. Mr. Wilson's experience is not so set apart; its setting is the city of London, to which we have already been introduced, and it points out continuities between the different periods and places in which the book's action occurs, and offers reassurance as to possibilities of the resolution even of apparently hopeless dilemmas. In addition, the position of the tale, coming towards what we know must be the novel's close, obtains for it a greater attention than might at first be attracted even by its considerable length, its vivacity and emotional power, and its many glancing links with other aspects of Fielding's narrative. Also, there is a kind of breathlessness to the account, and a plaintiveness to the tone, which work well in gaining our sympathy—a sympathy confirmed by Parson Adams's bell-wether condemnation of the dunning tailor who has Mr. Wilson thrown into prison. In terms of plot, then, Mr. Wilson's story implies hope for the future and an optimism as to cheerful outcomes that we may recollect when it later seems that Joseph and Fanny are, unmarriageably, brother and sister; in thematic terms, it lends force to Fielding's upholding of honesty and country living as against duplicity and urban folly, and suggests the need for determination and good luck in one's encounters with a world in which security can be bought only at the price of bitter experience. But, more than either of these, it stops in its tracks the headlong rush of Fielding's picaresque, and forces the reader, willy-nilly, to move aside into a different, if still affecting, realm, in which are encapsulated those exemplary general truths which the action itself has not adequate means to foster.

The last of the book's interpolated tales, and the least interesting, is the story of Leonard and Paul, read by Parson Adams's son Dick, and forming a single chapter, with another, more strenuous, in coda, towards the end of the novel. It describes the sad experience of the soldier, Paul, who rediscovers in the East Indies his former school-friend, Leonard, now properous and married. Paul stays with Leonard and his wife, finds himself awkwardly embroiled in their many arguments, and escapes from this difficulty by secretly agreeing with each of them about every topic of dissension. The ruse is discovered, and is just provoking yet another quarrel, though this time between Paul and Leonard, when the recital of their story is interrupted. The foppish Beau Didapper, having 'offered a rudeness' (p. 301) to Fanny, is soundly boxed on the ear by Joseph, and a general fight only just averted; then, after Joseph and Fanny have left, there is a good deal of discussion of charity, in both its practical and its theological aspects, terminated agreeably by the proposal of a shared ' "piece of bacon and greens" ' (p. 304) at the local alehouse. The first usefulness of this tale lies in its obstruction of the hastening conclusion of the novel's plot-line; it holds up the acceptance of Joseph's and Fanny's impending wedding, and also provides an interlude of calm and diversion before the pedlar's incidental remark, branding them brother and sister, appears to preclude any chance of marriage. As for the tale itself, critics have always been doubtful as to its function and quality.[12] It has a throw-away air, as of something incidental which is employed to set up a barrier against the too easy flow of the narrative, and the fact that it remains unfinished makes it difficult for us to feel sure as to its purpose. Its manner is that of a formal exemplum, lucid, uncoloured and literary: a manner that can remind us only of the tale of Leonora. Like that story, it has an obvious point, and one that it makes with a suspiciously solemn eighteenth-century decorousness—that there is a need for choosing, for supporting what is right, even in the most pressed of circumstances. In the light of the situation of Joseph and Fanny, this may confirm the reader, indirectly, in his or her view of the justice of the young couple's joint affection and firmness in remaining together. But in fact the value of this tale of Leonard and Paul comes more from its separateness from its context than from its rather slight integration into it. The alteration of tone and style from the robust social comedy which precedes it, to the conventionality and emotional lifelessness of the tale itself, is marked. I think that it is in this sort of contrast, rather than in its content, that the usefulness of this interpolation really lies. Like its peers, it is 'literature', in some sense; like them, too, it is interrupted, and placed and implicitly judged, by energetic reminders of the present, actual circumstances from which it is both a relief and an escape. Firstly, this is done by the paternal, if pedantic, voice of Parson Adams, correcting his son's pronunciation; but, more important, it comes with the provocation of genuine feeling, and authentic, immediate action, in Beau Didapper's affront to Fanny. The vigour of these scenes, the colloquial salubriousness of their presentation and their revelations of emotional truth, tellingly set off the artifice and equivocation of Paul's relations with his old friend. And the sharpness of this breaking in of the actual upon the exemplary, the clash of these two modes, is highlighted further by Parson Adams's principled support of Joseph, and the values he stands for, against the calumnies of the fashionable group by which he is surrounded.

As I suggested at the beginning of this essay, few critics now complain of the irrelevance or brusqueness of Fielding's interpolated tales in *Joseph Andrews*, although both the critic's ingenuity and the reader's belief have been stretched by some remarks, particularly on the story of Leonard and Paul. I have agreed that there are a number of quietly indicative thematic links between the interpolated tales and the main body of the novel, and have pointed to the explanation of these links in the need that Fielding feels to provide more distanced exempla, apart from the engrossing charivari of the picaresque life of the road, brief interludes that can offer a commentary on the action which is less immediate and local than can arise easily out of the action itself. But it is more significant, I think, that we are strongly aware of the interruptingness of these stories, and little, and obliquely, of their hidden continuities with the foreground of the book. Their main function is to disturb, and to do this in both moral and stylistic ways. They interrupt the flux of life, but are themselves constantly interrupted by it; they pinpoint precisely Fielding's primary struggle in *Joseph Andrews*, the need to accommodate his impulses simultaneously towards a rather generalized didacticism and towards a pure, unformed recreation of moments of everyday experience. What they subtly achieve, with an unassumingness which detracts not at all from the charm of the novel, is a dialogue where the 'literary' is upstaged by the 'actual', the remote by the immediate, the abstract by the concrete. Thus, in one sense, the use of the interpolated stories seems fairly unsophisticated; but in another, it enables Fielding to combine a well-directed moral design, demurely, with a nice permissiveness as to vagary of action and realism of texture. It has been felt that 'we pay too high a price'[13] for these stories; on the contrary, it seems to me, they are among the best instances that I know of the ingenious effectiveness of Fielding's art.

Henry Fielding: Justice Observed

NOTES

1. This criticism of the novel has been given impetus by the highly influential moralistic reading offered in Martin C. Battestin, *The Moral Basis of Fielding's Art* (Middletown, Conn.: Wesleyan University Press, 1959).
2. Battestin, p. 90.
3. The fullest such vindication to date, and a mine of interesting material on the novel, is Homer Goldberg, *The Art of 'Joseph Andrews'* (Chicago: Chicago University Press, 1969).
4. The fullest confirmation of this view appears in Michael Irwin, *Henry Fielding: The Tentative Realist* (Oxford: Oxford University Press, 1967).
5. All page references in the text are to Henry Fielding, *Joseph Andrews*, ed. R. F. Brissenden (Harmondsworth: Penguin, 1977).
6. There is a brilliant study of this artistic self-consciousness in Robert Alter, *Fielding and the Nature of the Novel* (Cambridge, Mass.: Harvard University Press, 1968).
7. Cf. Irwin, p. 74: 'The schematic approach which derives from Fielding's moral intention has an alienating effect. It constantly puts the narrative interest at the mercy of the didactic.'
8. Ibid., p. 64: '[Fielding] was trying to produce work at once formalized and realistic.'
9. There are two important articles on the interpolated tales: Homer Goldberg, 'The Interpolated Stories in *Joseph Andrews* or "The History of the World in General" Satirically Revised', *Modern Philology*, LXIII (1966), 295–310, and Douglas Brooks, 'The Interpolated Tales in *Joseph Andrews* Again', *Modern Philology*, LXV (1968), 208–13.
10. J. Paul Hunter, *Occasional Form* (Baltimore: Johns Hopkins University Press, 1975), p. 160.
11. Cf. Goldberg, p. 105: 'The mature Wilson functions as the novel's central norm of sensible humanity.'
12. Cf. Alter, p. 110: 'the truncated tale of Paul and Leonard, read by little Dick toward the end of the book, can be connected to the plot of the novel only by the most determined overinterpretation.'
13. Ibid., p. 112.

7

Out of the Thicket in *Tom Jones*

by MARK KINKEAD-WEEKES

> Prudence, of old a sacred term, implied
> Virtue, with godlike wisdom for her guide;
> But now in general use is known to mean
> The stalking-horse of vice, and folly's screen . . .
> —Churchill, *Night*, 1762.

The seventh chapter of Book III in *Tom Jones* proclaims itself the one 'In which the Author himself makes his Appearance on the Stage'. This is of course a tease, since he has been overtly conducting the entire performance ever since the opening sentence. Nevertheless the message he has apparently come to deliver—about Tom's essential need for prudence—has been taken very seriously indeed, especially of late. 'Prudence', says Martin Battestin in a scholarly article,[1] '(together with the more or less synonymous word *discretion*) is the central ethical concept of *Tom Jones*.' It may be true, as Eleanor Hutchens had noted in her study of Fielding's irony,[2] that the term and its derivatives 'are used unfavourably three times to every one time they are used favourably'. (I would put the proportion very much higher, myself.) 'Nearly every unadmirable character in the novel is described as prudent or is shown as advocating prudence'—and none more so, of course, than Blifil. 'It is one of the larger ironies of the novel', she goes on, 'that part of the task of the hero is to acquire one of the chief traits of the villain.' If, nonetheless, she remains

137

sure that Fielding approved of prudence, indeed that 'The
necessity for prudence as a concomitant of goodness is one of
the major themes of *Tom Jones*', it is because

> Fielding announces it early in the novel, and carries it through
> to the last page, where he notes that the mature Tom has
> 'acquired a discretion and prudence very uncommon in one of
> his lively parts'.

The Author's Appearance on the Stage has clearly been
decisive. Glenn Hatfield[3] draws what would seem the logical
conclusion:

> The central moral term which Fielding sets out to purify and
> define in *Tom Jones* . . . is not 'charity' or 'virtue', nor is it
> 'honour' or 'good nature'. It is 'prudence'.

The entire novel is seen, now, as concerned to bring about an
ironic disinfection of prudence, allowing for the implications of
self-seeking and worldly calculation that had begun to cluster
around the word by making the unadmirable characters
exhaust them, but doing so in order to rehabilitate the sense in
which Prudentia was defined by Cicero as the first of four
Cardinal Virtues. In this sense Prudentia was Christianized
by Aquinas and Ambrose, painted by Titian in a famous
allegory, and acknowledged through centuries of the Christian
Humanist tradition as that Wisdom which enables Man to
distinguish Good from Evil. It is a rational faculty, whose
parts, said Cicero, are Memory, Intelligence and Foresight—
hence Titian's three faces. Memory enables us to learn from
the past, intelligence to see things as they are in the present,
and foresight to judge the future consequences of things done
now. Indeed, say Battestin and Hatfield, Prudence equals
Sophia—or rather, Sophia is Prudentia in action and in
emblem. So when Tom Jones marries Miss Western, we can
be sure not only that he has at last acquired the prudence he so
signally lacked, but also that Prudentia has been restored to
her True Beauty, the Platonic ideal added to the Ciceronian
concept.

   It is an impressive argument, and there is some truth in it.
But I am very much afraid that when I turn back to the
Author's Appearance, the corners of my mouth begin to

twitch. For he begins by showing that Mr. Allworthy—the
most impeccable preacher of Prudence to have appeared so
far—has been neither All-Wise in his treatment of young
Tom and Blifil, nor even rational at all, since his favours
have in fact gone up and down like a pressure gauge in
reaction against the prejudices of his sister. (Perhaps one
remembers that grandiloquent simile comparing Allworthy
with the sun, which ended so bathetically—though without
in the least damaging our warm sense of his benevolence—by
showing him orbiting at the immediate behest less of Heaven,
than of Mistress Bridget?) However, as the Author ruefully
concedes, Tom does make things far worse for himself 'by his
own Wantonness, Wildness, and Want of Caution'.

> In recording some Instances of these, we shall, if rightly
> understood, afford a very useful Lesson to those well-disposed
> Youths, who shall hereafter be our Readers: For they may
> here find that Goodness of Heart, and Openness of Temper,
> tho' these may give them great Comfort within, and
> administer to an honest Pride in their own Minds, will by no
> Means, alas! do their Business in the World. Prudence and
> Circumspection are necessary even to the best of Men. They
> are indeed as it were a Guard to Virtue, without which she
> can never be safe. It is not enough that your Designs, nay that
> your Actions are intrinsically good, you must take Care they
> shall appear so. If your Inside be never so beautiful, you must
> preserve a fair Outside also. This must be constantly looked
> to, or Malice and Envy will take Care to blacken it so, that the
> Sagacity and Goodness of an *Allworthy* will not be able to see
> through it, and to discern the Beauties within. Let this, my
> young Readers, be your constant Maxim, That no Man can be
> good enough to enable him to neglect the Rules of Prudence;
> nor will Virtue herself look beautiful, unless she be bedecked
> with the outward Ornaments of Decency and Decorum. And
> this Precept, my worthy Disciples, if you read with due
> Attention, you will, I hope, find sufficiently enforced by
> Examples in the following Pages. I ask Pardon for this short
> Appearance, by way of Chorus on the Stage. It is in Reality
> for my own Sake, that while I am discovering the Rocks on
> which Innocence and Goodness often split, I may not be
> misunderstood to recommend the very Means to my worthy
> Readers, by which I intend to shew them they will be
> undone.[4]

And so, full of excuses, he bows himself off. . . .

Can we really be meant to take this voice as seriously representing Fielding's own view? This talk of maxims, precepts, rules? That ironic gap that is opened between 'outside' and 'inside' in the very act of apparently attempting to close it? The sly tone of bluff condescension to our youth and inexperience? Those sneaky digs about reading with due attention, understanding rightly, and not mistaking an intention for its opposite? The associations of doing Business in the World are highly equivocal. And if we do happen to have paid any attention to the uses of 'prudence' in the novel so far, there have been nine unmistakably ironic references, and only one, from Allworthy, suggesting that 'Worldly Prudence' is not to be despised. Unfortunately, it occurs in the context of the marriage of Captain Blifil to Bridget, in which, to say the least, there is no danger of it being despised; and Dr. Blifil listens to Allworthy's sermon 'with the profoundest Attention, tho' it cost him some Pains to prevent now and then a small Discomposure of his Muscles'.[5] (Allworthy is, of course—though again I stress that this is without at all damaging our sense of his benevolent goodness—a delightfully comic character . . . whenever he tries to be sagacious.)

Most telling of all, however, is the imaginative picture that builds up, of someone constantly looking to their appearance, and bedecking their outside to make sure they look good— while the words 'prudence' and 'decency' echo in our ears. Surely this reminds one of something? It does, of course. For such were the actions of Deborah Wilkins at her mirror and just these the words associated with them, in that great comic episode in Book I, where she was so unutterably shocked at finding Allworthy in his shirt, gazing at the baby in his bed and caring absolutely nothing for his own appearance, because he was so wholly taken out of himself in loving feeling. If he is funny when trying to be wise, he is here in the classic position of farce, without his breeches; yet it is impossible for him to be ridiculous. If our imaginations had been truly caught by the difference between Allworthy and his 'prudent housekeeper' then, we could hardly be taken in by 'the Author's' teasing now.

Yet, can we afford to hear that performing voice—for the Author is now 'on' the stage as well as showing it to us—as straightforwardly ironic, either? Are 'Goodness of Heart, and Openness of Temper' a sufficient guard to virtue? They may have seemed so in that far simpler-minded novel *Joseph Andrews*, where the good-hearted Innocents led a charmed life on the Road of Experience; but the world of *Tom Jones* already suggests otherwise. Indeed it must be because this is already so obvious, that so many critics by no means lacking in sensitivity and intelligence have been persuaded to take 'the Author' straightforwardly. The good heart is surely not enough?—something else *is* surely necessary, some kind of disciplinary or cautionary wisdom?—necessary perhaps to Allworthy in his 'sagacity' as well as to Jones in his wildness and wantonness? It cannot be any rule, or maxim, or precept. It cannot be any calculating kind of prudence concerned with appearances. What, then? In the act of apparently offering an 'authorial' key to the novel, Fielding is actually raising a question for the reader to puzzle over. Faced with two unsatisfactory positions, is there a better one? There surely must be . . . but he has not told us what it is. When we have finished applauding a comic parody, of the moralizing author of a conduct book for young people, we had better turn the page and read on with a question in mind—yet certain that it has been asked and will probably be answered *comically*.

Behind the argument about prudence, then, there has arisen a bigger one: about the kind of author Fielding is, the kind of experience the novel offers, and above all the kind of reader one is invited to be. The Author's Appearance on the Stage has shown that the narrative voice is to be regarded as a performance, like all the other characters. At one end of the spectrum that voice may approach Fielding's, sharing with the reader, much of the time, his humanity and good sense. But otherwise it proliferates comic and ironic rôles, in order to tease, and to test the reader. . . . The big difference moreover, between authorial commentary and authorial irony on the one hand, and the kind of double irony in which both apparent ways of reading are unsatisfactory, is that the latter throws the reader on his own resources and forces him to question his own response, as well as the comic texture out of which the questions arise. And that response cannot be merely a matter of concepts, even moral ones. It must also be a matter of the reader's comic imagination and sense of fun, as well as the writer's. If we seek to discover from the novel what Fielding himself, at his most creative,[6] really thought about Prudence, it may be a poorish start not to re-imagine Deborah Wilkins, or not to find 'the Author's' performance funny.

Moreover the experience of *Tom Jones* is of on-going process, of continuous comic contrivance and discovery. I do not think it does Fielding or the pleasure of reading him any justice to think of his novel as though it were spread out flat on some big table, so that a whole preconceived design can be exposed at once. (Even the famous plot has to be worked out stage by stage, and the pleasure of seeing it brought off is by no means unconnected with the sense of difficulty, and the creaking noises that are made from time to time.) To illustrate how Fielding's reader is taught to read, through an imaginative process, let us consider the crucial episode which causes Tom's expulsion from Paradise Hall, and see how both the comedy, and the creation of a reader capable of judging it, are carefully developed.

It begins in the tenth chapter of Book V with Tom, having drunk too much in his joy at Mr. Allworthy's recovery, wandering out into a pastoral landscape which soon raises thoughts, and then alas! practical possibilities, of 'love'. The languages which collide so comically, before Tom vanishes into the bushes with Molly Seagrim, proclaim their artificiality, so the ironies are comfortably authorial and plain. The first joke is to find in the language of pastoral, normally so genteel, a sexual innuendo which makes the effect of drink on Tom Jones abundantly clear. ('In this Scene, so sweetly accommodated to Love, he meditated on his dear *Sophia*. While his wanton Fancy roved unbounded over all her Beauties' . . . etc.). The next joke is that his 'Ejaculation' about his love and constancy already holds the subconscious giveaway about the Circassian Maid.

> Was I but possessed of thee, one only Suit of Rags thy whole Estate, is there a Man on Earth whom I would envy! How contemptible would the brightest *Circassian* Beauty, drest in all the Jewels of the *Indies*, appear to my Eyes! But why do I mention another Woman?

Why indeed?—except that he is feeling very sexy and is not possessed of Sophia. So we are prepared for the third joke, as the passionate vows of constancy intensify:

> 'Sophia, Sophia alone shall be mine. What Raptures are in that Name! I will engrave it on every Tree.'
> At these Words he started up, and beheld—not his *Sophia*—no, nor a *Circassian* Maid richly and elegantly attired for the Grand Signior's Seraglio. No; without a Gown, in a Shift that was somewhat of the coarsest, and none of the cleanest, bedewed likewise with some odoriferous Effluvia, the Produce of the Day's Labour, with a Pitch-fork in her Hand, *Molly Seagrim* approached.[7]

And so, after that parley which the Author does not feel obliged to relate, they vanish into the thicket. The overt manipulation of style sets the reader at a distance, comfortably uninvolved, so that he easily takes the point of the comic clash between heroic/romantic pretension and the somewhat begrimed sexual reality, and finds Tom laughable.

As the Author proceeds to account for what has happened, however, one kind of reader will begin to rebel against his flippancy and oversimplification. Is it enough to laugh the whole thing off with that cynical arithmetic about Jones thinking one woman better than none and Molly two men than one; or smilingly to excuse Tom on the grounds of his drunkenness? The so stagey stage-management, the so obvious manipulation of style for distance, begins to look like a kind of moral dishonesty, preventing the reader from experiencing Tom's consciousness with the inward attention that is necessary for any kind of moral judgement. Conversely, the authorial sensibility we are given instead, and expected to share, is coarse as well as flippant, and the author seems prepared to stoop to some pretty crude devices to keep us on his hero's side. The plea of drunkenness makes the case worse rather than better, for has not the Author just been making a claim for Tom in the previous chapter, on the grounds that drunkenness merely opens out what people are really like? The Author cannot be allowed to have it both ways. . . .

But this reader's voice—do I hear another reader beginning to murmur?—is starting to sound a little over-emphatic, not to say thumping. Does not that sort of reaction take the whole episode much too seriously? Is Tom's lapse so important? Was it not in fact, considering the world as it actually is, a natural thing to have happened? Is anyone really the worse for it? Is not the mature and humane response precisely the author's frank, but warm-hearted recognition of sexuality, and his insistence on the comedy of the case?

It is only now, however, that the comic exploration really begins—because Fielding is not all that interested in what goes on inside his characters, but is very much interested in what goes on inside his readers. So what he does, now, is take up just these two readers' voices and ways of looking, in order to expose the implications of their opposition. For to insist that Tom's actions were natural is in fact to reduce him—as the tremendous simile which opens Chapter II of Book V sets out precisely to bring about—to a rutting stag. His 'good-nature' has, inherently and instinctively, an overflow of animal spirits, a natural, energetic, and masculine sexuality—but if natural propensity operates unchecked, *this* is what it looks like. Moreover the good qualities also visible in Tom: his loyalty, so fiercely guarding his female against hurt and insult, are exercised on behalf of Molly not Sophia, who could well be betrayed, hurt and insulted if she knew. One sort of reader ought to be a little crestfallen. It is not only Tom who, in the language of sportsmen which the book bids us use, has been *found sitting*—a posture which cannot fail to remind us of one of the funniest scenes in the novel, the exposure of the 'natural philosophy' of Square.

But the other kind of reader will of course fare no better—for the second half of Chapter 11 suggests that he was an associate of Thwackum. If there is an awkward connection between good-nature and animality, there is a no less awkward connection between moral stricture and ill-nature. And moral indignation is an especially treacherous emotion, which may contain a care for moral good and truth, but only too easily accommodates the impulse to thwackum; rooting the sinner out to denounce and to pound, giving the double satisfactions of self-esteem and the gratification of power over others. Again and again in the prefatory chapters, so much concerned with judgement, Fielding returns to this connection between the critical impulse and ill-nature. All the world's a stage, but when one looks at the audience watching (for instance) Black George, why is it that nobody cares about the state of his heart? Why is it that nobody judges with humanity? If we find Tom-as-rutting-stag dehumanized, is not the infuriated parson just as brutal? . . . as indeed the pitched and bloody battle between them proceeds immediately to show.

Once again we are confronted with a choice between alternative readings, each of which is useful to expose the defects of the other, but neither of which is satisfactory. As they come to blows there seems no room to compromise either; but the conflict itself gets more and more destructive. Though I have used Professor Empson's term 'double irony'[8] for the technique, I cannot agree that it suggests tolerance for both positions, or any degree of relativity or pluralism in Fielding. Rather, as it seems to me, it is a challenge to find another way: not a compromise, but a different way of looking altogether, in another dimension. It is a challenge to the reader. We will not find our way by simply enjoying the battle, like Squire Western, or jumping in on whatever side seems to be having the worst of things. Indeed Western's position is the least viable of all. Nor is the author going to tell us how to respond. But the answer is going to have to come from our response, for that is where the real battlefield has now been located. Thwackum and Square have up till now been characters having arguments in the fiction. Now they have become internalized, by the Author's deliberate provocations, as conflicting impulses *within the reader*. Can we find a mode of responding that is neither thwackum nor square?

We can. For Fielding does not in fact leave us without help. As his final move in the episode, there is made to arrive into the scene itself the one factor that has not been operative at all. There arrives Sophia. Immediately the rutting stag and the outraged parson, the faces covered with blood and bruises, cease to look either funny or enjoyable. She is so upset that she faints away, 'from the Sight of the Blood' suggests the Author 'or from Fear for her Father, or from some other Reason'. He cannot fool us, and does not really mean to. To think for a moment is to realize that the reason is her love for Tom and

145

her fear that he has been hurt. The more loving the heart, the more horrible the sight. Yet she does not have any idea what they are fighting *about*; if she did, she would be even more upset. But as it is, the mere sight of her immediately brings Tom to his senses, and restores the perspective that should have been there all the time. Nothing else counts beside the fact of having been the cause of pain to her, and seeking to undo it. Nothing else exists, as he runs to her and carries to the brook. The water is not only to revive Sophia, but to wash the muck off. I don't think there is any ambiguity now. What have we discovered, in responding to the whole developing process of comedy and analysis over four chapters? The basis of an entirely different kind of discrimination and judgement is *Love*. One can now see that Tom's failures are not to be described in terms of a basic good-nature, only requiring to be guarded by greater prudence. Nor will his defects strike one, now, as being even mainly of the head: of the rational faculty of prudence, cautionary memory, intelligent circumspection and foresight. His real failure is in the heart, he has failed to love *enough*. With real love, as we have just seen, come greater imagination and sensitivity, the entire Being of the true lover absorbed in caring about the beloved; and with love, too, comes an altogether wiser vision and perspective of value. But as Tom responds spontaneously to Sophia—and there is little sense of prudence in his instantaneous, heartfelt reaction—he is also very different from the 'ejaculator' and the stag in the thicket. So it is that a reader, having found in his developing response to the whole complex episode the way out of that thicket, can join Fielding in the celebratory Preface to Book VI, 'Of Love', which follows immediately, with its sharp distinction between love and appetite. True love calls in the natural and animal, and heightens them to a degree the purely sensual can never know; but its basis is esteem and gratitude, and above all the desire to make the beloved happy. It is because he did not feel these things sufficiently for Sophia that Tom behaved as he did—and the judgement of him is as free from ambiguity as the judgement of 'hunger'. But unless and until we make these points our own, they judge us too.

> Examine your Heart, my good Reader, and resolve whether you do believe these Matters with me . . . if you do not, you

have, I assure you, already read more than you have understood. . . .[9]

If we could fall into flabby and dehumanizing talk about nature, or ill-natured denunciation in the name of morality, or talk of the centrality of prudence, we did not understand either the pure moral wisdom of love, or the need for judgement to be loving. But 'Fielding' himself only emerges at the very end of this long and complex *process*, having forced the reader to grow towards him under the provocations of 'the author', stage by stage. To have tried to extrapolate attitudes, or conceptual language as 'his' at any point would have been to distort. He is to be found in the reader's response to the *whole* imaginative and evaluative process of the fiction—and only there.

But before we leave the thicket: a last point about Sophia. I hope it is clear that her rôle is not that of an exponent, still less an emblem of Prudentia. It would be odd to display a rational faculty in terms of a young girl fainting! Yet Sophia is indeed Wise in a deeper and less conventional sense. Even as a child her judgements about Tom and Blifil were unerring. Unlike Allworthy, using his mind about what Blifil says and does, for instance in the affair of Sophia's pet bird, Sophia is not taken in. Her wisdom is not a rational quality, but a perceptiveness of the heart. She trusts to her feelings about the boys, and their relationship with her, and that tells her the truth about their motives. So in the scene we have just considered, the joke and the wisdom, are precisely in the fainting. Her intense feelings for Tom, so intense they *literally cause her to lose consciousness of herself*, produce the wisest of all comments on his behaviour, going spontaneously to the heart of the matter. Now if we actually go back to Cicero, the interesting fact is that he is to be found distinguishing in the *De Officiis* between 'prudentia' and 'sophia' in a way that may well have influenced Fielding.

> And then the foremost of all virtues is that wisdom which the Greeks call *sophia*; for by prudence, which they call *phronesis*, we understand something else, namely, the practical knowledge of things to be sought for and of things to be avoided. Again, that wisdom which I have given the foremost place is the knowledge of things human and divine, which is concerned also with the bonds of union between Gods and men and the relations of man to man.[10]

147

I think the kind of Wisdom Fielding wished to embody was indeed a 'sancta sophia', closely related to the love which links God and human beings, and springing essentially from the relations of the heart rather than the rational activity of the head.

Which is not to suggest, of course, that the heart in itself is wise. For only now can one see the full irony of Allworthy's misjudgement of Tom. The essence of Wisdom, as of Love, is unconsciousness of self. But the central charge against Tom, which Allworthy cannot even bring himself to express, so that Tom can make no defence against it, is the horrible belief planted by Blifil, that Tom cares nothing for his benefactor. The sentence of banishment is not, then, a judgement on Tom's imprudence, but the product of Allworthy's bruised heart; it is not a rational but an emotional decision, and it comes about because on the one occasion since the adoption of Tom that Allworthy judges from his own heart, his ego has distorted and reversed the direction of his feelings. Not that we can blame him. Indeed, Tom is not even innocent, if the charge were failing to love enough to be imaginative and sensitive about what his actions might mean to those who love him. But by the end of Book VI it is I think clear that the novel is not about Prudence, but about the need to acquire wisdom through loving *more* and *better*.

In the middle six books, Fielding extends this analysis in a new process of discovery, re-orchestrating the challenge to characters and reader in the complex series of events at Upton. Ideally one would have to carry through the same kind of stage-by-stage account in order to bring out the comic richness, and the wisdom, and show how inseparable these are. But since this is impossible in the space I have, I would like to try instead to suggest—albeit by brutal summary— how the architectonics of *Tom Jones* are not merely matters of plot, but of further exploration of the Loving Wisdom that has already been discovered. That crucial Preface to Book VI, which was the product of one process of comic imagination, can be seen to provide, one by one, all the roads that lead to Upton, and that must come together for us to be able to judge what happens there.

The central contention of the Preface is of the real existence of good nature, and this is the main road to Upton, easily followed, which establishes the huge contrast between the good nature of Tom as Book VI defines it, and the misanthropy and self-enclosure of the Old Man of the Hill. Titian's painting of Prudentia, as often with the iconography of the virtue, shows the backward-looking one of the three faces as an Old Man; but what the past had taught this one, is solipsism and contempt for his kind. His mental studies of philosophy and theology have not produced 'sophia'; his experience of human faults and betrayals has atrophied in him all affection and desire for relationship. While he sits on his hill, 'with great Patience and Unconcern', Tom rushes spontaneously down at the cry of human distress, and of a very different kind of philosophy and Christianity from those governing the Old Man's Prudence.

But in the impulsive human warmth of Tom, as we saw in the thicket, there is a vulnerability—and the Preface to Book VI was also crucially concerned to distinguish Love from Appetite. So the second road to Upton is the one Tom walks with Mrs. Waters, towards that great comic scene of appetite at the inn. This is a splendid imaginative realization of how sex is indeed like hunger (and also like fighting, again). We have to take the measure of juxtaposing the 'hearty' sigh for Sophia, the hearty appetite for beef, and the irresistibility of those two white breasts. Tom (like Orpheus) looks back in Hunger—and will lose his Sophia. It needs no more now than her muff on his empty bed to make the point her unconsciousness made before, and to produce the same instantaneous restoration of perspective in Tom.

Yet Fielding insists on making things more complex for his reader, to test whether he has learnt to judge both with honour and with love. There is a basic good nature and generosity in Mrs. Waters, and an element of the Preface's gratitude and esteem—though there are also many other factors to complicate our response, as almost everyone in the inn sets up in judgement in her bedroom. Our concept of Honour had certainly better not be the worldly, self-centred and ill-natured one ensconced by the fire and keeping the warmth from everyone else. But what kind of Honour should accompany our 'sophia'?

The roads to Upton have to come to a trial; so Fielding contrives one which is based on the wrong questions, about the wrong kinds of responsibility, and before a magistrate so incapable of justice that the verdict is bound to be wrong whether Tom is condemned or acquitted. Squire Western is as grotesque a parody of Tom's impulsive nature as his sister is of Sophia's wisdom. The question is whether the *reader* has learnt the right kind of judgement: selfless, loving, wise, honourable? But this time, we cannot rely on Sophia herself to guide our response. For she is now in the position of Allworthy before: incapable of judging what Tom actually did, because her whole vision is taken up with a lying story that suggests he never cared for her. Her heart's wisdom is clouded by her bruised ego. And though there is again no question of blaming her, the last of the Preface's points is made as she leaves Upton with Mrs. Fitzpatrick. Sophia is not taken in by her cousin, not because she has the radical suspicion of a bad heart, and not merely because she has the intelligence to see what is before her as the Irish peer gives Harriet's game away. At a deeper level there is no concealing the difference between the essential selflessness of the loving heart, and what the Preface to Book VI calls putting 'the World in our own Person'—the habitual self-centredness that permeates Harriet's vision. Yet a trace of this in Sophia—unusually, and only because of Partridge's lies—is enough to cloud counsel. Even more slyly than before, then, in the eighth chapter of Book XII, Fielding's double irony throws the question on the reader's lap.

> For Instance, as the Fact at present before us now stands, without any Comment of mine upon it, tho' it may at first Sight offend some Readers, yet upon more mature Consideration, it must please all; for wise and good Men may consider what happened to *Jones* at *Upton* as a just Punishment for his Wickedness, with Regard to Women, of which it was indeed the immediate Consequence; and silly and bad Persons may comfort themselves in their Vices, by Flattering their own Hearts that the Characters of Men are rather owing to Accident than to Virtue. Now perhaps the Reflections which we should be here inclined to draw, would alike contradict both these Conclusions, and would shew that these Incidents contribute

only to confirm the great, useful and uncommon Doctrine, which
it is the Purpose of this whole Work to inculcate, and which we
must not fill up our Pages by frequently repeating. . . .[11]

If I am right, the first joke is that there has been no
'repeating' at all, since he has *not* been concerned with the
wholly commonplace doctrine of prudence. The second joke is
that he is not concerned with 'Doctrine' either, since the
fiction is essentially aimed at creating a reader who will
discover in his own *response* the sensitivity and judgement
Fielding wishes him to have. Can he now respond in a
dimension quite different from the cynic or relativist on the
one hand, or a punitive morality on the other?—and judge
absolutely, but also lovingly? But, thirdly, the imaginative
vision Fielding has been creating *is* 'uncommon': much more
challenging, I believe, than the safely orthodox idea of
correcting nature by prudence—and he has made the thicket
more difficult for himself and his reader at Upton than it was
before.

In his final six books, re-orchestrating the challenge for a
third time, he makes it more difficult still. For the benefit of
those 'good and wise' people who want punishing consequences, Tom's road from Upton leads to the condemned cell,
since Fielding's challenge must not evade the worst that could
be said of Tom's behaviour and the worst imaginable results.
So what had been comically metaphorical, Tom's inability to
resist a challenge from man or woman, becomes literal, as he
appears to have killed Fitzpatrick, to have become the gigolo
of Lady Bellaston, and to have committed incest with his
mother, in sleeping with Mrs. Waters. The whole ethos of
duelling, both martial and sexual, in being converted from a
comic trope into apparently literal sins of the blood, is shown
to rest on a false code of honour, to be wholly unchristian, and
to result in a degradation that Tom's conscience recognizes
very clearly. We surely cannot make light of this? Yet
consequences so punitive seem wildly out of proportion, at
worst the product of sheer ill-fortune? Only, if we take it all as
mere comic plotting, contrived by the author for the sheer
pleasure of then untangling what has been tangled, do we not
enrol ourselves among the 'silly and bad' who treat moral

problems in terms of relativities of circumstance, or mere accident? Tom himself is not consoled, in the court of his conscience, by pleas of ill-luck or provocation. How can we neither exaggerate nor trivialize, avoid both moral over-emphasis and amoral permissiveness, be neither too serious nor too flippant?

I think that if we have grasped Fielding's central concern with the heart, the joke is that the wildest of the 'con-sequences'—the incest—will suggest a proportion, somewhere between the merely literal and the merely metaphorical, for dealing with the rest. When the bizarre might-have-been turns out to have been only a jest of the plot, there is still a suggestiveness in the sense of taboo. At its most shocking, incest is the prostitution to one's self of what is of one's own blood, and should be most revered. The point is that there has indeed been the closest relation between Tom's vice and the source of his virtue—not his mother, by happenstance, but his own blood certainly. His guilt is no mere matter of imprudence, but of having prostituted the Love (as Book VI defined it) which is the source and dynamic of his own true being. When all the accidental literalisms are cleared away, the suggestive verdict on the un-Loving relationships remains quite clear and serious, confirmed by the wholly justifiable rejection of Tom by Sophia.

Yet just because Tom's virtue and vice are so intimately related, are of the same blood, Fielding believes that the basically good-natured heart, in its very impulsiveness, *can correct itself.* In the first place the apparently complete loss of Sophia finally opens Tom's eyes to the disease of his heart. We have seen, twice before, how the realization of what his conduct means to her has restored perspective. Now the worst realization produces the clearest insight. Moreover, the road from Upton has produced a redemptive chain of actions as well as the damning ones, starting, to make the point again, from the selfsame impulsive act in the rescue of Mrs. Waters. As he did not fall through mere imprudence, so he does not rise again by learning prudence, but by acting out the Great Commandment, to Love. As he forgives and rehabilitates the 'highwayman' and saves Nancy and Nightingale from them-selves, so he finds the friends who (with Jenny) will help bring about his own rehabilitation, and the language in which to clarify his own failure to love, and to extricate himself from further unloving relationship. The diseases of the heart begin to be cured by learning to love better, more truly, more unselfishly, and, as a character in Saul Bellow puts it, 'learning to do things *for*'. It is not a question of using the head to correct the heart, but of letting the heart go with its full intrinsic 'charitable' force, and developing a loving intelligence and discrimination in so doing. Though Allworthy will preach prudence to Tom again, on their joyful reconciliation, Tom is already demonstrating a wisdom more forgiving, sensitive and imaginative than his. It is by learning to love, and to serve others, better, that Tom has learnt judgement.

But he cannot fully or securely redeem himself. He needs Sophia, not just her forgiveness, and certainly not as an emblem of Prudence, but herself. The final scene[12] is no mere conventional happy ending, neither is it concerned to create the lovers' feelings, dramatically—its point returns us to the Author's first Appearance. Partridge's lie about Upton, and the proposal to Lady Bellaston, have of course been cleared up; what Sophia must be concerned with now is the essential question: 'Can I believe the Passion you have profest to me to be sincere? Or if I can, what Happiness can I assure myself of with a Man capable of so much Inconstancy?' There is only one answer in prudence: that Tom must prove himself over a considerable length of time, and only when she is convinced that he deserves her confidence, will he obtain it. But Tom has a better guarantee than his word, 'a better Security, a Pledge for my Constancy, which it is impossible to see and to doubt'. He shows Sophia her own reflection in the mirror—and *there* is all the difference between prudence and love. Instead of carefully looking at his own reflection in the eyes of the world and the lady Prudentia, Tom is insisting that his love will grow stronger, and will learn true constancy, delicacy, and indeed prudence and discretion, *by loving and being loved*, through the relationship and security of love itself. It is deftly done; but it is no mere flattery, romantic conceit, or trick of wooing, but has the weight of the whole novel behind it. It is Tom's wisdom, and turns out to be Sophia's too. As I have tried to argue, hers has always been a wisdom of the heart, whose perceptiveness and judgement come from feeling, and through relationship.

When the basic 'to do things *for*' quality of Tom's love is shown by his confidence in a day 'when Fears shall be no more; when I shall have that dear, that vast, that exquisite, *extatic* Delight of *making my Sophia happy*' (my italics), she can easily be persuaded to marry him the next day. I need hardly labour the point that this is not prudent, indeed runs directly counter to what Memoria, Intelligentia and Providentia would have to say on the evidence—for Tom is as impulsive and spontaneous a creature now as he has ever been. But if it is not Prudentia, it is a higher Wisdom springing from that disposition to give happiness to others that Book VI held to be the essence of Love, and confident that a heart truly devoted to the happiness of another *must* develop self-control, sensitivity, and prudence too. And so it is that Fielding can conclude—at last, and for the first time without a trace of irony:

> Whatever in the Nature of *Jones* had a Tendency to Vice, has been corrected by continual Conversation with this good Man, and by his Union with this lovely and virtuous *Sophia*. He hath also, by Reflexion on his past Follies, acquired a Discretion and Prudence very uncommon in one of his lively Parts.

In the story, Tom has shown himself a creature of the heart rather than the head at the end, as at the beginning; but because his love has transformed itself, and been secured in relationship, the virtues of the head can be added. The order however is significant: first feeling, then true relation, then reflection and discretion 'also', and thereby.

Yet Fielding's main creative purpose, as we have seen, was to create a *reader* whose 'Sophia' is in the quality of his response. And here, if I may, I borrow an insight from an essay I much admire: John Preston's 'Plot as Irony: The Reader's Rôle in *Tom Jones*'.[13] It is of course only on a second reading that the full richness of the reading experience becomes possible; but this is not simply because we now 'know all', and so can share all the plot ironies, and the extra dimension of comedy that springs from them. For, Preston argues, though we may feel objectively possessed of a completed design, we cannot but recognize that the sense of *process* is intrinsic to the fiction. So we also have to become imaginatively involved again in a process of discovery, the

other half of our minds retaining, as it were, the blindness of a
first reading. 'That is,' says Preston,

> we have a sense of duality not only in the book itself but in our
> response to it. We recognize our 'blindness' just because we no
> longer suffer from it. We know and do not know simul-
> taneously. . . . [The reader] is the observer of his own ironic
> mistakes. Our responses to the book are, we may say, part of
> the reason for Fielding's laughter, a laughter in which we share.

I want only to add something about the *quality* of that
laughter. When I re-read, for example, the chapter whose
heading gruffly insists that it contains 'such grave Matter, that
the Reader cannot laugh once . . .'—the chapter in which
Allworthy preaches to Jenny Jones on incontinency, believing
her to be Tom's mother (Book I, Chapter 7)—I remember
that I did laugh once, even on a first reading, when he insisted
so solemnly that love was a rational passion. But on re-reading
it becomes marvellously funny throughout, because Allworthy
in all his prudence and sagacity is so splendidly adrift, and so
wonderfully unconscious of the significance of Jenny's
responses. Yet my laughter, which includes my own first-
reading fallibility as well as Allworthy's, remains affectionate,
and never damages my sense of his worthiness and benevolence. I am made both to know and to imagine his unknowing,
both to judge him and relish him just as he is, to fuse laughter
with affection. I part just a little with Preston in suspecting
that something of this 'Sophia' ought to go even into one's
response to Fielding's villain. One of the finest double-takes,
on second reading, comes when Blifil angrily rejects Tom's
apology for having forgotten in his drunkenness the news of
Bridget's death. 'It was little to be wondered at', said Blifil,

> if tragical Spectacles made no Impressions on the Blind; but,
> for his Part, he had the Misfortune to know who his Parents
> were, and consequently must be affected with their Loss.[14]

When we know he has just concealed from Tom that Bridget
was *his* mother too, the sneer is outrageous—as Preston says.
Yet it is so outrageous, in its plotting inventiveness, and the
primness of its deliberate irony, that a purely moral response
even to such inhumanity will not quite do. Dare one confess it?
One's lips begin to twitch again, sharing Fielding's *enjoyment* of

his villain. But there is more, also. Blifil's taunt of blindness has its irony for us too. It is not wholly untragical to have heard that one's mother bore a bastard, and that one's hated rival is actually one's elder brother. To have turned *that* into such comic impudence, so outrageously, that is Blifil. He is a great performer, whom I cannot help enjoying, as I judge. But by including my own fallibility in laughing at his, I laugh with charity too. It will not do to reduce Fielding to moral patterns, let alone prudential ones. His 'Sophia' depends on the creation of readers whose moral judgement has become inextricably fused, through his art, with laughter, affection and imagination.

NOTES

1. Martin Battestin, 'Fielding's Definition of Wisdom', *E.L.H.* XXXV (1968), 188–217; subsequently incorporated into his book *The Providence of Wit* (Oxford: Clarendon Press, 1974), pp. 166–92. I am encouraged to see my scepticism about the rôle of prudence in *Tom Jones* shared to a considerable extent by Claude Rawson; see his 'Order and Misrule: Eighteenth Century Literature in the 1970s', *E.L.H.* XLII (1975), 484–86. We are however lonely figures!
2. Eleanor Hutchens, *Irony in Tom Jones* (Alabama: University of Alabama Press, 1965), Chapter 5.
3. Glenn Hatfield, *Henry Fielding and the Language of Irony* (Chicago and London: University of Chicago Press, 1968), Chapter 5.
4. *Tom Jones*, ed. Fredson Bowers, with an Introduction and Commentary by Martin C. Battestin (Oxford, 1974), pp. 141–42. All subsequent page references will be to this, the 'Wesleyan Edition'.
5. Wesleyan Edition, pp. 71–2, Book I, Chapter 12.
6. Fielding's attitude outside the novel seems to have changed. From *The Champion*, 22 November 1739: 'I would . . . by no Means recommend to Mankind to cultivate Deceit, or endeavour to appear what they are not . . . I would only convince my Readers, That it is not enough to have Virtue, without we also take Care to preserve, by a certain Decency and Dignity of Behaviour, the outward Appearance of it also.' From *The True Patriot*, 10 June 1746: 'There is nothing so oppugnant to True Virtue, and true Understanding, as Ostentation. The innate Dignity which always attends these, will not stoop to mean and laborious Acts to inform others of what they conceive must be sufficiently apparent to them.' It is however the novelist's imaginative insight that is important when we discuss his fiction. Richardson, in the continuation of *Pamela* which he had neither intended nor wanted to write, concluded by having his heroine identified with Prudentia. In the original *Pamela*, he

imagines the crucial action on which her happiness will depend as a conscious and explicit rejection of prudence for love. (See my *Samuel Richardson: Dramatic Novelist* (London, 1973), pp. 42–55.)

7. Wesleyan Edition, p. 256.
8. William Empson, *'Tom Jones'*, *Kenyon Review* XXX (1958).
9. Wesleyan Edition, p. 271.
10. Princepsque omnium virtutum illa sapientia, quam *sophia* Graeci vocant—prudentiam enim, quam Graeci *phronesis* dicunt, aliam quandam intelligimus, quae est rerum expetendarum fugiendarumque scientia; illa autem sapientia, quam principem dixi, rerum est divinarum et humanarum scientia, in qua continetur deorum et hominum communitas et societas inter ipsos . . . Cicero, *De Officiis*, tr. Walter Miller, Loeb Classical Library (London, 1913), p. 157. I have very slightly modified the translation to conform more closely to the Latin emphasis.
11. Wesleyan Edition, pp. 651–52.
12. Wesleyan Edition, p. 970ff. Book XVIII, Chapter 12.
13. John Preston, 'Plot as Irony: The Reader's Rôle in *Tom Jones*', *E.L.H.* XXXV (1968), 365–80; subsequently incorporated into his book *The Created Self* (London: Heinemann, 1970).
14. Wesleyan Edition, p. 254.

8

Technique as Judgement in *Tom Jones*

by K. G. SIMPSON

In the novels of Fielding, as in those of Sterne, technique functions as a medium of judgement. In *Tom Jones* style, narrative mode and plot reflect attitudes on the part of Fielding. The concern of this essay is to investigate the degree of consistency amongst these attitudes and, further, to consider whether the values implicit in the various uses of technique are consonant with the values rendered by the subject-matter.

To the reader whose expectations of a novel are conditioned by experience of the mainstream of fictional realism two features of Fielding's practice as novelist in *Tom Jones* are immediately striking—the blatant and recurrent presence of the narrator, and the use of a style which draws attention to itself as style rather than to the material which it renders. Such a novel presents obvious problems for the reader who has been weaned on the 'impersonal' theory of Henry James and encouraged to judge the novelist in terms of his success in creating the 'illusion of reality'. For James,

> In proportion as in what [Fiction] offers us we see life *without* rearrangement do we feel that we are touching truth; in proportion as we see it *with* rearrangement do we feel that we are being put off with a substitute, a compromise and convention.[1]

158

And according to Stendhal, 'One should not write unless one
has important or profoundly beautiful things to say, but then
one must say them with the utmost simplicity, as though one
were trying to get them by unnoticed.'² To turn to Fielding's
novels after a diet of the worthily earnest realism of much of
the nineteenth century is to be reminded forcibly of the verve,
energy and unorthodoxy of the eighteenth-century English
novel. That these should be the characteristics of the work of
an author who sanctioned the Augustan ideal of society and
the neo-classical emphasis on the general rather than the
particular ('not men but manners; not an individual but a
species'³ were his concerns in *Joseph Andrews*) is not the least
of several paradoxes that surround this remarkable writer.

Both his intrusive presence and the self-advertising nature
of his style have made Fielding's narrator in *Tom Jones* a focus
of critical interest. If Henry James felt the inadequacies of the
psychological portrayal of Tom he found compensation in the
engaging presence of Tom's creator. Quite at variance with
his customary distaste for the authorial presence is James's
contention that

> [Tom's] author—he handsomely possessed of a mind—has
> such an amplitude of reflexion for him and round him that we
> see him through the mellow air of Fielding's fine old moralism,
> fine old humour and fine old style, which somehow enlarge,
> make every one and every thing important.⁴

More recently, Henry Knight Miller, in viewing Fielding as
'the "actual" hero (the mind in which we are interested) in
Tom Jones', has claimed:

> Fielding is the focus of interest, not because he displays for our
> delectation the intimate operations of a self-absorbed psyche,
> but rather because he has a unique view of objective reality,
> and what one is interested in (or, at least, what I find myself
> interested in) is that reality, as seen through the narrator's eyes,
> as conceived, vivified, and integrated by his superb command
> of language.⁵

Common to these—as to most—views is the identification of
the narrative voice in *Tom Jones* with Henry Fielding himself.
From Wayne Booth, however, came the suggestion that
Fielding might just as readily have created an independent

narrative *persona* in *Joseph Andrews* and *Tom Jones* as he did in *Jonathan Wild*. 'A great artist', wrote Booth, 'can create an implied author who is either detached or involved, depending on the needs of the work in hand.'[6]

In fact, at first glance, there is much to encourage a straight identification of narrator with author. Most obviously, there are the contemporary and personal references (to 'my Charlotte' (687)[7]; to Mrs. Whitefield of 'The Bell' at Gloucester; the tribute to Ralph Allen via the praise of Prior's Park; the confusion of Sophia with Jeannie Cameron, mistress of the Young Pretender). Such references aid the process whereby fiction is transformed into 'history'. As befits the 'historian' that he regularly claims to be, the narrator introduces Allworthy as a gentleman who 'lately lived (and perhaps lives still)' (53) in Somersetshire. In the statements made by the narrator there recur the authority and assurance that are readily associated with the pronouncements of an Augustan essayist. 'Nothing can be so quick and sudden as the operations of the mind, especially when hope, or fear; or jealousy to which the two others are but journeymen, set it to work' (96), the narrator assures us, and we readily accept the wisdom of the man of the world who knows human nature, the sage magistrate, Henry Fielding. The narrator is ever on hand with a precept, homily, or generalization ('. . . there is no conduct less politic than to enter into any confederacy with your friend's servants, against their master' (100); 'Nothing more aggravates ill success than the near approach to good' (612)). When the narrator pronounces that the effect of drink is to reveal the true personality which the guard of reason normally conceals (236), or when he detects in the behaviour of the doctors who attend the dying Captain Blifil the characteristics of their profession (117–18), he appears as a shrewd, urbane, and decidedly trustworthy ironist—all that one conceives Henry Fielding to have been.

Further support for the belief that Fielding and his narrator are one and the same may be found in the extent to which the novel reflects its author's range of literary interests. Paradoxically, the distinctiveness of *Tom Jones* derives largely from the use which Fielding makes of various existing literary examples. Creatively eclectic, Fielding takes considerable

160

licence in his use of sources and, in so doing, stresses the possibilities and the flexibility of the novel form. The pairing of Tom and Partridge, for instance, owes something to the example of Don Quixote and Sancho Panza. In the endorsement of Tom's feeling heart ('though he did not always act rightly, yet he never did otherwise without feeling or suffering for it' (168)), which requires only the tempering of prudence to entitle it to the name of true goodness, there are signs of that same reaction against the restrictive nature of Richardsonian didacticism that had helped prompt Fielding to write *Joseph Andrews*. There are clear indications, too, that one of Fielding's intentions in *Tom Jones* was to parody some of the conventions of popular romance. Despite protestations that they are the author's favourites, Tom and Sophia are called into service to fulfil this function. On finding Sophia's pocketbook, Tom 'opened [it] a hundred times during their walk, kissed it as often, talked much to himself, and very little to his companions' (563); his response to the discovery that Partridge is to blame for Sophia's having taken offence is to wish instantly to put him to death (647); and finally hearing from Sophia, he spends 'three hours in reading and kissing the aforesaid letter' (756). There is an occasion when Tom is invested, rather unexpectedly, with melancholic sensibility (396–97); and the running joke about the muff suggests more than a tilt at sentimentality. The superbly comic account of the meeting of the lovers by the canal (222–24) confirms E. M. Forster's identification of the implications of the use of parody with regard to characterization:

> Parody or adaptation have enormous advantages to certain novelists, particularly to those who have a great deal to say and abundant literary genius, but who do not see the world in terms of individual men and women—who do not, in other words, take easily to creating characters.[8]

As regards character, Fielding's fondness for parody has a levelling effect—the principal characters cannot escape unscathed from the reductive process, whereas the conventionally 'low' characters have their status inflated by their participation in the comic-epic. The former point is exemplified well by the opening to Book X, Chapter 5:

As in the month of June, the damask rose, which chance hath planted among the lilies with their candid hue mixes his vermilion: or, as some playsome heifer in the pleasant month of May diffuses her odoriferous breath over the flowery meadows: or as, in the blooming month of April, the gentle, constant dove, perched on some fair bough, sits meditating her mate; so looking a hundred charms and breathing as many sweets, her thoughts being fixed on her Tommy, with a heart as good and innocent, as her face was beautiful: Sophia (for it was she herself) lay reclining her lovely head on her hand. . . . (482)

Now Fielding was obviously enjoying himself at the expense of the exponents of the stock pastoral, but can it really be claimed that his beloved heroine escapes unscathed from her appearance in the same context as the playsome heifer's odoriferous breath? Fielding exploits the traditions of genre and decorum as sources of comedy. He feigns adherence to the tradition of decorum but the intention is to amuse; the heroine cannot be introduced at the end of a book, but in protesting that he cannot introduce her Fielding effectively and comically does just that (149).

Such instances make it difficult to support the claim of Henry Knight Miller that

By Fielding's time, it is true, the whole tradition of literary 'decorum' was becoming somewhat academic, old-fashioned, like the hierarchical conceptions that it mirrored; and it is one of the measures of his separation from his own age, his attachment to an earlier day, that he should have held so tenaciously to the tradition.[9]

Rather than adhering closely to the tradition in the spirit in which it had been practised, Fielding mimics it for manifestly comic purposes. Likewise, the principal motive for juxtaposing the prefatory exercise in the sublime and the description of the 'middle-sized woman' that is Sophia (153–55) is entertainment. Both R. P. C. Mutter, with his assertion that 'Sophia has been introduced in a glowing prose, through which one can feel the pulsation of Fielding's undying love and esteem for his dead first wife Charlotte',[10] and Miller, with his contention that 'the style, in all its complexity makes the point: Sophia is merely a human being; but, seen through the eyes of love, she is, like all fortunate creatures, a very paragon',[11] place undue emphasis on Fielding, the lover of the lady, to the neglect of Fielding, the self-delighting stylist. Similarly, the cumulative effect of the sequence of comic-epic similes in Book VI, Chapter 9 ('As when two doves or two wood-pigeons . . . Or as when two gentlemen, strangers to the wonderous wit of the place, are cracking a bottle together at some inn or tavern at Salisbury . . . So trembled poor Sophia . . .' (278–79)) is to distance the reader from Sophia while feeling strongly the presence of the narrator.

Equally, with the account of the battle in the graveyard, 'A battle sung by the Muse in the Homerican Style, and which none but the classical Reader can taste' (172), one suspects that the author's prime intention was to entertain. Yet here, conversely, one of the effects of the application of the heroic mode to 'low' matter is to aggrandize both the contest and its participants to the level of the archetypal (it is, for Miller, '*The Country-Churchyard Brawl*').[12] Old Echepole, the sow-gelder, is comic certainly, but there is no denying the stature of a man who 'fell with almost as much noise as a house' (174). The account of the fate of Jemmy Tweedle is highly amusing:

> Recount, O Muse, the names of those who fell on this fatal day. First Jemmy Tweedle felt on his hinder head the direful bone. Him the pleasant banks of sweetly winding Stower had nourished, where he first learnt the vocal art, with which, wandring up and down at wakes and fairs, he cheered the rural nymphs and swains, when upon the green they interweave the sprightly dance; while he himself stood fiddling and jumping to his own music. How little now avails his fiddle? He thumps the verdant floor with his carcass. (173–74)

The discrepancy between matter and manner is decidedly comic. That one sentence, 'He thumps the verdant floor with his carcass', with sound reinforcing the contrast of pastoral and mundane diction, epitomizes Fielding's method. But are we laughing solely, or even principally, at Jemmy? I believe, rather, that one of Fielding's aims is to invite the reader to note the comic irrelevance of stylized modes—heroic and pastoral— to the representation of ordinary rural life in the eighteenth century. Paradoxically, the outcome of using a blatantly self-advertising style, a style far removed from that neutrality or self-effacement beloved of later orthodox realism, is realism of attitude.

There is an obvious alternative to the view that Fielding, as a realist confronting eighteenth-century life, delights in parodying the conventions of heroic literature in order to show their irrelevance, even their absurdity, as vehicles for rendering just such eighteenth-century life. It is that the nostalgic arch-conservative laments the demise of the world of heroic values and, by employing heroic modes, demonstrates how far men and values have declined from those of the golden age. But the effect of the many examples of mock-heroic embellishment (e.g. 'Aurora now first opened her casement, *Anglicè*, the day began to break ...' (440)) would seem to argue for a common-sense realism of attitude to both experience and the means of representing it. Particularly telling in this context is that passage where the narrator, regretting that Homer thought fit to send his gods on trivial errands, comments, 'Lord Shaftesbury observes, that nothing is more cold than the invocation of a muse by a modern; he might have added that nothing can be more absurd' (362).

If the effect of Fielding's stylistic expertise in parodying heroic modes is to represent him as a modern and a realist, his use of plot reveals him in a somewhat different light. Perhaps understandably, given its complexity, the plot of *Tom Jones* is resolved only with some strain. With the discovery that Allworthy now smiles on Tom, Western's steadfast opposition melts. The spirited Sophia, who has defied her father and fled from his house, and then consistently refused to marry Tom, asks her father what his wish is and duly complies with it. Even the necessary release of Tom from prison has demanded something of a volte-face on the part of Fitzpatrick and Lord Fellamar. But Fielding is much more interested in recording behaviour than attempting to account for it. Even granting Coleridge's judgement that Fielding was 'a master of composition' and *Tom Jones* was one of 'the three most perfect plots ever planned',[13] there is substance to Ian Watt's challenge,

> Perfect for what? we must ask. Not, certainly, for the exploration of character and of personal relations, since in all

three plots (the others are *Oedipus Tyrannus* and *The Alchemist*)
the emphasis falls on the author's skilfully contrived revelation
of an external and deterministic scheme.[14]

The behaviour of the characters is governed by this 'external
and deterministic scheme'. Insofar as the didactic terms of the
dedication have been met by the action of the book, the
inference that might be drawn would be that the open-hearted
should acquire prudence and trust in providence.

The resolution of the action gives rise to a problem that is
difficult to resolve: the conclusion seems to amount to an
endorsement of the *status quo*, yet the action of the book is
punctuated with satirical comment underpinned by a righteous
indignation at society's values. Here is an early account of the
fate of Partridge:

> Partridge, having now lost his wife, his school, and his annuity,
> and the unknown person having now discontinued the last-
> mentioned charity, resolved to change the scene, and left the
> country, where he was in danger of starving with the universal
> compassion of all his neighbours. (109)

It is difficult to discern there any lack of commitment, such as
might support Andrew Wright's contention that 'Fielding's
comic novels [are] as splendid—and, because comic, as
disengaged—as any in the language.'[15] Both Tom's journey
from Somerset to London and his experience of the *beau monde*
(with which is ironically juxtaposed the natural kingdom of
the gypsies) afford abundant instances of the various mani-
festations of hypocrisy, which Fielding was so intent on
exposing. And, as Mutter rightly noted,[16] rural life, as Fielding
depicts it, has its share of snobberies and affectations. Yet the
conclusion sees Tom accepted by polite society and elevated to
his rightful place in a rigidly hierarchical social structure. As
Watt observed, 'Fielding portrays the successful adaptation of
the individual to society'[17]; and this despite his intermittent
and strong censure of the values of that society (an early
footnote, for instance, glosses 'the mob' as 'persons without
virtue, or sense, in all stations, and many of the highest rank
are often meant by it' (73); a landlord is described as 'bred as
they call it, a gentleman, that is, bred up to do nothing' (385)).
Such censure implies the desirability of change, yet the nature

165

of the conclusion is such as to countenance no more than goodness's accommodation of discretion. Mutter shows awareness of the problem when he writes, 'We are made very much aware of the class system throughout *Tom Jones*, but the system is, on the whole, accepted.'[18] The resolution of the plot would seem to indicate that, in terms of values, Fielding ultimately reaffirms a hierarchical version of the neo-classical social ideal.

Yet plot in *Tom Jones* assumes a further dimension: it embraces narrator-reader relations. So obtrusive is the presence of the narrator that the reader develops an interest in the course that relations between himself and the narrator will take and the basis on which they will conclude. Though acknowledging that 'in *Tom Jones*, the "plot" of our relationship with Fielding-as-narrator has no similarity to the story of Tom', Wayne Booth went on to claim that 'somehow a genuine harmony of the two dramatized elements is produced' and that 'we move through the novel under [the narrator's] guidance'.[19] The nature of that guidance requires careful scrutiny, and the shifting stance of the narrator and his capacity for self-contradiction are such that the reader might well refuse to accept that his voice could feasibly be that of the wise author, Henry Fielding.

Fielding's narrator states that his provision 'is no other than HUMAN NATURE' but at the same time acknowledges that 'the excellence of the mental entertainment consists less in the subject, than in the author's skill in well dressing it up' (51–2). The same duality informs a later attempt to distinguish 'this heroic, historical, prosaic poem' from both romance and history:

> . . . truth distinguishes our writings from those idle romances which are filled with monsters, the productions, not of nature, but of distempered brains. . . .
> . . . That our work . . . might be in no danger of being likened to the labours of these historians, we have taken every occasion of interspersing through the whole sundry similes, descriptions, and other kind of poetical embellishments. (151)

While the narrator regularly proclaims his status as historian, he also recognizes, in Book II, Chapter 1, that his method is necessarily and justifiably, given the need to interest the

166

reader, that of the selective historian. Later he is to admit that

> tho' the facts themselves may appear, yet so different will be the motives, circumstances, and consequences, when a man tells his own story, and when his enemy tells it that we scarce can recognize the facts to be one and the same. (379)

The narrator claims to have a realistic attitude to his subject—man. Yet for all the apparent emphasis on the rendering of the recognizably human, he behaves, as Henry Knight Miller notes, 'as a rhetorician, presenting an interpretation of experience along with the experience, rather than as a reporter setting down neutral facts'.[20] No historian ever fussed so blatantly and persistently around his readers; yet, paradoxically, the effect is not to provide the reader with consistent or reliable guidance.

In the area of narrator-author relations ironies abound. After an account of Bridget's response to Allworthy's decision to adopt the infant Tom has prompted a short discourse on the nature of obedience, the narrator then warns the reader,

> As this is one of those deep observations which very few readers can be supposed capable of making themselves, I have thought proper to lend them my assistance; but this is a favour rarely to be expected in the course of my work. Indeed I shall seldom or never so indulge him, unless in such instances as this, where nothing but the inspiration with which we writers are gifted, can possibly enable any one to make the discovery. (62)

As the reader soon discovers, the narrator in fact rarely misses an opportunity to intervene with 'assistance', and the reader has to remain ever on the alert in order to distinguish literal from ironic guidance. Often what has initially the appearance of authoritative judgement is found to contain an element of qualification. 'Perhaps' is probably the favourite word of the narrator of *Tom Jones*. It invariably appears when he seems to be offering assistance to the reader (e.g. 'The infidelity of Molly, which Jones had now discovered, would, perhaps, have vindicated a much greater degree of resentment than he expressed on the occasion; and if he had abandoned her directly from that moment, very few, I believe, would have blamed him' (219)). One of the prefatory chapters, in which he is wont to lay down the law, carries the admission, 'it seems, perhaps, difficult to conceive that anyone should have had enough of impudence to lay down dogmatic rules in any art or science without the least foundation' (199). Yet Chapter 1 of Book IX begins with the claim that one of the purposes of the introductory chapters is to serve as 'a kind of mark or stamp, which may hereafter enable a very indifferent reader to distinguish, what is true and genuine in this historic kind of writing, from what is false and counterfeit' (435).

One of the narrator's habits is to disclaim any capacity for judgement. Of Dr. Blifil he comments, 'Whether his religion was real, or consisted only in appearance, I shall not presume to say, as I am not possessed of any touchstone, which can distinguish the true from the false' (75). Another tactic is to profess that he is at the mercy of events or the whim of his characters. Tom Jones, we are informed, 'bad as he is, must serve for the hero of this history' (123). And here he both claims a desire that he be not misunderstood and offers an apology for his appearance to say so:

> I ask pardon for this short appearance, by way of chorus, on the stage. It is in reality for my own sake, that while I am discovering the rocks on which innocence and goodness often split, I may not be misunderstood to recommend the very means to my worthy readers, by which I intend to shew them they will be undone. And this, as I could not prevail on any of my actors to speak, I was obliged to declare myself. (142)

Why does Fielding offer us a narrator who is so strongly and persistently present but so capable of self-contradiction? Can it be that he has created in the *persona* of his narrator another instance (albeit more complex and interesting than the characters) of human limitation? Is it really the case that Fielding deliberately presents us with a narrator whose fondness for irony (possibly a refuge for one baffled by life's enigmas?) leads him into inconsistency and self-contradiction? Dorothy Van Ghent made an admirable attempt to show how Fielding's narrator communicates with his reader in coded fashion by applying morally approbatory terms in such a way as to systematically identify them with hypocrisy.[21] This explains references to 'good' Master Blifil and comments such as this (on Partridge): 'a strict adherence to truth was not among this honest fellow's morality, or his religion' (830). But there are times when the addiction to verbal irony is hard to justify. For instance, when Bridget Allworthy's lack of beauty has been established at the outset (54), what purpose can be achieved by opening Chapter 2 of Book II with the statement that 'Eight months after the celebration of the nuptials between Captain Blifil and Miss Bridget Allworthy, a young lady of beauty, merit, and fortune, was Miss Bridget, by reason of a fright, delivered of a fine boy' (89)? Who is the source of this comment and who or what is the target of the irony? From Henry Knight Miller came the suggestion that 'an allusion to Bridget's wedding calls forth the formulaic voice of the newspaper-announcement.'[22] Even if the voice can be identified thus, the irony loses some of its force because of the vague nature of the target.

The foremost instance of the problems with irony is in the presentation of Allworthy. His treatment of Partridge and Black George and his championing of Blifil versus Tom belie the claim that he was 'as great a pattern (of true wisdom) as of goodness' (262). The narrator makes various attempts at explaining the nature of Allworthy's judgements: regarding the treatment of Partridge, he assures us, 'Certain it is, that whatever was the truth of the case, there was evidence more than sufficient to convict him before Allworthy; indeed much less would have satisfied a bench of justices on an order of bastardy' (107); he warns against condemning 'the wisdom or penetration of Mr. Allworthy' and, in so doing, making 'a very bad and ungrateful use of that knowledge which we have communicated' (137); and he protests, 'we do not pretend to introduce any infallible characters into this history' (137). But despite the combined effect of these, and other similar defences, doubts remain concerning the behaviour and the judgement of the symbolically-named magistrate.

Does Fielding deliberately create a narrator who gets into difficulties because, like Allworthy, of the limitations of his judgement? The 'plot' of narrator-reader relations leads to the conclusion that any fixed and single view-point is necessarily inadequate to cope with judgement of the complexity and flux of experience. Such are the discrepancies between the narrator's evaluations and the behaviour of the characters that it is impossible that he could be unaware of them. It may be that such disparities reflect the polarization of language and action, but they cannot have escaped the narrator's notice. It seems impossible that someone who has proved to be such an accomplished stylist could be such a naïve and fallible judge of human behaviour.

In fact what is happening is that Fielding's narrator is engaging in a sophisticated game which involves subtle flattery of the 'knowing' reader. In a perceptive essay Ian Ross observes that in *Tom Jones* 'the stance adopted towards the world is that of a humorous ironist, rather than that of someone who despairs of making sense of the world'.[23] It remains to be added that one of the tactics of the humorous ironist is to adopt the stance of one who despairs of making sense of the world and of his own capacity to guide the reader ('I think, I can with less pains write one of the books of this history, than the prefatory chapter to each' (739)).

One of the justifications of the time-gaps in the narrative is, allegedly, that they offer the reader 'an opportunity of employing that wonderful sagacity, of which he is master, by filling up these vacant spaces of time with his own conjectures' (121). There follows the crucial caveat, 'for which purpose, we have taken care to qualify him in the preceding pages'. (This is not unlike Sterne's having Tristram leave space for the reader to draw the Widow Wadman, but at precisely the point which *he* chooses.) On a later occasion the narrator promises 'proper assistance in difficult places', but instantly warns,

> . . . yet we shall not indulge thy laziness where nothing but thy own attention is required; for thou art highly mistaken if thou dost imagine that we intended, when we begun this great work, to leave thy sagacity nothing to do, or that, without sometimes exercising this talent, thou wilt be able to travel through our pages with any pleasure or profit to thyself. (546)

Habitually the narrator plays to the vanity of the 'knowledge-able' reader, as here, for instance:

> This unexpected encounter surprised the ladies much more than I believe it will the sagacious reader, who must have imagined that the strange lady could be no other than Mrs.

Fitzpatrick, the cousin of Miss Western, whom we before-mentioned to have sallied from the inn a few minutes after her. (510–11)

The intention is that the reader should be flattered by being treated as an equal by the urbane narrator who is capable of such comments as 'We shall therefore take leave at present of Sophia, and with our usual good-breeding, attend her ladyship' (750). Implicit in all of this is the assumption that the 'sagacious' reader will enjoy sharing with the narrator the jokes at the expense of the hypothetical 'foolish' reader. Fielding's narrator encourages divisions amongst his readers. His account of Tom's kindness to the highwayman, on learning of his wretched circumstances, is followed by the statement, 'Our readers will probably be divided in their opinions concerning this action' (605). The 'foolish' reader is presumably supposed to be taken in by such comments as 'A most dreadful Chapter indeed; and which few Readers ought to venture upon in an Evening, especially when alone' (350). The same reader is expected to rush off and reserve his seat at Tyburn when confronted by this assertion:

> This I faithfully promise, that notwithstanding any affection, which we may be supposed to have for this rogue, whom we have unfortunately made our heroe, we will lend him none of that supernatural assistance with which we are entrusted, upon condition that we use it only on very important occasions. If he doth not therefore find some natural means of fairly extricating himself from all his distresses, we will do no violence to the truth and dignity of history for his sake; for we had rather relate that he was hanged at Tyburn (which may very probably be the case) than forfeit our integrity, or shock the faith of our reader. (777–78)

Instances such as this give rise to the question of the distance at which Fielding stands from his narrator. That distance fluctuates, just as the target of Fielding's irony can expand to include 'sagacious' reader and, at times, narrator himself, before narrowing to focus on the hypothetical 'foolish' reader.

It becomes plain that Fielding, always in control (and this quality is reflected in the stylistic mastery), assumes the voice of the fallible, and thus manifestly human, narrator. In

Chapter 1 of Book VII, 'A Comparison between the World and the Stage', is this key passage:

> Some have considered the larger part of mankind in the light of actors, as personating characters no more their own, and to which, in fact, they have no better title, than the player hath to be in earnest thought the king or emperor whom he represents. Thus the hypocrite may be said to be a player; and indeed the Greeks called them both by one and the same name. (299–300)

Paradoxically, the author who has made the hypocrite the prime target of his censure has exploited precisely that capacity for personation in himself by his donning of the mask of the fallible judge. The magisterial author, the god of the world of his novel, 'gets down into the arena'[24] himself (to borrow James's phrase) by feigning human weakness in his rôle as narrator. He has, he protests, 'done great violence to the luxuriance of [his] genius' (558): he has omitted passages which the reader would skip over, which is exactly what he admits to having done himself when confronted by the works of 'voluminous historians'. And, he assures us, 'there are some incidents in life so very strange and unaccountable, that it seems to require more than human skill and foresight in producing them' (682). Earlier he has made it plain that his duty is to relate the accidents of Fortune (190). Despite his apparent readiness to countenance, through the *persona* of his narrator, both the flux and complexity of experience and the limitations of man's attempts to evaluate experience, Fielding emerges finally and clearly as the source of the allegedly providentially-ordered world of his novel. This reflects, as Martin Battestin demonstrated,[25] his belief in the providential ordinance of the macrocosm.

NOTES

1. Henry James, 'The Art of Fiction', in *The House of Fiction: Essays on the Novel*, edited with an introduction by Leon Edel (London: Rupert Hart-Davis, 1957), p. 38.
2. Stendhal, Letter to his sister, Pauline, 20 August 1805, *Correspondance* (Paris: Editions Louis Conard, 1908); cited Miriam Allott, *Novelists on the Novel* (London: Routledge; New York: Columbia University Press, 1959), p. 128.

3. *Joseph Andrews*, Book III, Chapter 1.
4. Henry James, Preface to *The Princess Casamassima*, The Bodley Head Henry James, Vol. X, with an introduction by Leon Edel, p. 22.
5. Henry Knight Miller, 'The Voices of Henry Fielding: Style in *Tom Jones*', in *The Augustan Milieu: Essays presented to Louis A. Landa*, edited by Henry Knight Miller, Eric Rothstein, and G. S. Rousseau (Oxford: Clarendon Press, 1970), p. 267.
6. Wayne Booth, *The Rhetoric of Fiction* (Chicago and London: University of Chicago Press, 1961), p. 83.
7. References are to *The History of Tom Jones*, edited by R. P. C. Mutter (Harmondsworth: Penguin Books, 1966).
8. E. M. Forster, *Aspects of the Novel* (Harmondsworth: Penguin Books, 1962), p. 125.
9. Miller, p. 270.
10. *TJ*, ed. Mutter, p. 14.
11. Miller, p. 272.
12. Ibid., p. 275.
13. Cited Frederic T. Blanchard, *Fielding the Novelist: A Study in Historical Criticism* (New Haven: Yale University Press, 1926), pp. 320–21. The definitive study of the plot of *Tom Jones* remains R. S. Crane, 'The Concept of Plot and the Plot of *Tom Jones*', in *Critics and Criticism, Ancient and Modern*, edited with an introduction by R. S. Crane (Chicago: University of Chicago Press, 1952).
14. Ian Watt, *The Rise of the Novel: Studies in Defoe, Richardson, and Fielding* (Harmondsworth: Penguin Books, in association with Chatto and Windus, 1963), p. 280.
15. Andrew Wright, *Henry Fielding: Mask and Feast* (Berkeley and Los Angeles: University of California Press, 1966), p. 17.
16. *TJ*, ed. Mutter, p. 25.
17. Watt, p. 282.
18. *TJ*, ed. Mutter, p. 19.
19. Booth, *The Rhetoric of Fiction*, pp. 216–17.
20. Miller, p. 263.
21. Dorothy Van Ghent, *The English Novel: Form and Function* (New York: Harper and Row, 1961).
22. Miller, p. 278.
23. Ian Ross, 'Philosophy and Fiction. The Challenge of David Hume', in *Hume and the Enlightenment: Essays Presented to Ernest Campbell Mossner*, edited by W. B. Todd (Edinburgh: Edinburgh University Press, 1974), p. 64.
24. Henry James, Preface to *The Golden Bowl*, The Bodley Head Henry James, Volume IX, with an introduction by Leon Edel, p. 16.
25. Martin Battestin, '*Tom Jones*: the Argument of Design', in *The Augustan Milieu*, ed. Miller, Rothstein, and Rousseau; later incorporated in *The Providence of Wit: Aspects of Form in Augustan Literature and the Arts* (Oxford: Clarendon Press, 1974).

9

Lying and Concealment in *Amelia*

by DONALD FRASER

In the first line of *Amelia*, Fielding defines his subject matter as 'the various Accidents which befel a very worthy Couple' (I, 1, 15),[1] and promises to demonstrate that these events will serve to display not the power of fortune but the greater efficacy of wisdom and virtue. He concludes his first chapter with a celebrated analogy between the novel, as a pattern of significant occurrences, and human life, which if viewed correctly presents a similarly meaningful design:

> As Histories of this Kind, therefore, may properly be called Models of HUMAN LIFE; so by observing minutely the several Incidents which tend to the Catastrophe or Completion of the whole, and the minute Causes whence those Incidents are produced, we shall be best instructed in this most useful of all Arts, which I call the ART of LIFE. (I, 1, 17)

Fielding's stress here on the importance of minute detail as a guide to the causes of events, which individually produce results and ultimately a conclusion (i.e. 'Completion of the whole'), may be taken as a pointer to readers about to embark on their experience of this 'Model of HUMAN LIFE'. It will be the duty of the reader who wishes to understand the shape of human life by means of this fiction, to examine closely its incidents, to consider what brings them about, and what results they produce.

At the beginning of his last book, Fielding is still encouraging his readers to attend closely to the causes and explanations for *all* the happenings of his story. Fielding takes two pages to explain elaborately, almost laboriously, *why* Colonel James had challenged Booth, and the mechanics of *how* Booth came to be arrested yet again. He then justifies his provision of so much detail of *'polite History'* (XII, 1; chapter heading):

> These were several Matters, of which we thought necessary our Reader should be informed; for, besides that it conduces greatly to a perfect Understanding of all History, there is no Exercise of the Mind of a sensible Reader more pleasant than the tracing the several small and almost imperceptible Links in every Chain of Events by which all the great Actions of the World are produced. (XII, 1, 495–96)

There is of course a mildly ironic self-deprecation here, since the high purpose of the novel as model of human life is presumably meant to offer more than a pleasant mental exercise for the reader, but there remains a pointed significance in Fielding's assertion. Fielding wishes the reader to know these 'facts', in order to recognize how complete is his grasp over all the details, and if the reader has been following 'the thread of [the] story' (III, 5, 115), he assuredly will wish to be privy to the full provenance of all the incidents. That such study is *not* simply an intellectual entertainment, but a means to greater understanding, is shown by the placing of this remark; it immediately precedes the chapter where Booth at last confesses to Amelia his adultery with Miss Mathews, together with 'all that he had done and suffered, to conceal his Transgression from her Knowledge' (XII, 2, 498). For it has been the concealment of Booth's adultery, with the subsequent lying and deceit this entails, which has been a major cause of the 'Distresses' and 'extraordinary Incidents' which make up our couple's history.

It is this issue of lying, deception and concealment which is persistently questioned by Fielding in *Amelia*, and it is by the close examination of causes and events, and of the story-teller's control and presentation of those events, that Fielding leads his readers to consider the complex issues that surround such themes.[2] Such an investigation will reveal important ways in which the notoriously intricate contrivance of the plot, often presented as a major reason for the 'failure' of the book, does have an aesthetic and moral function. As J. Paul Hunter comments, 'The problem is not in contrivance *per se*, but rather in the supporting tone and the novelistic vision that generates the tone.'[3] That tone is usually agreed to be one of more 'general darkness' (209) than in *Joseph Andrews* and *Tom Jones*, and it is in keeping with such comparative sombreness, and the sense of 'remorse' (212) and 'renunciation' (216) which Hunter finds in the book, that Fielding should so determinedly attempt to align his own sense of earnest truthfulness in the story with the high standard he sets for his characters.

Two episodes, the first reasonably minor, the second crucial, will serve as preliminary demonstrations of how Fielding makes minute details of cause and effect in his plot manifest the centrality which I am claiming for notions of truth and falsehood in the action of the work. In Book V, Chapter 5, Booth and Colonel Bath fight a duel, for reasons which are still, in Book V, Chapter 8, not fully explained to Booth or the reader, though it is understood (by both) to be about something Colonel James said of Booth. When Booth next meets Colonel James, in the presence of the wounded Colonel Bath, James is surprisingly friendly to him; we are told that Colonel James 'whispered *Booth* that he would give him all the Satisfaction imaginable concerning the whole Affair' (221–22), and they go out, leaving Colonel Bath convinced because of the ambiguity of 'satisfaction' (i.e. reparation through duelling) in this context, that they have gone to duel, while the reader is left uncertain about why James has reacted so apparently heartily (i.e. a satisfactory explanation). In fact, it turns out that they are (temporarily) reconciled, but readers cannot understand this at once, because the narration stays with Colonel Bath until later in the chapter.

Towards the end of the chapter, Fielding undertakes to 'account for an Incident which we have related in the very Chapter, and which we think deserves some Solution' (224): that is, James's unexpectedly friendly behaviour. The account is as follows: Miss Mathews (IV, 8, 186) told James that Booth traduced his character, and this lie, which Colonel Bath believed, aroused his anger: hence the original duel. A false report of this duel gave out that Booth was killed by a Colonel, and this untrue rumour caused Miss Matthews to relent of her rage against Booth, transferring it to James, whom she has made 'the Instrument of Mischief' against her real beloved. She therefore writes to James, confessing her 'Falsehood' about Booth, and James accordingly forgives him.

If the causes and effects of this complicated (and rather trivial) *imbroglio* are examined, it becomes clear that a lie (about Booth) leads to a catastrophe (the duel), and a further untruth (the rumour) then produces a solution of Booth's immediate difficulty. It may perhaps seem a trifling incident on which to base a 'model of human life', but it is interesting that Fielding goes to such trouble to tease out the connections. It is also interesting that he presents this *éclaircissement* to the reader as a directly addressed explanation of a puzzle, rather than dramatizing it in the next chapter, when James is said to 'acquaint *Booth* with all that which the Reader knows already' (V, 9, 226). This of course leaves space in the chapter for the thematic debate on constancy, but it also serves the purpose of not obscuring any of the details of events, which are supposed thus to carry symbolic ethical significance.

My second example of a lie and its consequences is an event which acts as a powerful lever in the plot, bringing about the resolution of the Booth family's financial problems. This takes place in Book XII, Chapter 3, immediately after Booth has revealed his adultery to Amelia. The pawnbroker tells Amelia that a man (who will be Robinson) recognized her in the portrait (itself the object of a trail of curious clues) which she had pawned the day before. The pawnbroker claims that he told the man he had never seen Amelia before, but Fielding tells the reader that in this 'he made a small Deviation from the Truth' (506), having actually told the man that she was 'some poor undone Woman' who was pawning the very last of her property. Fielding adds: 'This Hint we thought proper to give the Reader, as it may chance to be material.'

It is indeed material, and the reader will be alert for further revelation on this basis. The revelation comes (after Booth's statement of his repentance of his religious doubts) in

Book XII, chapter 6. The man at the pawnshop is (of course) Robinson, who in his 'deathbed' confession feels that the 'Hand of Providence' (516) led him to the pawnbroker where he discovered that his fraudulent alteration of the Harris family will had brought about the 'undoing' of Amelia. So the pawnbroker's deviation from the truth actually produces in Robinson a shock which compels him to repent, and to seek to redress the injury he had done. When Dr. Harrison tells Booth that 'Providence hath done you . . . Justice at last' (XII, 7, 522), the reader who has taken Fielding's earlier 'hint' recognizes that Providence has operated, in this great culminating resolution, through a petty falsehood, which Fielding has been careful to point out, not through specific commentary, but by alerting the reader to details of plot which seem to be merely incidental.

These examples, which manifest a deliberate contrivance of plot elements around questions of truth and falsehood, also serve to point up the ethically ambiguous properties of lies, in their ability to produce providentially sound results despite their moral reprehensibility.

Fielding's explicit purpose to investigate the workings of Providence through the theme of lying and deceit is signalled thematically in the very first chapter of narration, with its concentration on perjury and evidence in the legal system. The history begins in a J.P.'s court which, Fielding tells us, constitutes a typical and unhappy sample of his belief that all human institutions (in this case the law) are subject to 'small Imperfections' (I, 2, 19). The imperfection lies less in the laws themselves, than in their execution, in the person of Mr. Justice Thrasher. This magistrate's first victims are all committed because of various lies by their accusers, and the same unjust conclusion is then reached on Booth, who is charged with assaulting a watchman. 'This was deposed by two Witnesses' (24), and the magistrate will not believe 'the bare Word of an Offender', refuses to send for other witnesses, and has 'too great an Honour for Truth' to believe she could appear in that 'sordid Apparel' which is the mark of Booth's poverty. Fielding has to certify explicitly the accused's truthfulness, saying that Booth's account 'was in Reality the Case',[4] because this is our first introduction to the hero, but such asseverations also serve thematically, directing attention towards the question of how to uncover lying and discover truth.

It is pointed out that Booth's accusers perjure themselves, and the question of perjury is discussed shortly in Book I, Chapter 4, by Robinson and Booth; the former significantly remarks that perjuries in civil matters are not so very criminal, 'for what is taking away a little Property from a Man compared to taking away his Life, and his Reputation, and ruining his Family into the Bargain?' (34–5). Although readers cannot know it, the destiny of the will and a major slice of the action of the story exactly depend on such a question.

The perjury that sends Booth to Newgate Prison is a matter of false evidence: 'The shattered Remains of a broken Lanthorn, which had long been preserved for the Sake of its Testimony, were produced to corroborate the Evidence' (24). Fielding posits, and points out, the centrality of evidence in this case, and on several later occasions raises the topic again. Murphy declares, in considering how to mount Miss Mathews's defence: 'The Chapter of Evidence is the main Business. . . . Evidence is indeed the Whole' (I, 10, 61). There is also in Book XI, Chapter 3, a brief debate on the difficulties occasioned for courts by the complexities and confusions of the law of evidence.

If evidence plays such a crucial part in determining the truth of disputed matters, by what means can magistrates hope to distinguish truth from falsehood? A corrupt justice like Thrasher is obviously unable and unwilling to try, but Fielding suggests a quality which would have enabled him to perceive Booth's 'Air of Truth and Sincerity' (24). That quality is 'Sagacity', which together with 'another Quality very necessary to all who are to administer Justice' (perhaps industry, or patience), would have enabled him to penetrate nearer to the truth in this matter.

This quality, which Johnson defines as 'quick in thought; acute in making discoveries',[5] seems to have been highly valued by Fielding, for it is striking that on at least three important occasions, he employs the concept of sagacity with specific relation to his readers. In Book V, Chapter 9, when

179

Booth begins to suspect the womanizing peer, Fielding, without being at all explicit, alerts the reader thus:

> Yet some Chimeras now arose in his Brain, which gave him no very agreeable Sensations. What these were the sagacious Reader may probably suspect; but if he should not, we may perhaps have Occasion to open them in the sequel. (228)

When Mrs. Bennet's maid inadvertently addresses Atkinson as 'my Master', 'a Secret is . . . innocently blabbed out' (VII, 8, 300), the secret marriage of the Atkinsons. Fielding tells us that Amelia began to guess something; 'what that is the sagacious Readers may likewise probably suggest to themselves; if not, they must wait our Time for disclosing it.' And when Amelia reluctantly reveals her secret, that James has been pursuing her, Booth's extremely passionate response goes beyond mere anger at the slight on his honour, or shame over the loss of a huge sum at the gaming table; we are told that 'poor *Amelia* generously forgave a Passion, of which the sagacious Reader is better acquainted with the real Cause, than was that unhappy Lady' (X, 6, 438), and this seems to invite us to recall Booth's sense of guilt at the continuing concealment of his adultery.

At each of these points, Fielding hints at a development which he has *not* made explicit, but one which could reasonably be sorted out by a reader who has been attending to the precise incidents which precede it. The 'sagacious reader' will sift evidence, as a worthy judge should do, and hence should be able to arrive at the truth. For this purpose it is of course essential that the evidence should not be perjured, and hence the reader is entitled to expect that the author will tell the truth and not seek to deceive or mislead; it is fascinating to see how Fielding's concern with truth and falsehood in the invented world of his novel extends by such analogies to the notion of truth and lying in the very structure of his fiction.

There is plenty of falsehood, at various levels of intensity, to be found in the action of the story. Many of the characters are variously dissemblers, deceivers and outright liars, and as Booth says: 'Sometimes one would be almost persuaded that there was Pleasure in Lying itself' (VI, 4, 242). Miss

Mathews, described in elaborately sarcastic similes (I, 6) as the epitome of deception, specializes, as we have seen, in downright lies, as well as in histrionic displays of love and fury. Mrs. Ellison, who shows at first as 'a very good-humoured Woman' (IV, 9, 189), and seems to admire Amelia's beauty without jealousy (perhaps in itself a danger sign?), is ultimately revealed as a dissembler whose plots are unambivalently evil. Even Mrs. Bennet misleads the company by her opposition to second marriages (VI, 7), for although the failure of her father's second marriage (described in Book VII, Chapters 2 and 3) seems to explain this hostility, the revelation in Book VII, Chapter 10, that she is already secretly married to Sergeant Atkinson casts an interesting backlight on her vehemence. There is presumably at least some force in Mrs. Ellison's declaration that it is 'a certain Sign that she intended to marry again soon' (VI, 8, 259), and hence is intended to produce misunderstanding.

Deception obviously is not confined to the female characters. Among Booth's acquaintance, Robinson, Trent and the noble Lord live by plots, deceit and lying. Colonel James, who behaves very properly, and says 'every Thing which became the Mouth of a Friend on the Occasion' (VIII, 5, 330), frequently betrays Booth's friendship, and we are encouraged to endorse Mrs. Bennet's view that, as with Lord —, 'what the World generally calls Politeness, I term Insincerity' (V, 3, 203). With these men, elegance and *politesse* are deceit, to gain their sexual ends.

Nor, furthermore, can Booth be omitted from the list of dissemblers. As a man of good nature he plainly takes no pleasure in lying, but much of the action does stem from his failure to tell Amelia the truth about his adultery, thus subjecting himself (and her) to torments which the plot finally demonstrates to have been unnecessary; he really would have been forgiven, as the narrator confidently conjectures ('in great Probability he would have received immediate Forgiveness from that best of Women' (IV, 5, 176)), and as Amelia's ultimate reaction proves (XII, 2).

By contrast with the rest of the characters, Amelia and Dr. Harrison make every effort to avoid lying and to preserve themselves innocent of deceit. (They both, however, have significantly ambivalent attitudes towards what they define as 'stratagems', a point to be dealt with later.) Amelia tells the maid, who has lied about the break-in to the apartment, to confess the truth, 'for I mortally hate a Liar, and can forgive any Fault sooner than Falsehood' (VI, 4, 245). She even disapproves of concealments designed to avoid giving others pain or uneasiness, replying to Booth's excuse that 'these are called the pious Frauds of Friendship' with this assertion: 'I detest all Fraud . . . and *pious* is too good an Epithet to be joined to so odious a Word' (VI, 6, 249). As concomitant to this strenuous and virtuous adherence to truthfulness, Fielding arranges events so that goodness is at times imposed on by those who are natural deceivers. The comment on Amelia's reluctance to believe the worst of Colonel James, that 'it is not Want of Sense, but Want of Suspicion by which Innocence is often betrayed' (VIII, 9, 347), is frequently reiterated as commentary, and demonstrated in the action.

Dr. Harrison describes Amelia as a true Christian, in the biblical phrase: 'I may call her *an* Israelite *indeed, in whom there is no Guile*' (IX, 8, 387). The compliment could also be applied to the Doctor himself, and Fielding says that he was 'no Dissembler (indeed he was incapable of any Disguise)' (XIII, 5, 510). Dr. Harrison tells Amelia, when she admits she is afraid to tell him the truth about Booth's enormous gambling debt, that 'Any Prevarication . . . will forfeit my Friendship for ever' (XII, 3, 502).[6] Again, continuing to draw on Biblical allusions, Dr. Harrison objects to being called 'wise . . . as the World understands the Phrase'.[7] His 'modesty' in this is immediately justified, as he fails to credit Amelia's 'strong reasons' for refusing to agree to stay at home if Booth is posted abroad, and is forced in the next chapter to concede that he did not perceive Colonel James's villainy. Fielding informs us that Dr. Harrison is duped by his country friend (IX, 10), and that the regrettable task of the faithful historian is 'to describe Human Nature as it is, not as we would wish it to be' (X, 4, 429).

How can such innocent beings survive in a world of plots, deceit and lying? They can, and do, trust in Providence to redirect events, bringing good from evil by ensuring that the plots of the deceivers ultimately miscarry. They also at times resort to virtuous stratagems or devices, which sometimes temporarily rebound on them, but are always ultimately resolved into good conclusions. And they continue to cling, often with amazing and amusing ingenuity, to their principles of truthfulness, for although they may not always rigorously tell all the truth, they are never formally or literally dishonest.

Here, too, the analogies with Fielding's procedures as a writer of fiction continue to hold good. Fielding (notoriously) ensures that the plot is manipulated in such a way that Providential justice is seen to be done. The structure which manifests this symbolic ordering is of course Fielding's plot, which consists of a series of incidents, at first unclear, but all tending towards ultimate clarification and resolution. And, in arranging this action, Fielding is careful to ensure that the reader is never actually, actively, deceived. There may be many instances of apparent misleading, but these can be explained as acts of misreading, by readers who are not sagacious enough to test every word of the narration for its truth. Fielding never actually 'lies' to create the surprises he springs on us, and he makes efforts which are both strenuous and subtle, to observe a literal veracity in the presentation of the story, and the reader's progressive understandings.

It is now worth analysing a couple of episodes, in terms of events and their consequences, to see how this concern with truth and lying is managed in the story and in Fielding's construction and control of the story. The episode of the break-in and its consequences provides a nice little nexus of mysteries and misleading information, kept reasonably straightforward by the fact that the stratagems and concealments here are largely in the narration, rather than in the action. The masquerade will present a much more complex interweaving of deceits by the characters, with authorial dissembling; there, narration and action are permeated with falsity, from which Amelia and Fielding, with great difficulty and ingenuity, just manage to distance themselves.

On their return from a pleasant walk, Booth and Amelia discover that their apartment has been ransacked; the maid at first tells them a man burst in with pistols, but later modifies this, confessing that she admitted the man, who suddenly began searching through their possessions, muttering like a madman, and eventually ran off. The odd thing is that nothing was actually stolen, not even the valuable gold watch. So this remains an unresolved puzzle, leaving Booth with his 'Curiosity' roused, and 'several Doubts and Apprehensions of he knew not what' (VI, 4, 245). The occurrence is similarly mysterious to the reader, who is alerted by Booth's fears to expect some further development.

After three more chapters, there is an explanation. Sergeant Atkinson warns Booth that Murphy knows about Booth's possessions, and is about to mount an action for recovery of some debts; it therefore seems obvious that Murphy or one of his investigators broke in, to ascertain whether Booth is sufficiently well-off to be worth proceeding against. The mystery apparently now solved, two books pass by. In Book VII, we hear Mrs. Bennet's history, and are astonished at the end by the news of Booth's arrest at the suit of Dr. Harrison! In Book VIII, Chapter 1, Fielding offers to explain the 'Circumstances, which led to the Catastrophe' (308), but he only describes the immediate details of the arrest, leaving Booth and the reader, without the aid of any commentary, to wonder at the strangely 'barbarous Action' (VII, 9, 307) of a man we have expected to be a person of charity.

It is not until the start of Book IX that the story

> looks back a little, in order to account for the late Conduct of Doctor *Harrison*; which, however inconsistent it may have hitherto appeared, when examined to the Bottom, will be found, I apprehend, to be truly congruous with all the Rules of the most perfect Prudence, as well as with the most consummate Goodness. (IX, 1, 357)

The reader still has no reason to connect Dr. Harrison with the break-in, and at this point is simply expecting enlightenment about the apparent oddities of his recent conduct. So it comes as a surprise when Fielding reveals, quite casually and without any apology for allowing us to believe otherwise, that the Doctor himself was responsible for the intrusion, 'concerning which the Reader may be pleased to remember so many strange and odd Conjectures' (358).

How could Fielding have so led us astray? The author plainly feels no shame or sense of responsibility for having done this, so perhaps he did *not* mislead us. A return to the scene of the crime provides evidence which even the sagacious reader could not have interpreted correctly at the time, but which absolves Fielding from any charge of deliberate, or literal, deception. The maid eventually reports that the intruder was gentlemanly, that he talked to himself and spoke many strange words, behaving like a madman, and in 'very ill Words, he said *he would do for him*' (VI, 4, 244). The maid's account is the *evidence*, all of which can now be seen as legitimately (and credibly) applicable to Dr. Harrison's outrage at the Booths' apparent extravagance.

There are then two interesting points in the 'explanation' which is accepted in Book VI, Chapter 9. A close reading reveals that the conjecture is made through Booth's understanding, and that Fielding as narrator stands back from the solution, locating it only in Booth's mind:

> He now *plainly perceived, as he thought,* that Murphy himself, or one of his Emissaries, had been the supposed Madman; and *he now very well accounted to himself in his own Mind,* for all that had happened, *conceiving* that the Design was to examine into the State of his Effects, and to try whether it was worth his Creditors while to plunder him by Law. (261)

This does appear a very thorough explanation, but it is clear, from my italicized phrases, that Fielding is not endorsing this conclusion himself, however much the reader is seduced by its probability. He is careful not to propagate an outright untruth himself, despite his willingness to leave readers with Booth's impression. The second part of the sentence is also effectively true. Although it is not by design, the *effect* of Dr. Harrison's break-in is that Booth *is* again pursued by Murphy and the creditors for his debts.

In Book IX, Chapter 1, the question of evidence is again brought before our eyes. It is because of 'gross and scandalous Lies' (357) and exaggerated accounts of Booth's extravagance that Dr. Harrison comes to London, resolving nevertheless that he 'would not absolutely condemn him without ocular Demonstration'. Now the gold watch was an innocently accepted present, but, provoked by lies, the doctor misreads this evidence, seeing it as a sign of extravagance; hence, he sets the action for debt into motion, Booth is taken up by the bailiff, and the next cycle of catastrophe begins. In a world of deliberate falsehood, and misleading evidence, Dr. Harrison's lack of guile seems to be a handicap. But this of course is not the end of the story, and Dr. Harrison's relationship with truth and concealment will yet be shown as more complex.

A masquerade is by definition, and in its symbolism, an occasion of deceit and intrigue, where people formally pretend to be what they are not, and may furthermore seek to gain advantage by it. How can the innocent survive, or even avoid the taint of deceit, in such a place? And what good can an honest author hope to produce through such a complex of falsities? Booth objects to the first (Ranelagh) masquerade (VI, 6) on the grounds that men gave ladies tickets in order to achieve assignations with them, and Mrs. Bennet, for reasons that are discovered later and which support Booth's objection, grows 'particularly grave at the Mention of the Masquerade' (VI, 8, 259). Its dangers are confirmed by Mrs. Bennet's history, and the realization that an identical plot to ruin Amelia is being prepared by the lecherous peer, comes about when the ladies 'compared Notes' (VII, 7, 296); the reader, too, has been comparing the manifest similarities between Mrs. Bennet's history and Amelia's previous connection with Mrs. Ellison and the Lord. Amelia, and the reader, then have every reason to be suspicious in Book X, Chapter 1, when it is discovered that Colonel James has sent Booth and Amelia two tickets for another masquerade. Even when the events of this masquerade are re-read with hindsight, they are quite difficult to analyse, and some elements (such as who is the blue domino?) are left unexplained after the basic discovery in Book X, Chapter 3, without even a hint for the future.

Ironically, Booth insists on going to this masquerade, and Amelia refers her problem to Dr. Harrison: 'I really do not know how to refuse, without giving him some Reason; and I am not able to invent any other than the true one' (X, 1, 406). She cannot tell Booth about James's pursuit of her, can think of no other reason, and is not willing to make up a false reason (i.e. to lie). Even Dr. Harrison is completely puzzled by this, but promises to think about it. Meanwhile, Mrs. Atkinson enters, and though they come to no resolution on the matter, she encourages Amelia by saying, 'Fear nothing, my dear *Amelia*; two women will surely be too hard for one Man' (407), instantly launching into a quotation from the *Aeneid*. This is the only clue that there will be a stratagem, and it is quickly masked, first by its obscurity. Who is the one man? Colonel James? Booth? Perhaps it is Dr. Harrison, whose perspicacity may on this occasion be trumped by the two women? The second means by which Fielding diverts attention from the clue is by side-tracking into the long debate on female learning which occupies the rest of the chapter.[8] So we arrive at the masquerade in Book X, Chapter 2, with no further information, assuming that Amelia has submitted obediently to Booth's insistence.

Readers certainly have to believe that Amelia *does* attend the masquerade, and that she even spends some time with Lord —. She certainly seems to have entered into the spirit of deceit and lying. It does seem surprising, however, and the uncovering of the stratagem (disguise added to disguise) in Book X, Chapter 3, brings a sense of relief that Amelia has *not* so thoroughly abandoned her principles. Fielding's ambiguous language similarly preserves him from any charges of lying, though (like Amelia) he has arranged for us to be misled. 'The four Masques then set out together in several Chairs' (X, 2, 410) and on arrival, 'nor did *Booth* and his Lady remain long together, but were soon divided from each other by different Masques' (411). The 'false' Amelia (i.e. Mrs. Atkinson) is generally described as 'the Lady' or with a pronoun, and the would-be seducers are rewarded only by mistaking their prey, because of the disguise, which is actually expected to enable their conquest.

Towards the end, we are told that '*Booth* had not yet seen his Wife' (417), and Colonel James leads him to 'the Peer and *Amelia* (such he was now well convinced she was) sitting together' (418). The lady is then described as 'the supposed *Amelia*', because she had earlier denied being she to James, but both of the men (and the Peer), and undoubtedly the struggling reader, take the supposition for the fact. On the return home, 'The Lady getting first out of her Chair ran hastily up into the Nursery' (X, 3, 419), whence Amelia shortly comes down into the dining-room. At no point, in fact, has Fielding ever stated that Amelia was present at the masquerade. No explicit lie has left his pen.

187

In the chapter of consequences (X, 3), attention focuses more on Amelia's strategic responses to Booth's jealous accusation. In a striking analogy with Fielding's literal truthfulness, Amelia, though she seems to be lying to Booth, utters not a single falsehood in the dialogue by which she leads him actually to state that he wishes she had never gone. Here are some of her most pertinent (and surprising) remarks: 'I did not know one Person at the Masquerade'; 'you know we were not together'; 'can I tell People in Masques?'; 'I know nothing of the Methods of a Masquerade; for I never was at one in my Life.' The last remark is particularly neat, as the contemporary syntax could produce either of these meanings: 'I have never been (before) . . .' or 'I have never been (yet) . . .'. Each of these remarks is accurate, though ambiguous enough in the context to be thought by Booth and unsuspecting readers to be remarkably prevaricative. Booth makes this point, when he cries, 'Can I suspect you of not speaking Truth?' (X, 3, 420).

Amelia then ceases to tease Booth ('I do not jest with you', 421), confessing that she was not there: 'Forgive me this first Deceit I ever practised, and indeed it shall be the last; for I have paid severely for this by the Uneasiness it hath given me' (421). The substitution of Mrs. Atkinson for Amelia is then described variously as a 'Secret', 'the Imposition', 'the Deceit' (421) and finally a 'Stratagem' (X, 4, 422). This more neutral word is introduced as Dr. Harrison's definition of the affair, and is an interesting mark of the way in which such devices of dissembling may legitimately play a part in the virtuous person's struggle against evil. However, although Dr. Harrison is pleased with the success of the stratagem and presumably agreed to it, there is no indication in the text that he actually invented this device. For there will turn out to be further consequences of the deceit, which will prove much more awkward to handle.

One further result of the masquerade itself is the web of misunderstandings over Dr. Harrison's letter on adultery, which eventually persuades Booth that James is not to be trusted, a strand which continues to animate the plot and requires Amelia to exercise the most exquisite delicacy in her relations with both men. The details of this I forbear to follow. More significant are the further problems generated by Mrs.

Atkinson's bold opportunism in her rôle as 'Amelia'. When
Mrs. Atkinson recounts her experiences at the masquerade,
Fielding refuses to say whether she told all, thus warning us to
suspect some further development. 'Whether she told the
whole Truth with regard to herself, I will not determine' (X, 4,
425). Her personal sub-plot brings a love-letter from the Lord
to Amelia, containing a commission for Sergeant Atkinson,
but Amelia is outraged that any favours should have been
granted 'in my Name',[9] now repenting entirely of the stratagem:

> I am heartily sorry I ever consented to practice any Deceit. I
> plainly see the Truth of what Dr. *Harrison* hath often told me,
> that if one steps ever so little out of the Ways of Virtue and
> Innocence, we know not how we may slide; for all the Ways of
> Vice are a slippery Descent. (X, 8, 445)

Thus the final consequences of the stratagem, designed to
protect Booth from the knowledge that James is a traitor
(information that he nevertheless gains only three chapters
later in Book X, Chapter 6), is an estrangement between the
ladies, and the revival of Booth's quiescent suspicions about
the Lord: hardly a straightforward conclusion, despite the
temporary success of the device.

The masquerade is the most questionable example of the
stratagem perpetrated by virtuous characters for honest
purposes, but there are a number of other occasions where
similar devices are attempted, with results that vary
interestingly. In Book V, Chapter 4, the honest sergeant
uncovers the momentarily useful information that Murphy
expects to be able to arrest Booth very shortly, by pretending
to Murphy that Booth owed him a small debt. Nothing comes
of this threat, but because of it Atkinson is invited into the
back parlour as a porter/guard, where 'he had sometimes the
Company of Mrs. *Ellison*, and sometimes of *Booth, Amelia,* and
Mrs. *Bennet*, too; for this last had taken as great a Fancy to
Amelia, as *Amelia* had to her . . .' (V, 4, 206). It is here, of
course, that his acquaintance and courtship of Mrs. Bennet
presumably begins; note how Fielding makes available this
information (which we nevertheless have no way of using),
and then immediately side-tracks us from it, by pointing out
that the attraction is between Mrs. Bennet and Amelia.

Though we could not know this, a consequence of Atkinson's little ploy is his successful courtship and marriage.

Two chapters later, Atkinson confides to Booth that 'he had had an Offer of Marriage from a Lady of his Acquaintance, to whose Company he had introduced him' (V, 7, 219). Booth, Amelia and the reader all assume this means Mrs. Ellison, about whose lack of probity we are all still unsure, and Atkinson's secretiveness produces a series of misunderstandings and offences, which eventually pass off 'in apparent good Humour' (V, 4, 241). But Mrs. Ellison's animus against Booth is further provoked by his continuous, tactless (and mistaken) teasing of her on this account.

Dr. Harrison, as we have seen, is not a natural plotter. When faced with a morally awkward situation, such as Amelia's justifiable unwillingness to stay with Colonel and Mrs. James, the reasons for which she cannot reveal, he proposes to remove her from the moral complexities of the London scene and take her to the relative simplicity of the country (IX, 8). Thus the problem would be evaded rather than solved. He does, however, early in the story, try to help Booth and Amelia to their chaste elopement by his attempted hamper-trick. This is defined as 'a Conceit' (II, 5, 81), but, perhaps significantly, the device is a failure, since the servant that Booth blackmails into silence is later 'unable to devise any Excuse' (II, 6, 83) and feebly confesses the truth.

Similarly, early in Booth's history, he tells how his deceptive attempt to conceal his love from Amelia (for honest reasons) results in his real passion overcoming him, and is thus a greater recommendation to Amelia, who becomes determined to have him (II, 2). Miss Mathews calls this behaviour 'almost beyond the Reach of Humanity' (II, 2, 73), and the narrator too asks the reader to consider whether this conduct was natural or not. It does reflect interestingly the deviously testing means by which Booth and Dr. Harrison finally reveal to Amelia the good news about the estate.

It is Amelia, though, who faces the most problematic moral choices in the story, and Fielding provides a number of stern tests of her integrity and adherence to the truth, in order to try to demonstrate how virtue may operate unsullied in a world of deceits. She is regularly placed in situations where the principle of truth seems to clash with the instinct of self-preservation, or, more difficult, with the genuine interests of others. These pressures are forced on Amelia by Fielding with the aim of bringing her virtues to light, and showing them at work in a complex world. Amelia's virtues, including her truthfulness, are without stain, but, like Fielding's devices, they are not always without subtlety.

It is worth noting here how often the virtue of the Booths is tested when they venture out from the safety of their accommodation. London itself is plainly a place of moral insecurity. Events such as card-parties (IX, 7) or dinner at the Colonel's (IX, 4), a walk which may end up at a tavern (X, 5), an oratorio, and perhaps less surprisingly, a masquerade—each of these leads to personal, social and often moral entanglements in which the upholding of truth and avoidance of deceit become extremely difficult tasks. Fielding's (traditional) point is that moral virtue must be seen to operate in the world if it is to be a worthy exemplar, and his own insistent plotting devices are designed to provide severe examinations of the quality of Amelia's veracity in a world permeated with deceptions.

Two minor occasions in Amelia's early history can serve as examples of her virtuosity in the maintenance of truthfulness. At her elopement, her old nurse is justifiably suspicious of 'this fine young Gentleman' (II, 6, 85) who arrives with Amelia, soaking wet and in the middle of the night: ' "I am afraid Madam knows nothing of all this Matter".' Amelia immediately replies: ' "Suppose he should be my Husband, Nurse" ', an answer which does not lie (implying 'if he were my husband, would that be all right?'), but which the nurse is able to take as a hint that they *are* actually married. Anyway, Amelia is already absolved from any taint of lying by Dr. Harrison's previous assurance that they 'ought to be esteemed Man and Wife', because free and mutual consents had previously been given.

Her local verbal prowess is matched by her interpersonal skills. When pursued by Booth's friend Bagillard, at Montpelier, Amelia has to pretend she is jealous of Booth's friendship with the Frenchman; she cannot risk telling him the real reason, even though this entails her being at least civil to the suitor, thus allowing him to think he may succeed with her

(III, 8, 9). This little *imbroglio* is a paradigm of many of Amelia's later problems, when she is forced to conceal the real faults of Booth's rivals in order to forestall any dangerous effects from perceived threats to his honour. This is why, for instance, in Book IX, Chapter 2, Amelia has to exercise 'great Prudence and Delicacy' over Colonel James's potentially embarrassing dinner invitation. When Booth persuades himself that her objections are to *Mrs.* James, Amelia 'was highly pleased when she saw him taking a wrong Scent. She gave, therefore, a little into the Deceit ...' (IX, 2, 362). Though this is not a deceit she has herself engineered, it does still leave her with her awkward secret about James, and the necessity of counterfeiting a proper civility towards him.

In fact, secrets of this type, being kept for virtuous purposes, seem to escape Fielding's censure, and Dr. Harrison on hearing of Amelia's difficulty, does not refuse to continue to conceal it from Booth (IX, 5). Amelia is still engaging with the problem of this concealment even after Booth's complete confession to her of his guilt. In order to prevent Booth from seeing James,[10] and thus discovering about his challenge, which is still extant, Amelia is forced to tell her husband that she has 'had Dreams last Night about you two' (XII, 2, 500). She must be in desperate straits here, for she refuses to describe 'one [dream] too horrible to be mentioned', and is even willing to be regarded as 'unreasonable' if it will gain his agreement. This difficult discussion is cut short by the bailiff and not renewed later, for 'Booth was going to speak' and his continued resistance to Amelia's plea could have proved damaging either to her truthfulness or to her powers of secrecy. As it is, there seems no sign in the text that Amelia did have a dream: Fielding perhaps means readers to recall Atkinson's dream (IX, 5) of James's treachery, which so nearly precipitates a discovery by Booth.

The aftermath of the revelation through Atkinson's dream provides a further sample of Amelia's brilliant manoeuvrings to maintain her secret without departing from the truth. Booth, now beginning to suspect Colonel James, asks why she is so frightened at his mention of the Colonel's name (IX, 6, 381). First, she changes the subject, by reverting to the spurious horrors of last night's bedroom scene (where cherry brandy was taken for blood!). She is then able to reply to his further questioning only with questions of her own: 'Why should you suspect it?' 'Can you imagine I should dislike a Man, who is so much your Friend?' (382). 'Do you think . . . that I have any Objection to him?' She finally deflects Booth's interrogation by insisting that she will never permit Booth to go (abroad) without her. Amelia does prevaricate here, in the sense of 'speaking evasively', but even though she will not quite answer Booth's questions, nevertheless she does not quite lie, either. Fielding shortly releases Amelia from this difficulty, by allowing Booth to understand only that James had insulted Mrs. Atkinson. The narration recalls that 'the Discernment of *Amelia* was extremely quick', and she is relieved finally to be able to humour her husband by agreeing with him on one of James's minor misdemeanours.

The unhappiest secret in the book is the fact of Booth's adultery. The principal concealment is of course Booth's, but once Amelia finds out it becomes a further awkward secret for her, and it is not remarkable that she does keep it to herself. After she receives Miss Mathews's letter, she keeps this painful knowledge to herself (though the reader cannot know this for sure), presumably waiting in hopes that Booth will confess to her on his own initiative. (It is said that Amelia 'pretty well guessed the obscure Meaning' of Booth's letter (XI, 9, 492), though readers have to assume this is through quick discernment rather than hard information.) When he does confess, Amelia produces Miss Matthews's letter, saying 'I am likewise capable of keeping a Secret' (XII, 2, 498). This of course enhances Amelia's act of forgiveness, and heightens Booth's sense of gratitude.

In the next chapter Amelia again conceals Booth's affair with Miss Mathews, for reasons that are obviously virtuous and legitimate, though distinctly underplayed by Fielding in his narration. She first tells the whole of 'the gaming Story' (XII, 3, 502); after Dr. Harrison has absorbed this and offered the solution of flight to the country, Amelia then raises the matter of James's challenge: ' "That wicked Colonel . . hath picked some Quarrel with my Husband," (for she did not think proper to mention the Cause) "and hath sent him a Challenge" ' (503). Amelia thus hides Booth's guilt from Dr.

Harrison, as Fielding does in the next chapter, by making Colonel James himself ashamed to reveal the cause of the 'quarrel' in front of the doctor, and his brother-in-law, Colonel Bath. So Booth is protected from further public humiliation for his marital infidelity. This is presumably not an improper concealment, as his confession and repentance of his theological infidelity (XII, 5, 511) entitle him to such an absolution.

What becomes a virtuous secret for Amelia, is however a deceitful concealment for Booth, and occasionally an absolute lie, as when he declares his surprise at being handed Dr. Harrison's letter against adultery: 'I do not think I deserve the Character of such a Husband' (X, 4, 423).[11] Booth's reasons for concealment, and the means he employs, now deserve some examination. Although Booth has every reason to fear that Miss Mathews will 'effect the Discovery of that which he would at any Price have concealed' (IV, 5, 171), and foresees that this crime 'would occasion him many Difficulties and Terrors to endeavour to conceal' (176), he nonetheless decides, for reasons of pride, as Fielding explains it, not to confess to Amelia. Fielding assures us that he would 'in great Probability' have been immediately forgiven by Amelia, and we perhaps have reason to believe this, as we have already seen her excuse him for concealing his illness in Gibraltar (IV, 6); her reaction there is a paradigm of her need to *know* unhappy facts and her real ability to act for the best under such circumstances. Booth acknowledges to himself, much later in the story, that he could still confess to Amelia, 'from whose Goodness he doubted not but to obtain an absolute Remission' (XI, 7, 487).

But Booth does not come clean, and is forced into a series of little lies and deceits in order to account for Miss Mathews's letters, until for a time she is taken off his hands by Colonel James. From the end of Book IV until the masquerade (X, 2), Booth is more occupied with his financial problems, but his guilty secret remains as a time-bomb; after the masquerade, Booth and the reader again have to dread and expect the aggrieved mistress to reveal all.

Booth's lies are often hasty and ill-prepared, and it may be that Fielding is seeking ways of at least partially excusing them. As was the case with his denial of guilt in response to the letter on adultery, these lies are not always commented on in the narration. Fielding stresses his fears and anxieties about possible discovery in Book IV, Chapter 5, but does not remark his lies to Amelia. In Book V, Chapter 6, after the duel, Booth shows he is neither a natural liar, nor a skilled one: 'In short, he made many shuffling and evasive Answers, not boldly lying out, which perhaps would have succeeded, but poorly and vainly endeavouring to reconcile Falsehood with Truth' (213). It does appear that Fielding is concerned to preserve the reader's sympathy for Booth, by underplaying his lies and heightening our sense of the awfulness of a discovery, as at the end of the masquerade, where Fielding insists that Booth had 'no Fear upon Earth equal to that of *Amelia*'s knowing what it was in the Power of Miss *Mathews* to communicate to her, and which to conceal from her, he had already undergone so much Uneasiness' (X, 2, 419).

Even once Booth has resolved to resist finally Miss Mathews's blackmail (XI, 8), he finds it impossible (perhaps not unreasonably) to confess his guilt explicitly in his letter to Amelia (XI, 9). This, however, can hardly be defined as a concealment, except from the reader, who still does not know that Amelia knows, and is in for a surprise as great as Booth's own, when he finally uncovers this fact. After this clarification and justification of righteous veracity, one might expect no more devices, stratagems or concealments, but interestingly the absolutely final dénouement turns on one further concealment, practised again on Amelia by her husband and Dr. Harrison.

Dr. Harrison is afraid that the sensationally good news about the restoration of the estate will be too much for Amelia, 'for this wise and good Man was fearful of making such a Discovery all at once to *Amelia*, lest it should overpower her' (XII, 7, 525). This reason is legitimate enough, for Amelia has nearly fainted simply on finding Booth at liberty; but it does not really suffice to explain why Booth and Dr. Harrison continue to say nothing of the grand affair even when she has become calm. The next morning Booth postpones the revelation by setting out, most unjustifiably, one feels, to test Amelia's obedience and stoicism. He insists on borrowing hard-saved money from the 'poor and generous' (XII, 8, 526) Atkinsons, embarrassing Amelia by his confidence about repayment; testing her stoicism, he makes up a dream of their coming into their fortunes, asking her how she would support such a transition, if it were real; Dr. Harrison then repeats, with the addition of some Homeric verses, this querying of her stoical powers.

He then takes out the day's newspaper ('after I have put on my Spectacles I will try you', 529), and reads an item about Murphy's commitment for forgery. This information, as Dr. Harrison sarcastically comments, is remarkable for being true, but even this does not clarify the situation entirely, and the Doctor produces his own addendum to the printed account, pretending it is a learned gloss, which at last reveals the *names* of Miss Harris, Booth and 'an old Parson, call'd Dr. Harrison'.

At last, there is nothing further to be concealed from anyone, but such a lengthy test seems scarcely necessary, and is in fact an insult to Amelia's indubitably equitable temperament. For Fielding as writer the delay serves to bring together sufficient of his cast to make the discovery by the heroine more dramatic, and the reader is also teased into waiting for the final emotional release. The postponement of the names should perhaps be related to Fielding's odd habit of making the reader wait, sometimes for a long time, before divulging the actual name of characters who are coming to be quite important in the story.[12]

Despite the emotional manipulation this trickery by delay seems to entail for Amelia, it seems that Fielding has designed the delayed revelation as a 'good' stratagem, perhaps to be paralleled with the 'honest' deceit by which Booth first won Amelia's heart (II, 2). Concealment, then, is a device which may climactically be employed for the ultimate purposes of truthful revelation, as fiction itself, with its progressive sets of mysteries and clarifications, may also be a servant of moral truth, and immune to accusations of lying. But the fiction writer, especially in a world as comparatively sombre as that of *Amelia*, must also display total probity in the stratagems by which he leads his readers towards the Providential dénouement, and that is why Fielding's strategy in *Amelia* deploys plentiful concealment and an amount of dissembling, but literally no lying.

Lying and Concealment in 'Amelia'

NOTES

1. All references to *Amelia* are to the Wesleyan Edition of the Works of Henry Fielding, *Amelia*, ed. Martin Battestin (Oxford: Clarendon Press, 1983).

2. Sissela Bok in *Lying: Moral Choice in Public and Private Life* (London: Quartet, 1980) points out (13–14) that lying is only a part of the much larger question of deception (with its own relationship to secrets); she also claims, interestingly, that very few contemporary philosophers, and not many since the Renaissance, have engaged with this issue, although it was an important topic in classical and medieval thought (xix–xx).

3. J. Paul Hunter, *Occasional Form: Henry Fielding and the Chains of Circumstance* (Baltimore and London: Johns Hopkins, 1975).

4. As with the woman charged with being a strumpet: 'She pleaded in her Defence (as was really the Truth) that she was a Servant' (I, 2, 22).

5. Samuel Johnson, *Dictionary* (1755), 'SAGACIOUS, 2'.

6. Johnson defines 'prevaricate' as 'to cavil, quibble, or shuffle'; nonetheless, Amelia 'did not think proper to mention the Cause' (503) of James's challenge, thus concealing from Dr. Harrison the fact of Booth's adultery. See below.

7. Cf. Luke 16:8: 'For the children of this world are in their generation wiser than the children of light.'

8. Fielding uses this device of an interruption on several occasions, sometimes to postpone moments of enlightenment for the characters, as in Book VIII, Chapter 8, when Sergeant Atkinson's arrival twice distracts Amelia from further consideration of the possibility that James hopes to seduce her.

9. There are parallels here with Amelia's total refusal to gain preferment for Booth by *any* morally dubious concession (VIII, 3) and with Dr. Harrison's indignant refusal to vote corruptly in order to procure Booth's reinstatement in the army (XI, 2). Compare the willingness of James (V, 9) and Trent (XI, 3) to exploit the sexual favours of women to gain advancement.

10. Asking Booth and the bailiff to 'deny' that Booth is in the house could presumably be regarded as the contemporary formality by which is indicated unwillingness to be disturbed, though it does appear that Amelia hopes that James would actually believe that Booth was not there.

11. Compare this with another sign of Booth's lack of self-awareness. Just after he has lost £50 by gambling, and spent Amelia's hard-gained cash on bribery, he lectures the thieving maid in terms that ought to be remarkably relevant to himself: 'You should not have thought of robbing your Mistress, particularly at this Time. . . . You have robbed the best and kindest Mistress in the World . . . a felonious breach of Trust; for . . . everything your Mistress had, was intrusted to your Care' (XI, 7, 485).

12. Amelia, though she is in both protagonists' thoughts throughout Book I, is not named until Book II, Chapter 1; Atkinson first appears in Book II,

Chapter 6, as the son of Amelia's nurse, in Book III, Chapter 3, he is 'my Man', Amelia's foster-brother, and only in Book III, Chapter 5, is he named as 'Atkinson'. This odd practice certainly makes the reader attend closely to each new figure, trying to work out his or her moral potential, lest he or she should turn out to be significant.

Notes on Contributors

BRYAN BURNS is a lecturer in English literature at the University of Sheffield, and has written the forthcoming *Novels of Thomas Love Peacock* and articles on the cinema and on fiction in the Romantic period.

LANCE ST. JOHN BUTLER, who studied at Pembroke College, Cambridge, and the University of East Anglia, is a lecturer in English Studies at the University of Stirling. He is the author of *Thomas Hardy After Fifty Years* (with others) (1977), *Thomas Hardy* (1978), and *Samuel Beckett and the Meaning of Being* (1984). At present he is working in the areas of the Victorian loss of faith and the philosophy of literature.

DONALD FRASER was born in Wellington, New Zealand, and studied for his first degree at Victoria University of Wellington. His Ph.D., on Pope's poetry, was taken at Birkbeck College, University of London. He has published articles on Pope and on film criticism, and has compiled the *Collins Concise Dictionary of Quotations* (1983) and a *Dictionary of Musical Quotations* (1985). He is a lecturer in English Studies at the University of Strathclyde.

MORRIS GOLDEN, Professor of English at the University of Massachusetts, Amherst, has been trying, since the mid-'50s, to catch aspects of eighteenth-century literature and society in a number of articles as well as *In Search of Stability: The Poetry of William Cowper* (1961), *Richardson's Characters* (1963), *Thomas Gray* (1964), *Fielding's Moral Psychology* (1966), and *The Self Observed: Swift, Johnson, Wordsworth* (1972). For the last few years, Golden has searched the chaos of eighteenth-century English journalism for light on how prominent events and people can have affected the novels of Richardson and Fielding. As his recent work has argued, the forms of political life and their conceptions of themselves have fused to shape their best fiction.

199

Henry Fielding: Justice Observed

MARK KINKEAD-WEEKES, born in South Africa, is Professor of English literature at the University of Kent. He is best known for (with Ian Gregor) *William Golding, A Critical Study* (1967; revised 1984) and for his *Samuel Richardson, Dramatic Novelist* (1973). He has also published on nineteenth- and twentieth-century fiction and on African and Caribbean literature. Currently he is at work on a biography of Lawrence and is completing an edition of *The Rainbow*.

DONALD LOW is Reader in English Studies at the University of Stirling, where he directs the University's Robert Burns Project. In 1981 he published *Thieves' Kitchen: The Regency Underworld*, which describes attempts to deal with crime and delinquency in London in a period directly influenced by its varied inheritance from the age of Fielding and Hogarth. Donald Low's publications on eighteenth-century literature include *Robert Burns: The Critical Heritage* (1974), and the first separate annotated edition of Burns's *Kilmarnock Poems* (1985). He has in preparation a biography of Burns and an edition of his songs.

PATRICK REILLY was storeman, soldier, salesman, labourer and lamplighter before going to Glasgow University as a mature student. He took a First in English and went to Oxford to complete a B.Litt. on Swift. He then worked as a schoolteacher before joining the English department at Glasgow where he is now Senior Lecturer. Married with six children, he has written two books (*Jonathan Swift: The Brave Desponder* and *George Orwell: The Age's Adversary*) and contributed to three others (*Modern Scottish Catholicism*, and two volumes of *Literary Criticism*). He has published articles on Joyce, Orwell, Dickens, and aspects of contemporary culture, religion and education.

NEIL RHODES was a Scholar of St. Catherine's College, Oxford, from 1971–74, where he took the degrees of B.A. and D.Phil. From 1977–79 he was a lecturer in English at the University of Strathclyde, and he is currently a lecturer in English at St. Andrews University. He is the author of *Elizabethan Grotesque* (1980) and *John Donne: Selected Prose* (1985).

K. G. SIMPSON was born in Ayrshire and graduated M.A. (Glasgow), Ph.D. (Strathclyde). Since 1969 he has been a lecturer in the Department of English Studies at Strathclyde University, specializing in the teaching of the development of the novel and the literature of the period 1900–50. He has contributed to the Critical

Studies volumes on Smollett, Sterne, Burns and Stevenson, and has published articles on Galt, Home's *Douglas*, and various aspects of Scottish and eighteenth-century literature. Recently he has completed a study of the literature of the Scottish Enlightenment.

Index

Index

Fielding, John, 17, 32n
Fielding, Sarah, 110; *Adventures of David Simple*, 40, 110
Fielding, William, 17
Foord, Archibald S., 54n
Ford, Ford Madox, 91
Forster, E. M., 161, 173n
Frederick, Prince, 49

George, Dorothy, 33n
George II, 48, 50
Gide, André, 78–9
Glover, Richard, 37
Godden, G. M., 54n
Goldberg, Homer, 136n
Goldgar, Bertrand A., 54n, 55n
Golding, William, 112; *Rites of Passage*, 113, 118n
Grundy, Isobel, 54n

Hardy, Thomas, 95–6; *Tess of the d'Urbervilles*, 95, 100n
Harrison, Bernard, 56, 68–9, 73n
Hatfield, Glenn, 138, 156n
Hawkins, Sir John, 56
Hoadly, Benjamin, 56, 62, 65, 111
Hogarth, William, 8, 18–20, 50, 114; *The Rake's Progress*, 115
Humphreys, A. R. (ed.): *'Jonathan Wild' and 'The Journal of a Voyage to Lisbon'*, 32n
Hunter, J. Paul, 127, 136n, 176, 197n
Hutchens, Eleanor, 137, 156n

Irwin, Michael, 136n
Irwin, William Robert, 55n

James, Henry, 158–59, 172&n, 173n
Johnson, Samuel, 34–5, 90–2, 179, 197n

Kafka, Franz, 98
Kinkead-Weekes, Mark, 157n
Knapp, Lewis M., 12n
Kundera, Milan, 11, 12n

Lewis, C. S., 7
Linebaugh, Peter, 32n
Low, Donald A., 32n
Lyttelton, George, 15, 37, 64

Middleton, Conyers: *Life of Cicero*, 49
Miller, Henry Knight, 159, 162–63, 167, 169, 173n; (ed.) *Miscellanies* (Vol. I), 55n
Milton, John: *Paradise Lost*, 115, 118n

Monboddo, James Burnett, Lord, 76
Montagu, Lady Mary Wortley, 8, 23–5, 36, 90–1, 94
Mutter, R. P. C., 8, 162, 165; (ed.) *Tom Jones*, 12n, 32n

Newcastle, Duke of, 25, 51

Orwell, George: *Animal Farm*, 84–6

Paine, Thomas, 52
Paulson, Ronald, 11, 19, 32n, 99n
Paulson, Ronald, and Lockwood, Thomas, 11, 12n, 118n
Peel, Sir Robert, 18, 22
Pelham, Henry, 16, 35–6, 40–1, 50
Pitt, William, 1st Earl of Chatham, 37
Pope, Alexander, 36, 103–4, 114; 'Epistle to Dr. Arbuthnot', 103; 'The Rape of the Lock', 115
Preston, John, 56, 71, 154–55, 157n
Priestley, J. B., 7
Pritchett, V. S., 8, 12n
Pulteney, William, 35, 38, 40, 49

Radzinowicz, Leon, 22, 32n
Rawson, C. J., 73n, 99n, 100n, 118n, 156n
Richardson, Samuel, 8, 63, 75, 89–90, 94–5, 101–2, 105; *Pamela*, 9, 49, 63, 95, 101–3, 109, 122, 156n; *Clarissa*, 94–5
Rogers, Pat, 7, 10, 31n, 99n
Ross, Ian, 170, 173n

Sandys, Samuel, 36, 49
Scott, Sir Walter, 76
Shaftesbury, Anthony Ashley Cooper, 3rd Earl of, 9, 56–73; *Characteristics of Men, Manners, Opinions, Times, Etc.*, 56–73, 73n
Shakespeare, William: *The Winter's Tale*, 11, 105, 107–8
Sherburn, George, 99n
Sidney, Sir Philip: *Arcadia*, 117
Smollett, Tobias, 7–8, 34–5, 123; *Humphry Clinker*, 123
Spilka, Mark, 117, 118n
Steele, Sir Richard, 24
Stendhal (Henri Beyle), 159, 172n
Stephen, Leslie (ed.): *The Works of Henry Fielding Esq.*, 32n
Sterne, Laurence, 11, 158, 170
Swift, Jonathan, 8–9, 34, 52, 75–9, 88–9, 97, 99n, 100n; *Voyage to the Houyhnhnms*, 75; *Modest Proposal*, 75; *Argument Against Abolishing Christianity*, 75

204

Index

Thackeray, William Makepeace, 92
Thompson, E. P., 32n
Tillotson, John, 56, 62, 65, 78
Trentham, Granville, Viscount, 42

Van Ghent, Dorothy, 87, 100n, 168, 173n
Virgil: *Aeneid*, 187

Walpole, Horace, 21; *Memoirs of the Reign of George II*, 32n
Walpole, Sir Robert, 13, 35–7, 44, 48–50, 54n, 103–4

Warren, Robert Penn, 82; *All the King's Men*, 99n
Watt, Ian, 164–65, 173n
Welch, Saunders, 21
West, Rebecca, 99n
Whichcote, Benjamin, 56
Windham, William, 49
Woods, Charles B., 55n
Wordsworth, William, 95–6
Wright, Andrew, 165, 173n

Zirker, Malvin R. Jr., 32n